ARTHUR RANSOME
ON FISHING

'IT'S A SHARK!'
(Ransome's drawing from *Swallows and Amazons*)

ARTHUR RANSOME
ON
FISHING

Jeremy Swift

JONATHAN CAPE
LONDON

First published 1994

1 3 5 7 9 10 8 6 4 2

© 1994 by Jeremy Swift and the Arthur Ransome Estate

Jeremy Swift has asserted his right under the Copyright, Designs and Patents Act
1988 to be identified as the author of this work

First published in the United Kingdom in 1994 by Jonathan Cape,
Random House, 20 Vauxhall Bridge Road, London SW1V 2SA

Random House Australia (Pty) Limited
20 Alfred Street, Milsons Point, Sydney,
New South Wales 2061, Australia

Random House New Zealand Limited
18 Poland Road, Glenfield,
Auckland 10, New Zealand

Random House South Africa (Pty) Limited
PO Box 337, Bergvlei, South Africa

Random House UK Limited Reg. No. 954009

A CIP catalogue record for this book
is available from the British Library

ISBN 0–224–03555–X (hardback)
0–224–04236–X (paperback)

Typeset by Deltatype Limited, Ellesmere Port, South Wirral
Printed in Great Britain by
Mackays of Chatham plc

To Daniel

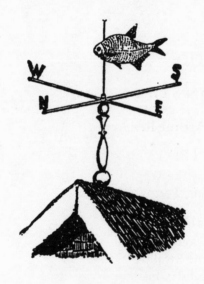

Contents

Illustrations

Charles Renold fishing on Loweswater
Ransome with a large salmon, caught near
    Cockermouth
Writing on board the last of Ransome's six yachts,
    Lottie Blossom, 1954
A wet day's fishing in 1954
Fishing the Derwent for sea trout, 1956

Text
drawings

'Its a Shark!', by Ransome (Frontispiece)
Ransome's puffin (dedication)
The weather vein from *The Big Six* (Contents)
Ransome, self-portrait sketch (p. 15)
Ransome's letter illustration (p. 17)
Feeling for trout, by Ransome (p. 19)
Another one to put back, from *The Big Six* (p. 58)
Clifford Webb's drawing of *Swallow* and *Amazon*
    (p. 66)
'It's a shark!' by Clifford Webb (p. 69)
Steven Spurrier's 'Roger and the pike' (p. 70)
'Roger fell on it', by Ransome (p. 72)
The big fish, Ransome's drawing for *The Big Six*
    (p. 77)
Fishing with the Renolds on the Norfolk Broads
    (p. 84)
Ransome's Christmas card drawing, 1938 (p. 85)
Woodcut by Eric Fitch Daglish of a salmon taking
    a fly (p. 89)
Ransome's drawing of the elver fly (p. 95)
Ransome's sketch 'Boiling with grayling' (p. 98)
The catching of the great trout, Webb's drawing
    for *Swallowdale* (p. 112)

All the decorative drawings among Ransome's pieces are his
own with the exception of Webb's on page 172.

Sir Henry Wotton . . . was also a most dear lover, and a frequent practiser of the art of angling; of which he would say 'it was an employment for his idle time, which was not then idly spent . . . a rest to his mind, a cheerer to his spirits, a diverter of sadness, a calmer of unquiet thoughts, a moderator of passions, a procurer of contentedness; and that it begat habits of peace and patience in those that professed and practised it.'

Izaak Walton, The Compleat Angler, 1653

INTRODUCTION

No. Not that photograph. Not the C.I.D.man, bootlegger or political tough and hi-jacker, but a benevolent baldheaded one, something like this

ARTHUR RANSOME had four lives. As a young man he wrote well-received works of literary criticism, including books on Oscar Wilde and Edgar Allan Poe. He was later a foreign correspondent, one of the few who knew Russia well and reported the Bolshevik revolution; he was personally acquainted with many of the leading revolutionaries, and he married Trotsky's secretary. He is best remembered now as the author of twelve children's books which redefined children's fiction and remained popular more than half a century later.

Pardoxically, his most lasting achievement, and certainly the one that gave him the most pleasure, is as a fishing writer. His masterpiece, *Rod and Line*, drawn from a fishing column of the same name in the *Manchester Guardian*, is one of the three or four most important fishing books of this century in any language. It has been reprinted many times and has given pleasure to countless people who know little of fishing.

Ransome wrote and broadcast regularly about fishing for much of his life, and yet only a small part of his fishing output has been kept alive in *Rod and Line* and *Mainly About Fishing*. His most ambitious work centred on fishing – an historical novel – was abandoned before it was finished, although fragments of it remain and are preserved with other unpublished fishing writing among his papers in the Leeds University library and elsewhere. This book brings together the best of this writing in order to make it available to readers in a permanent form.

In this book, I first describe Ransome's life as a fisherman and how writing about fishing became a corner-stone of his personal and professional life. I have built on and added to other accounts, notably his own autobiography and Hugh Brogan's comprehensive biography, so as to explore what fishing meant to him.

Fishing was, with writing, the one constant source of inspiration and strength to Arthur Ransome throughout his life, and writing about fishing was perhaps the thing he did with greatest pleasure. The second half of the book contains his own, largely unpublished, writing. Although the theme is fishing, the appeal of these pieces is much wider: here is an important twentieth-century writer at his best.

Jeremy Swift
March 1994

A FISHERMAN'S LIFE

by Jeremy Swift

BORN IN LEEDS in 1884, Arthur Ransome was a third generation fisherman. His grandfather, an unworldly scientist and inventor, was an excellent naturalist and a keen and original fisherman who made a small contribution to rod design. He had seen early on the advantage of stiffer, shorter, quicker-striking rods over the long whippy rods that were then in use. But such rods had the disadvantage that they easily broke the delicate horsehair cast when the fisherman struck too hard. He therefore added a foot of whalebone to the tip of his stiff rods; the stiff rod gave speed in the strike while the whalebone provided just enough give to save the horsehair from breaking.

His grandfather's favourite river was the Bela on the southern borders of the Lake District, which he fished in the 1870s. Arthur's father, Cyril, and Arthur himself both fished the same river, and Arthur later used the Bela as the model for the river in his great, unfinished, fishing book.

Cyril – Professor of History at Yorkshire College, later to become the University of Leeds – was less idiosyncratic, but no less enthusiastic about outdoor sports. Cyril disagreed with his father about almost everything except fishing and shooting, at which he himself excelled. He was one of

17

the first fishermen to introduce Halford's new upstream dry
fly methods to the traditional wet fly country of the North
of England, although after a year or two he gave up tying
dry flies because they demanded too much time compared
to the sparse northern spiders, and he was at heart a wet fly
fisherman.

As a small boy, Cyril Ransome had enjoyed fishing with
his father, and he took his son in turn to the Wharfe or on
holiday to Coniston. He had a passion for the Lakes and their
mountains, and carried Arthur to the top of Coniston Old
Man as an infant. Leeds in those days was a good place for a
keen countryman, and Cyril fished or shot every weekend
in term time. In the holidays, he took the whole family north
to the Lakes. 'Every Long Vacation,' Arthur records, 'he was
no longer a professor who fished, but a fisherman who wrote
history-books in his spare time.' Arthur himself was an
inattentive pupil, not at first very impressed by the claims of
trout over coarse fish.

> I was never content to watch him catching trout and so to
> learn to do as much myself when old enough to have a
> rod. He would turn, on hooking a trout, to make sure that
> his pupil was alert and watching, only to find that he was
> alone, and that his pupil had gone off down river and was
> paddling in the water, turning stones, to catch loaches by
> himself. It was different on Coniston where I had a rod of
> my own and an almost equal chance of catching perch. But
> for him trout came first, and my unwillingness to learn the
> mysteries by mere watching seemed to him little short of
> sacrilege.

Arthur's mother, Edith, was a water-colourist, a quiet but
determined woman who exercised a powerful influence on
him. She was the first of several difficult and strong-willed
women destined to have an indelible effect on his life. He had
a brother and two sisters.

Preparations for family trips to the Lakes began weeks
before. Flies were tied for himself and his friends, especially
the sparse and delicate northern wet flies described in the

FEELING FOR A TROUT (from *The Picts and the Martyrs*)

standard work by Leeds fisherman and angling journalist T. E. Pritt, whose book *Yorkshire Trout Flies* had been published in 1885, with a dedication 'To a Host of Yorkshire Anglers, Good Fellows, and Good Fishers All'. In his *Autobiography* Ransome describes how long before the day of the journey the wooden candlesticks in his father's study were festooned with newly-made casts, his rods were ready, his landing net mended, and he had inspected the children's perch floats. Bedding and clothes were packed in a portable bath with a lid, a padlock and a leather strap, and all the children had to sit on the lid to try to shut it before it could be locked. Usually it needed the large cook, Molly, to sit on the lid too before it would close.

On the railway journey north, Arthur's father pointed out the rivers they crossed – Wharfe, Ribble, Lune. The train went around the edge of Morecambe Bay to the little station at Greenodd, where the Crake and Leven ran into the sea, and they were met by one of the Swainsons from High Nibthwaite at the southern end of Coniston, and it was there that they spent the holiday.

Ransome attributes his love of the Lake country to these times at Swainson's farm, and to his father's passion for this countryside. From childhood this country was home for him, more than Leeds, and no other place in his life was ever as real as Swainson's farm and the Crake valley. He learned to handle a heavy boat and be at home on the water. Tutored by his father, an ornithologist and naturalist, he went for long walks, picked mushrooms, and had close and painful encounters with squirrels and a wounded heron. His father taught him to tickle trout – guddling in Lake dialect – under Nibthwaite bridge. They caught minnows in a small cut in the lake shore where the Swainsons kept their boat. The children were taken perch fishing, each one watching a float of a different colour. It was a good deal more fun than simply watching his father catch trout on the Wharfe.

More than thirty years later, in one of his Saturday articles for the *Manchester Guardian*, Ransome recalls the particular joy of these childhood expeditions in the countryside.

> There was a bridge over a very little beck. It used to be possible to crawl through underneath it. I used to crawl under other bridges. There was one under which I caught trout in a tin can by clapping it over the hole they bolted in to hide when startled by a confederate in the pool above.

These were the formative experiences for an important part

of his adult life, as much for the fishing as for children's adventures in boats. There is a nostalgic note in his *Autobiography*, when he talks about a childhood which he recreates in his children's books, but was unable to make in real life for his own child.

> Sometimes, when my father was fishing the lake for trout he would row the whole family up to Peel Island where we landed in the lovely little harbour at the south end (that some who have read my books as children may recognise borrowed for the sake of secrecy to improve an island in another lake). We spent the day as savages. My mother would settle down to make a sketch in water-colours. My father, forgetting to eat his sandwiches, would drift far along the lake-shores, casting his flies and coming back in the evening with trout in the bottom of the boat for Mrs Swainson to cook for next day's breakfast.

His father fought a losing battle to write on holiday at Nibthwaite. Swainson's farm was close to the place where the Crake leaves the lake, and he kept his rod ready leaning against the porch. The children were sent off to play by the boathouse and watch for the rise.

> The water would be as still as glass and then, suddenly, one of us would see rings spreading where a trout had come up and dimpled the surface in taking a fly. One such rise meant nothing. We waited, watching, and if the first was followed by another and then another, we would race off with the news, burst breathless but welcome into the farmhouse parlour where my father sat at work, and he, knowing that if the fish were rising there they would be rising in the river, would leave his papers, take his rod and hurry across the fields to the Crake. Hard worker as he was, he did not waste good fishing weather on writing history-books.

His father fished for sea trout in the Crake, and Arthur remembered all his life the scream of his father's reel when he once hooked a salmon there. He also fished for pike in the lake, and in Allen Tarn at the junction of lake and river. Cyril would put a spaniel ashore while he drifted down in the open water, and then whistle to bring it splashing through the reeds, driving the pike out into the open water where they could see his lures, made by himself and painted by Arthur's mother. Arthur was at the oars for the capture of a twenty pound pike, although he nearly lost it by rowing the wrong way. Allen Tarn was later to be the model for Octopus lagoon in the Swallows and Amazons books.

Arthur would return from these childhood holidays with a large collection of treasures, caterpillars, minnows, newts and lizards, together with heather, oak leaves and groundsel for them to feed on. Getting them back to Leeds was always a problem.

> One year I had packed all my creatures for the journey into a large cardboard box with partitions and smaller boxes within it. At Greenodd station we had to cross the line, and, just as we crossed it, the train from Lakeside already in sight, I slipped and fell, the box opened and all my livestock scattered in the path of the approaching train. 'Oh, my family! my family!' I cried and began desperately collecting them. As fast as I picked up one newt another made off. Caterpillars were crawling in all directions. That noble stationmaster, earning thereby more than sixty years of humble gratitude, instead of ordering a small boy off the line, himself reversed the signals, held up the train on the bridge a few yards away, came back and on all fours helped with the rescue of my menagerie.

Cyril Ransome was not an easy father. Hugh Brogan, Ransome's biographer, calls him 'oppressively imperceptive', sitting perpetually in judgement on his son. Cyril was both dauntingly severe and only occasionally supportive. Nevertheless Arthur hero-worshipped his father, and modelled himself on him for much of his life. One of the things which gave Arthur greatest pleasure in his old age was an honorary doctorate from Leeds University, a final link to his father's world and his own childhood. In contrast, his mother scarcely appears at all in his *Autobiography*, although in later life he maintained an intense correspondence with her, and early in his career he rarely embarked on a new undertaking without consulting her.

Arthur's own childhood reading included *Robinson Crusoe*, *Treasure Island* and Scott, which his mother read aloud to him. He loved the fairy tales of Andrew Lang, not much read nowadays, and collected them one by one at Christmas and birthdays. Surprisingly, he does not mention Lang's charming book of fishing stories, *Angling Sketches*, published in 1891 with a very Ransome-like first chapter, called 'Confessions of a duffer', wryly describing what a poor fisherman Lang felt himself to be; *Angling Sketches* is not in Ransome's list of favourite fishing books published by the National Book League in 1955, and after his death no copy was found in his library.

Much later in life he claimed that W. J. Collingwood's book about Coniston, *Thorstein of the Mere*, was also a key book of his childhood; the important role played by the River Crake in the book endeared it to him, since he 'knew every yard of the Crake itself . . . including the difficult footing of the river bed by the old Bobbin Mill where my father used to catch sea trout.'

★

ARTHUR STARTED writing early. He produced his first story – about two boys marooned on a desert island near Australia – at the age of eight, and already fishing plays a part in the story. The boys go out to sea to catch fish for food, and see sharks and brightly coloured tropical fish. They also, more surprisingly, catch plaice and a sea trout.

After a succession of tutors and day schools in Leeds, Arthur was sent to board at Old College at Windermere. One reason for this choice was probably that the headmaster was a keen fisherman, who took parties of richer boys fishing in Norway during the summer holidays, and who fished the Bela with Cyril Ransome. Arthur was unhappy there, although the nearness of Coniston and of an aunt who lived in Windermere were consolations. He was still able to collect caterpillars on school walks through the woods, and tickle trout in a beck near the school.

Best of all, he was at school for the Great Frost of 1895, when Windermere froze over for several weeks, and the headmaster wisely let the boys off school to skate and explore on the ice. Arthur and the others left the lake only at dusk, when fires were lit. He saw a coach and four driven across the ice, and an ox being roasted on Bowness Bay. He found a perch frozen in the ice, 'preserved as if in glass beneath my feet.' For once he was better at something than his fellow pupils, having been taught to skate in the countryside outside Leeds by Prince Kropotkin, the anarchist living in England in exile from Russia, whose great work, *Mutual Aid*, had been appearing in sections in a magazine since 1890. The memory of those weeks, frozen perch and his own unexpected skating skills included, provided a mass of material forty years later for *Winter Holiday*.

In the end, fishing cost Cyril his life. Fishing at night for sea trout in the Crake, he caught his foot under an old grindstone and fell on it. Thinking he had sprained an ankle, and in great pain, he forced himself to use the foot in case it stiffened and spoiled his holiday; he fished on and then walked back to Nibthwaite with a heavy catch. The foot had swollen very large. The doctor bandaged it, and for a long time he walked with crutches, but it never got better. After a long delay and several specialists later, the doctors found that he had damaged a bone and that the wound had become tubercular. The foot was cut off, but the leg grew no better and his leg had to be amputated, first at the knee, then at the thigh. For years he refused to accept what was happening, and continued to shoot and fish, although wading with a cork leg was not easy.

Cyril died in 1897, just after Arthur, now aged 13, had come bottom of the list for a scholarship to Rugby. He was devastated by his father's death. In his *Autobiography* he writes: 'I have been learning ever since how much I lost in him. He had been disappointed in me, but I have often thought what friends we could have been had he not died so young.' His immediate response was to give up all the things he had enjoyed with his father, especially fishing. It was fourteen years before he was to fish again.

Although he failed lamentably in the scholarship exam, Ransome passed into Rugby the year of his father's death. It was not a happy time. He was bullied because he was hopeless at sport. Very short sight made it difficult for him to see the ball at football or cricket, or to ward off his opponent at boxing. He fagged for R. H. Tawney, and met Ted Scott, son of E. P. Scott of the *Manchester Guardian*, who became one of his most important friends. He read voraciously, encouraged by a sympathetic master. His hobbies were those of a lonely child: walking and cycling, collecting ammonites for the school museum. He had started writing, and had a poem ('a dreadful piece of earnest doggerel' he records in his *Autobiography*) published by the local newspaper. He also showed some promise in science and engineering. In 1901, to everyone's surprise, especially his own, he passed in the first division into Yorkshire College to read science.

Ransome was already having second thoughts about becoming a scientist however. He collected books and read poetry, and decorated the walls of his lodging with portraits of Tennyson, Browning and Carlyle, rather than of scientists. For the first time in his life he had great freedom, and he celebrated it by going to a different church each Sunday. He started walking seriously, and this was to remain one of his chief pleasures for the next ten years. The crisis came one day in the College library where he was supposed to be working on magnetism but by accident came across a life of William Morris. He started to read it, and, as he recorded later in life, from that moment his fate was decided: he would be a writer. Even at this early stage he knew he wanted to write essays and stories for children. He stopped studying science and two terms later wrote to a London publisher, asking about jobs. When he got an offer of a menial office-boy position at eight shillings a week, he consulted his mother and accepted. His university life was over and a writing career beginning.

For the next ten years, Ransome lived a self-consciously

bohemian and literary life in London. He lived at first in Balham with his mother, who came to London to be with him, then moved to rented rooms of his own in Chelsea. He made friends who were living a similar life, especially the poet Edward Thomas, and writers Gordon Bottomly and Lascelles Abercrombie, and between delivering parcels from his office in Leicester Square bought second hand books in Charing Cross Road and St Martin's Lane. In 1903, he went on a walking and reading holiday at Coniston, where he met W. G. Collingwood, a formidable historian, artist and writer, who had been Ruskin's student, companion and biographer, and who lived near Ruskin's house, Brantwood, at the head of Coniston Water. The Collingwoods adopted Ransome, providing him with the secure, happy and challenging family life he had never previously had. He set up a pattern that was to organise his life for the next few years, spending the spring and summer in the Lakes, recreating with the help of the Collingwood children his own childhood of sailing and walking. Ransome often camped out in his own tent, and spent time with the charcoal burners in the coppice woods above Nibthwaite. He smoked the clay pipes they had baked in their kilns and left for him in the Red Lion pub at Lowick Bridge. In the autumn and winter he retreated to London to make money to pay for this idyllic life. From this time on he saw much less of his mother, although they exchanged letters often.

He was writing continuously, doing whatever he could find a commission to do. He had abandoned poetry, but was soon dashing off hack books: the first were *The ABC of Physical Culture*, and two books of romantic essays.

In 1906, aged 22, he started a more serious enterprise. He was commissioned to write five short books for children on country themes. The cast included two children, a gardener, Imp and Elf, two winsome creatures, and Ogre, a reasonable copy of W. G. Collingwood. The second in the series, after *The Things in our Garden*, was entitled *Pond and Stream*, and although it has very little literary merit as such (it starts 'This is a book about the things that are jolly and wet: streams, and ponds, and ditches, and all the things that swim and wriggle in them.') it is important in Ransome's development as a writer. The purpose of the book was to instruct children about natural history, and Ransome, writing in London, drew on Lakeland childhood memories of fishing to make an accurate portrait of the inhabitants of the water. The larval stage of the caddis or stonefly – a key fisherman's insect – is described in detail in its mobile shuck of sand and sticks, and freshwater shrimps, minnows and loach all make appearances. Stickleback behaviour is observed closely, as are various birds. Fish do not figure prominently, although rising trout are spotted briefly, and the fish that do appear are mainly coarse, especially pike and perch.

The main interest now of *Pond and Stream* is that it sketches out for the first time, with uncanny precision, much of the terrain Ransome was later to explore in detail in the Swallows and Amazons books.

> One month in every year the Imp and the Elf and I go to stay in a farmhouse close by the shores of a lake . . . Of course we are pirates, and Sir Francis Drakes, and vikings, and other sea rovers, from time to time. I often find I have been a villainous pirate mate, when, for all I knew, I had been peaceably reading a book in the stern . . . We row down the lake, lazily and slowly, past rocky bays and sharp-nosed promontories, and low points pinnacled with firs . . . We run the boat carefully aground in a pebbly inlet at one end of the island. We take the baskets ashore, and camp in the shadow of a little group of pines . . . When we have picked our way through to the other end, we climb upon a high rock with a flat top to it, and heather growing in its crevices; and here we lie, torpid after our tea, and pretend we are viking-folk from the north who have forced our way here by land and sea, and are looking for the first time upon a lake that no one knew before us.

It is hardly surprising that the publisher of the *Pond and Stream* series went bankrupt after three or four titles, but by then Ransome had embarked on a larger enterprise, a book of essays about London literary life. This was his first proper book, and was published in 1907 by Arthur Waugh at Chapman & Hall as *Bohemia in London*. Ransome himself had a mixed opinion of the book. 'It has much rubbish in it but is not wholly bad, though I should be sorry if it were to be reprinted.' Notwithstanding, it was reprinted by Oxford University Press in 1984.

Early in 1909 Ransome married Ivy Walker from Bournemouth, and his daughter Tabitha was born the following year. Neither of these were happy relationships for him, and both ended in disaster. Ivy became, after his mother, the second dominating woman in his life; she combined a sense of excitement and fun with a considerable talent for malice. At the same time he was doing well professionally. His critical study of Edgar Allen Poe received good reviews in late 1910, but characteristically, he was not happy with this book either.

★

IN LATE AUGUST 1910 a momentous event occurred. The Ransomes, with the three-month-old Tabitha, had taken lodgings for the summer at Milford near Godalming in Surrey while he finished Poe. He recorded, many years later in his *Autobiography*, that he made friends with the local postman, who persuaded him to go fishing on the River Wey, where he caught two roach. In one afternoon he rediscovered all the pleasure he had known as a small boy watching a perch float, but had not practised since his father's death more than a decade previously. He was hooked for the rest of his life.

Ransome described this episode somewhat differently six months after the event in his first piece of fishing writing. Among the magazines he wrote for regularly at this time was *The Tramp: An Open Air Magazine*, a glossy, illustrated monthly in the Georgian tradition of 'beer, dog roses and the open road', as Hugh Brogan calls it. It closely matched Ransome's interests of the time, a mixture of literature, new writing and travel. It published articles about England ('Round Devon on a Coaster'), abroad ('Weekends out of England III: Le Havre and Trouville'), fiction (including

Chekhov and Jack London), poetry and book reviews. Most issues had a sporting article, on climbing, winter sports or fishing. Ransome had contributed to several issues of the magazine, with articles on walking themes in a style that is witty and understated, a form he was beginning to perfect in journalism and which is most fully realised more than a decade later in his *Rod and Line* fishing articles. His piece of February 1911, called 'Fishing by the Way', gives a detailed description of this crucial event in his life which differs in significant ways from the account in the *Autobiography*.

In the article, he records walking in town one Saturday morning, and noticing fishing tackle in an ironmonger's window. He went in, and was particularly entranced by the large emerald and scarlet floats which reminded him of fishing for perch as a child. The shopkeeper sent him off to see the President of the B . . . (perhaps Byfleet?) Angling Society, Mr Martin the postman, who gave him a membership card, dug up worms in the back garden, and prepared bread bait. The ironmonger persuaded him to fish with a small nondescript quill rather than the large and gaudy float he coveted, and he eventually caught a small roach, which he returned. As he left the river he threw away the float. In the *Autobiography*, written over 40 years later, he records two roach; perhaps fisherman's licence had taken over by then.

The *Tramp* piece (reprinted later in this volume) is typical of Ransome's style of the period, more directly narrative than his later work, but with a wry and self-deprecating note. He had moved rapidly from the sentimentality of the Elf and the Imp, and from the self-conscious bohemianism of the London essays and criticism. He is well on the way towards the mature style of *Rod and Line* and the children's books.

Although promising much for the future, this episode did not end well financially. In his list of miscellaneous journalism at the front of his 1911 diary (total earnings for the year: 68 pounds four shillings and six pence), is an entry: 'Fishing by the Way', Tramp. The fee of two guineas is written in, then scored through and 'bad debt' written alongside. The magazine folded after the March 1911 issue, and presumably went bankrupt before he was paid. But he must have remained on good terms with Douglas Goldring, the editor, because Goldring was to play a key role in his life three years later when he offered him work in St Petersburg.

Ransome's life at this time was idyllic, despite the ties of an unhappy marriage and a tiny and rather difficult child. He was 27. He had been commissioned to write a book on roads and walking, with 'chapters on my Yewdale gipsies, my French bear-leaders, French roads, English roads, and so on.' This was never published, although his *Tramp* pieces were a start to this enterprise. He had a small light-weight tent that would stow in a knapsack, and, in the autumn of 1910, he walked around the lake country, setting up his tent here and there, and probably relearning to fish for trout, although he does not say so. He sailed on Coniston with Robin Collingwood, and camped on Peel Island, later a model for Wild Cat island in the Swallows and Amazons books, where Robin's sister Ursula swam out with the proofs of Poe fastened on her head. For the winter, he moved into the empty Collingwood house at Lanehead with Ivy, Tabitha and a Jamaican nurse. His marriage was already in trouble. Ivy, no doubt very unhappy, increasingly lived a fantasy life with which he found it difficult to cope.

In May 1911, the Ransomes moved to an old farmhouse at Hatch, near Tisbury in Wiltshire. It stood on a narrow lane which ran through the hamlet about a quarter of a mile above the river Nadder. Ransome walked a great deal with Edward Thomas and Lascelles Abercrombie, but he does not record much fishing at this time, despite the Nadder being a famous chalk stream. As a beginner he was probably unable to get access to such an exclusive trout stream. Later, in 1915, his autobiography mentions fishing in Wiltshire, perhaps on the Nadder.

The house at Hatch was a success for a short time. In his biography of Ransome, Hugh Brogan reports an unpublished memoir by Tabitha describing the house and the life they all lived there which sounds less frightful than Ransome's own description in the *Autobiography*. Ransome had by then acquired several fishing rods, which were hung from hooks along the stone-floored passages. One whole room was full of the mice Ransome bred, together with the certificates he won by exhibiting them. He charmed snakes with his penny whistle, once bringing one home and keeping it in the tea pot.

Making an effort at reconciliation, he and Ivy went out in boats and punts on nearby lakes, with Ivy baling while he fished in pouring rain. They had a monkey, Moab, which drew the cart that took them on fishing expeditions. There was sometimes trouble with the catch. On one occasion, Ransome decided to have mounted some perch and carp he had caught. To keep them fresh, he put the live fish into the bath until he could take them to London. When the day came, he asked the cleaning woman to put the fish in cans while he dressed. She couldn't cope, and the fish were soon all over the place and the woman flat on the floor.

Meanwhile Ransome was developing a style of writing all his own. His critical study, *Edgar Allen Poe*, was published by Secker in 1910 and he then thought about Hazlitt and Robert Louis Stevenson as suitable subjects for books. Although he wrote large sections of the latter, his publisher suddenly asked him to do a study of the more scandalous Oscar Wilde. While Ransome struggled with the book, feeling out of sympathy with the subject, he was also writing book reviews and articles about the countryside for *Country Life* and reading manuscripts for the publishers Macmillan. That year (1911), he records in his autobiography, he wrote on Kant, Peacock, Paraclesus and Stevenson. We now know from the recent discovery of 387 pages with the title 'RLS', handwritten on Russian watermarked paper and found among things left by his daughter Tabitha when she died in 1992, that he took his book on Stevenson a good deal farther than anyone had supposed. In an article in the *Independent on Sunday* magazine (27 March 1994) Christina Hardyment described the package that had passed from a London solicitor's office, where it had lain forgotten, to the Brotherton Collection at Leeds University.

It is scrappy, incomplete and unrevised, but the shape of the work outlined on the opening page is clearly recognisable. 'The book as I see it now should be really two books,' Ransome begins. 'The one should be a plain tale of an adventurous romantic's progress through life in the 19th century, and the other should be a kind of log book, kept by the clerk of a workshop, retaining perhaps a little of the hurried character of the whistle and hum of machinery ... It should I think retain the sharp clean smell of new sawdust.'

Stevenson's ideas, Ransome writes, 'were always those of the craftsman, not the systematic falsehood of the philosopher . . . Stevenson as craftsman knew how, but he did not always know why.' Ransome finished *Oscar Wilde* at Hatch and started translating Remy de Gourmont. It was the high point of his career as a literary critic. Disaster was just around the corner.

In March 1912 Lord Alfred Douglas sued Ransome for libel on the grounds that his book suggested Douglas had been responsible for Wilde's downfall. The publisher Martin Secker, the printers and the Times Book Club, which was distributing copies of *Oscar Wilde* to its members, were all dragged into the case. Printer and publisher soon settled out of court, leaving Ransome and the Book Club to face thirteen months of waiting and four days of trial alone. The Book Club was defended by F. E. Smith, whose main strategy was to defend Ransome and the book itself, which he did in style. The jury found in their favour. Ivy revelled in the limelight and drama, while Ransome, profoundly relieved by the outcome, vowed never again to write anything that could land him in such misfortune.

It was a small respite. Financial and emotional crises threatened. While awaiting the trial, Ransome's new publisher, in whose hands he had put all his current work, absconded and fled abroad with his secretary, accused of bigamy and embezzlement. During this time, too, Ivy told him she was sleeping with a friend of his. Probably relieved, Ransome immediately offered her a divorce, but she withdrew the claim. By the summer of 1913 they agreed, after huge scenes, to separate.

★

A NEW PERIOD was starting in Ransome's life. He had discovered a translated collection of Russian folk tales in the London Library, and this triggered an old plan for a collection of folk stories of his own. Russia sounded the right place, and was far enough away to be out of Ivy's reach. He surreptitiously got a passport and visa and in mid-1913 embarked on a cargo boat for Copenhagen. From there he travelled by ferry and train to Stockholm. He was in St Petersburg a month later, staying with an Anglo-Russian family of a bohemian friend. In no time he was learning Russian from children's reading books and newspapers, and travelling with an English flax merchant. He fished in lakes, and worked from time to time on his book on Stevenson. At the end of only a few weeks, he was filling notebooks with rough translations of a book of folk tales from the Caucasus he found in a shop on the Nevsky Prospect.

He returned to England in the autumn via Berlin and Paris and settled down to spend the winter writing two children's books. The following spring, Douglas Goldring, former editor of *The Tramp*, offered him a free hand to write a descriptive and historical *Guide to St Petersburg*. Ransome did not hesitate, and by mid-May 1914 was once again in Russia. He finished the book in two months, and although it was never published because of the revolution, it taught him more about the city than most Russians knew; it also meant that he was well-placed to chronicle the day-to-day events of the revolution. He reported that, in addition to general goodwill towards the English following a visit by the British fleet, he was particularly helped in his task by a most impressive letter on the embossed paper of the London Library, signed with the sprawling signature of the librarian, angrily demanding the return of some overdue books:

Whenever a policeman or a soldier or minor official tried to bar my way in St Petersburg (and later, on the Russian front or frontier), I found that letter with its crest and that determined signature far more useful than any other 'paper' I possessed. At the sight of it opposition wilted, hands shot up in awed salute, and on one occasion even a messenger was sent before me to warn others that they had better stand to attention. Sometimes, indeed, it did not seem to matter which way up the document was held.

In the weeks after he had finished the guide he relaxed, fished with friends in the Gulf of Finland, and started to work again on Russian folk-tales. Political events were speeding up. Archduke Franz Ferdinand was murdered in Sarajevo at the end of June 1914 by a young Serb. Russia was shaken both by the prospect of a European war, and also by rapidly increasing social unrest and street demonstrations. By the end of July Austria had declared war on Serbia, the Russians had mobilised in defence of their fellow Slavs, and Europe descended into war. Ransome decided that with his excellent Russian and knowledge of the country he would be best employed as a correspondent, and in August he returned once again to England to try to organise such an assignment.

It was not as easy as he had hoped. By the time he returned to England, all the major papers had their Russian correspondents in place. Ransome hung around, hoping something would turn up, wrote articles for newspapers in England and America, went on with his translations, and fished in Wiltshire and Norfolk. He was living at Hatch with Ivy in some sort of compromise, and when she showed an interest in fishing he gave her lessons. After that they fished together for the rest of the season. He even gave her a rod for Christmas.

Ransome returned to Russia in December 1914, by boat to Bergen, by rail across a snowbound Norway and Sweden, by sledge across the Finnish frontier near the Arctic circle with a Lapp driver sitting on his stomach to keep him warm, then train again to the newly-named Petrograd and, for the first time, on to Moscow. In Moscow, he found himself in a magic world. It was so cold his walrus moustache froze into a block of ice, but he drove about looking at the places he had long dreamed of. He became friends with the novelist Hugh Walpole, lodged with a Russian widow and her children near the Donskoi Monastery to improve his Russian, and went to the theatre to see Chekhov, Turgenev and Tolstoy. He was translating Russian folk tales for his intended anthology.

Now aged 30, Ransome felt liberated by Moscow. He walked at night in the Kremlin, read and wrote. His Russian was now good enough to talk easily to people. Early on he started fishing, despite the weather. His diary records:

Talked with tackle-maker by the river who told me there were six fishing-clubs in Moscow and sold me a fishing-rod for a rouble. Had it jointed for seventy kopecks. Fished through the ice under the Kremlin wall.

He was impressed by Hugh Walpole's ability to write rapidly and decisively, unlike his own endless polishing and rewriting. Walpole explained to Ransome that he used a loose-leaf book and, choosing an auspicious day, wrote 'Chapter I' at the top of a page and then simply started; he wrote all the way through until he came to the end, doing very little revision. Prompted by this, the idea came to Ransome for a fantasy story based on his earlier philosophical reading, and he determined to write it with the Walpole method, to prove to himself that he could.

One morning he worked out a synopsis of twenty chapters, and then drove into Moscow by sledge to buy typing paper. He started to write directly on his typewriter, and that afternoon completed six pages. Next day he again wrote furiously during the day and in the evening read the work aloud in Russian to friends. In a week he had written 20,000 words, the following week another 14,000. He was ill, and broke his glasses, but continued; within a month he had finished. He consulted Walpole, now in Petrograd, who approved. Ransome quickly revised the manuscript, and had it professionally typed. It was soon passed by the Censor, and within two and a half months *The Elixir of Life* was posted to Methuen in London.

In his *Autobiography* he records that he took the omens about the success of the book by going fishing. They were mixed. He went out of Petrograd to Lachta on the Gulf of Finland where he had previously noticed a wide river flowing into the gulf. He rowed up a small tributary and watched a hare dancing. Then, tying up at the pier of a railway bridge, he began to fish for pike.

> I hooked a large one and after a struggle brought him to the top and saw him bite through the gimp of the trace just as I had him alongside the boat. I did not know what to make of the omen unless not to be too sure that having finished one story I could write another. At the very last moment the gimp might part.

The Elixir of Life, published in 1915, was Ransome's first full-length novel. Set in the early eighteenth-century, it is a gothic horror story owing much to Poe. The central figure is John Killigrew who, two hundred years earlier, had obtained from an old alchemist the elixir of life, which rejuvenated those who drank it. A link is established between the elixir and Paraclesus and the other early philosopher-alchemists Ransome had been reading and writing about five years earlier. The hero, Richard Stanborough, a foppish young man concerned mainly with philosophy and clothes, is thrown out by his exasperated uncle, a solid Yorkshireman for whom fishing is the chief thing in life. Stanborough falls in with Killigrew, is tempted to drink the elixir, but is saved by falling in love with Rose, Killigrew's ward, and ends by destroying the elixir, marrying Rose and being reconciled with his uncle.

The uncle, who has the robust character tinged with sentimentality of Ransome himself in later life and is thus perhaps the first of several Ransome-figures to appear in his books, is the only real character in this melodramatic book; his reality is established largely though his love of fishing. In this book, fishing plays a small but key role. It provides a point of reference in everyday life for the far fetched events surrounding the elixir of life.

By 1915, fishing had become a symbol of the good life for

Ransome, the sort of life he hoped later to construct for himself. It was also his main anchor to reality in the increasingly unreal way he had lived in England with Ivy, and in Russia. This is the role fishing plays in *The Elixir*. At the end of an angry letter to his wayward nephew, starting 'Jacknapes, I have read your insolent epistle. If I were younger I would make the journey south with the especial purpose of chastising you', the uncle adds:

> P.P.S. The chub are feeding well, and on dull days I have done well with trout. It is a sad pity you do not take to angling.

At the end of the book, after a series of increasingly violent adventures, Stanborough marries Rose and is reconciled to his uncle, who sees the future largely in fishing terms. 'Dick, my lad' he said, 'now you are getting married, you'd best mend your ways and take up a rod'. When the housekeeper objects, the uncle sets out his philosophy for a happy life: 'A rod for fishing, and he must let me show him a cast or two, and how to tie a fly, and then they'll be the happiest married couple between York Minster and Skiddaw.'

Ransome's own marriage had not been much improved by his fishing, but *Elixir* finishes with what for Ransome was at that time a dream in his personal life. The young couple take up life in North Yorkshire, and live happily ever after.

> My uncle died some six years later, thanking God that his illness had come upon him at the end of the trout season, instead of at the beginning. He had the satisfaction of making a fisherman of me, and of fastening a bent pin on the end of a thread, and seeing his first great-nephew catch a minnow. I believe he never caught a salmon himself with greater pride.

The rapid completion of *Elixir* allowed Ransome to return to writing *Old Peter's Russian Tales*, which had been put aside. He moved to the countryside, staying with friends on an estate at Vergezha on the river Volkhov east of Petrograd. Although he was still unwell, he finished a first draft of the book in mid-

June. This time the omens were better; he celebrated, in his usual fashion, Hugh Brogan tells us, 'by going down to the river and offering an artificial fly to a number of rising dace, with the result that I pulled them out one after another, and only stopped because I was driven indoors by clouds of poisonous mosquitoes, who have made a most unholy mess of every visible part of me.'

On the surface, in 1915 the war still made little change in most people's lives in Russia. Ransome was happiest in the country, staying at Vergezha where his friends came to visit, writing *Old Peter* for part of each day, and fishing the rest of the time. He made himself useful by catching supper.

> If work had gone well I would take an hour or so off, to go fishing with some of the younger ones, catching perch, pike, bream, orfes, ruffes and the rarer burbots, all welcomed by the cooks preparing *ukha*, a sort of fish soup not unlike bouillabaisse.

But he knew that these summer days were unreal, and the outside world did not go away. The river, the forest and the long summer nights made everyone happy, but the boys with whom he was fishing would be called up if the war lasted.

Methuen accepted *Elixir*, and Ransome decided to have an operation – several times postponed – for piles. While convalescing he was asked to stand in temporarily for the Petrograd correspondent of the *Daily News*. Ransome accepted, despite his doctors' warnings that he should not work. His first telegram to his new employers was written lying flat on his back, and as a reward his friend Harold Williams bought him a delightful reprint of an old fishing book found in a second-hand bookshop. Although Ransome does not record what the book was, it is likely that it was Aksakov's *Notes on Fishing*, first published in 1847 and republished several times afterwards. Ransome thought it to be the best fishing book in Russian, and later in part translated and published it in England with his own first fishing book.

Ransome was in England again in September 1915, finishing his convalescence. He was given a boost when, between fishing in Wiltshire and on Coniston, he saw the bound copies of *The Elixir of Life* in a bookshop window. But his leave was short-lived. In early October he was told that the *Daily News* correspondent in Russia was still ill, and was invited to take his place as permanent correspondent in Petrograd. Ransome did not hesitate. By late October 1915 he was on his way back to Russia for the big show.

*

Of THE SMALL group of Englishmen in St Petersburg in 1915, Robert Bruce Lockhart was the one most like Ransome, although their acquaintance grew only slowly and in the end their political opinions diverged. A lowland Scot three years younger than Ransome, Lockhart was one of the most flamboyant figures of the time. He had had an uneasy career. Sent to Malaya at the age of 21 to administer a family rubber plantation, he fell in love with a Malay princess, creating a great scandal in both Malaya and Britain, and was invalided home to an unforgiving family. He redeemed himself by passing top of the list into the Consular service. By October 1914 he was Acting British Consul General in Moscow. He was in Moscow during most of the Revolution, like Ransome in daily contact with the Bolshevik leaders. Lockhart was also a committed fisherman, and this was one of the reasons for his friendship with Ransome.

Ransome and Lockhart were both sympathetic to the Russians who wanted political changes, and they were well enough informed to think revolution a possibility. If this happened, they wanted Britain to be on the side of change. Later, after the Bolsheviks took power, these British journalists and diplomats saw the futility of Allied intervention on the side of the White Russians, on the grounds that it would not work and was also wrong. They largely failed to persuade the British government or public of these views, and as a result Ransome was treated with suspicion in England.

Ransome was filing regular reports to his paper, but he did not want yet to abandon other forms of writing. Perhaps fired by the ease with which he had written *Elixir*, he started a new book. This time, fishing would be the point of the book, not merely something the main characters did for recreation. In his biography, Hugh Brogan describes how one day Ransome cornered Bernard Pares, the *Daily Telegraph* correspondent and made him listen to his idea for the new book. It was to be a story about the time of Izaak Walton, with a lot of fishing in it but without any plot or incident. He was finding it difficult to distance himself from the chaos of daily life and get on with it. Now that he was a full time correspondent, finding time for other things was not so easy.

Eventually he wrote over 40,000 words and gave the work a title – *Piscator and his Phillida*. Ransome described it to his mother as a 'Roger de Coverley sort of book'. He had encouraging reactions from some of the English colony in St Petersburg, but Harold Williams, the most influential of the English journalists and adventurers in Russia at that time and a strong father figure for Ransome, condemned the work. Just as he was to do 27 years later with his other major work of fiction on fishing, Ransome put aside the manuscript, and worked no more on it. He makes no mention of the manuscript in his *Autobiography*, and there is now no trace of it.

He was not greatly discouraged. His journalist's life was increasingly busy, with a trip to the front and another to Romania. He taught Hamilton Fyfe, the *Daily Mail* correspondent, to fish for tench in a horse-pond. *Old Peter's Russian Tales* had gone to the printer, but he was still translating, sometimes only a sentence a day, perhaps by this time already working on Aksakov's fishing memoirs. When the pressure became too much, he played chess or went a few miles out of the city to fish, finding the contemplation of a float a 'sovereign clearance for such mind as I had left.' In August he fished for chub in the Moscow river and had his first experience of fishing for large fish using cockchafers as bait.

Old Peter's Russian Tales was published in 1916. It was immediately popular, and has remained so. Ransome had taken a further important step towards establishing his literary identity. One of the stories – 'A Chapter of Fish' – uses his specialised knowledge of Russian fish, and probably could not have been translated and edited convincingly by a non-fisherman. Another chapter – 'The Golden Fish' – is a much more ambitious and better-known story, about a fish which grants wishes. The fisherman who triggers such generosity, by releasing the fish in the first place, reluctantly passes on his wife's increasingly demanding wishes, until at last she asks for too much and loses all she has gained. There is an echo of the character of Ivy, safely in England but not yet completely without the power to make Ransome's life a misery. He returned to England briefly in the autumn of 1916 and saw Ivy on a short trip to Wiltshire, where he spent two days fishing. Much of his time was spent in London trying to tell an obtuse Foreign Office that Russia was ready for revolution, and he also went to the Lakes. By early December he was back in Russia, where he was thrown straight into the rush of events by the murder of Rasputin. Revolution was clearly ahead.

It came in two stages, in February and October 1917. Ransome's reporting of the revolution was, unusually for a foreign journalist in Petrograd and Moscow at that time, sympathetic to the Russian people and, at least initially, to the revolutionaries themselves. His knowledge of Russian, of Russians and of Petrograd, stood him in good stead. His account, in his journalism and later books, is simple, factual, even matter-of-fact, but vivid and direct.

I worked my way through the crowd and came upon an orator much excited, yelling 'Bread! Bread!' He smote on the side of a tramcar and cried, 'Bread! Does the tramcar give us bread? No! Then let us overturn the tramcar!' What, in the end, happened to the tramcar I do not know, becoming more interested in keeping myself the right way up. A line of Cossacks had spread across the road, and, riding on the pavement, had begun to move steadily through the crowd. What interested me was the expression on their faces. It was hard to believe that these were the ferocious Cossacks. Benevolent and cheerful they moved along the pavements and though that night when I undressed I found myself bruised from being squeezed between two of their horses, it was clear that if the Autocracy thought that it could count on the Cossacks it was mistaken. 'Go for the police, not us,' shouted a woman. A Cossack shouted back 'Don't be afraid. We shall square accounts with the police later.'

Ransome reported the revolution for his paper, the *Daily News*, and also wrote pieces for the *Observer*, although J. L. Garvin, editor of the *Observer*, did not like his pro-Russian stance. Despite the efforts of Ransome and a handful of other journalists, people in England were badly informed about events in Russia and preoccupied with the war in Europe. Fighting had started in the streets in Petrograd by June 1917, and there was a food crisis. Ransome escaped occasionally to the suburbs to fish for roach and perch, and the fish he brought home were a welcome addition to the larder. But he rarely had time for this. He dreamed of going home to England and getting in some serious fishing; a letter to his mother around this time sums up his mood:

> Who cares for lack of printed books
> While there are fish in southern brooks?
> And who enforced oblivion recks
> With better fish in northern becks?

He finally got away in October 1917, missing the October Revolution. He caught a perch of over 3lb in Beckford's lake at Fonthill, and had a brief meeting with Ivy and Tabitha. Most important, he made friends with Francis Hirst, who had been sacked as editor of *The Economist* the previous year because of his anti-war views and the way he had used the *Economist* to oppose the war. Hirst was a passionate fisherman, with a stretch of the Meon, a small chalk stream in Hampshire, which was to become a haven for Ransome in the following years.

He returned to Russia in December and found Petrograd in chaos as the Bolsheviks tried to learn how to govern, though the city was quieter than it had been in the summer. By now he had excellent introductions and within a few days he had met Lenin and Trotsky. At Trotsky's office in the Smolny

Institute, a former girls' school and now the revolutionary headquarters, he met and soon fell in love with Evgenia Petrovna Shelepina, a 23-year old woman completely committed to the Bolsheviks who later became Trotsky's personal secretary.

Ransome's closest friend among the Bolsheviks at this time was Karl Radek, who was in charge of the Press Bureau at the Commissariat for Foreign Affairs. They met because Radek, in pursuit of his official duties, had opened a parcel of personal belongings Ransome had sent on from Stockholm; Radek had been intrigued to meet a person whose baggage consisted of a volume of Shakespeare, a folding chess board, and books on fishing, navigation and folklaw. They got on well, and Radek's wife was friendly with Evgenia. Through the Radeks, Ransome had better access to the Bolsheviks than any other correspondent, or most diplomats.

His influence as a journalist was never higher than at this moment. He saw Trotsky and the other Bolshevik leaders almost daily, and sometimes played chess with them; he was able to report their views to his paper often before the British Ambassador had reported back to the Foreign Office. At times it seems almost as though the Bolsheviks were using him as a channel of information to the west. But western governments did not share the view of Ransome and a few other journalists, such as Philips Price of the *Manchester Guardian*, that the Russians had no alternative but to make a separate peace with the Germans, and that western intervention against the Bolsheviks would be disastrous. Both these views turned out to be right, but Ransome and others who argued them gradually came to be considered dangerous reds.

At the start of 1918, with easy access to Trotsky and other leaders, Ransome was writing knowledgeably about the situation which faced the Bolsheviks when they began negotiating a separate peace with Germany at Brest-Litovsk. Ransome's articles were read by the War Cabinet in London as a message that Trotsky wanted to improve relations with Britain, and Lloyd George sent Robert Bruce Lockhart back to Russia at the head of a special mission to make contact with

the Bolshevik leaders. Ransome describes Lockhart, who was
by this time very popular in Russia, as 'a cheerful young man
with a taste for gipsies, wine and dancing'. This endeared him
to the Moscow society of the old regime, but he was a good
mixer and, 'with a red cloth-bound *History of British Socialism*
under his arm, was soon on better terms with Trotsky than I
was'.

Ransome and Lockhart now saw each other almost daily. In
his book, *Memoirs of a British Agent*, Lockhart's attitude was
admiring but a little patronising.

> Ransome was a Don Quixote with a walrus moustache, a
> sentimentalist, who could always be relied upon to
> champion the under-dog, and a visionary, whose imagina-
> tion had been fired by the revolution. He was on excellent
> terms with the Bolsheviks and frequently brought us
> information of the greatest value. An incorrigible roman-
> ticist, who could spin a fairy-tale out of nothing, he was an
> amusing and good-natured companion. As an ardent
> fisherman who had written some charming sketches on
> angling, he made a warm appeal to my sympathy, and I
> championed him resolutely against the secret service idiots
> who later tried to denounce him as a Bolshevik agent.

Ransome introduced Lockhart to his Bolshevik contacts,
especially Radek. On account of his pipe, pile of books always
under his arm, and huge revolver strapped to his side,
Lockhart thought Radek looked like a cross between a
professor and a bandit.

Stuck in Moscow in a deteriorating political atmosphere,
Ransome and Lockhart were brought together not only by
their common political views, but also by fishing. Like
Ransome, Lockhart was able to get out of the city occasionally
since he had access to the Bolshevik leaders who seem to have
had no trouble in accepting that these two wanted to fish in
the middle of a revolution.

> Once or twice during the summer of 1918 I stole away from
> Moscow to spend a quiet hour by the banks of the river.

My special pass from Trotsky gave me complete freedom, and with respectful awe the armed sentries, who guarded every exit from the city, raised the Schlagbaum and waved me through. In those turbulent days, too, I saw much of [Ransome] . . . His cheerful conversation, in which he always mingled politics with fishing, did much to keep me sane . . . I shall always regret that I never discussed fishing with Lenin. It might have been the best approach to that not unkind, but politically cold genius.

Ransome was a much more successful angler than he was. These short holidays were to remain among Lockhart's best memories of Russia. He records that Lenin was a fisherman, as was Chekhov, and quotes Gorki's account of Lenin in Capri being taught sea-fishing with a hand line by the local fisherman.

The Italians explained to him that the fish must be struck as soon as the fingers felt the vibration of the line. They gave him a practical demonstration and exclaimed: 'Cosi, drin, drin. Capisce?' A second or two later Lenin felt a bite, struck savagely, and hauled in a fish with a child-like joy and a shout of 'Drin-drin'. The Italians laughed and thereafter christened him Signor Drin-Drin. When he left Capri, they remembered him and used to ask Gorki: 'How is Drin-Drin getting on? The Tsar hasn't caught him yet, has he?'

Petrograd at this time was a turbulent town and Ransome was in the middle of revolutionary events. This was the most exciting moment of his life, and he joined in with enthusiasm, delighting in the small events as much as the large. He pointed out to a Menshevik delegate at one of the early assemblies, who had no spoons in his hotel, that even revolutionary peasants might lift the spoons in the hotel to show that they had really been to Moscow. He reported with satisfaction the case of the little Moscow fishing club which lost its boats in the first excitement of the revolution but had them very properly restored when the fishermen said they were a co-operative society whose object it was to increase the food supply of the population. He even applauded the Russian who, at the height of the revolution, when everything was impossible to obtain, contrived by the most elaborate methods to add to his already enormous collection of fishing tackle, without the slightest intention of ever going fishing with it. He felt at home with Russians of all sorts, and with the revolutionary atmosphere.

By now Ransome was an unofficial member of the British diplomatic mission. In February 1918 the Western embassies feared that Petrograd was about to fall to the Germans, and Lockhart, who wanted to stay behind with the Bolshevik last-ditch defenders, sent Ransome off with the diplomatic train to Vologda, three hundred miles to the east, with instructions to pick the best building in town and hoist a British flag on it. The only problem was that no British flag could be found, and Ransome had to make do with a Pilot Jack (a Union Jack with a wide white border) from a British ship on the forzen Neva. Little came of this, and by early March he was back in Petrograd. The flag was never flown at Vologda, but Ransome kept it, and later used it on his own sailing boat.

In April 1918 Evgenia was able to do Lockhart a service. Following the signature of the Brest-Litovsk treaty which ended Russian involvement in the war, a German ambassador, Count Mirbach, was appointed to Moscow. Britain and Germany were, of course, still at war. The Bolsheviks proposed to put him and his large party up at the hotel where Lockhart and Ransome lived. Lockhart complained furiously to Chicherin, the Commissar for Foreign Affairs, who was unable to help. In despair, he went to find Trotsky, who was at a meeting in the Kremlin. Evgenia came to Lockhart's rescue and got Trotsky on the telephone. He promised immediate action, and was as good as his word. The hapless Count Mirbach was moved to alternative lodgings; scarcely two months later he was assassinated by Maria Spiridonova of the Left Social Revolutionary Party.

Lockhart was able to return this service later in the year. In mid-1918 Ransome and Evgenia decided to leave Russia. By October, when there was a possibility that the White army might occupy Moscow, her life was in danger because of her position as Trotsky's secretary. Lockhart, as British Consul General, asked the Foreign Office in London to allow him to put Evgenia on Ransome's passport. They refused. Lockhart went ahead anyway and issued a passport to Ransome which included Evgenia as his wife although they were not yet married. In the event, Evgenia never used this passport, preferring to travel on her own Russian one until she married Ransome in 1924. But by this time they were more or less inseparable.

Ransome's position in Moscow grew more precarious. He had made no secret of his general support for the Bolshevik objectives, and after the Brest-Litovsk Treaty he believed that British policy should be to recognise that Russia was in no condition to fight Germany, and that for the British to join Germany to fight the Russians was not at all sensible. For the White Russians and some people in Britain, this was treachery, the sort of thing to be expected from a well-known red. Members of Lockhart's mission circulated wildly exaggerated accounts of Ransome's dealings with the Bolsheviks. Lockhart himself was more sensible, and brought Ransome together with the notorious and often ill-informed English spy Sidney Reilly, perhaps to show him Ransome didn't have a forked tail. The rumours became so incriminating that the Foreign Office investigated whether criminal charges could be brought against Ransome and his friend Philips Price. The verdict was that they could not.

One of the things which gave Ransome most pleasure during his time in Russia was his discovery of the books of Sergei Aksakov, combining as they do Ransome's own interests in literature and fishing. Sergei Timofeevich Aksakov was born in 1791 and brought up on family estates in the eastern Russian steppes. He briefly held civil service posts, but spent much of his adult life in and around Moscow. He became a writer late in life, under the influence of Gogol, and was well-known for three elegant books of memoirs about his grandfather and his own childhood and upbringing. He also wrote what is probably the first book about fishing in Russian, *Notes on Fishing*, in 1847, as well as several books of sporting memoirs.

Aksakov's three volumes of family life were published in English from 1915 onwards in a translation by J. D. Duff, and two of the volumes are still in print. Either Ransome was unaware of this, since he retranslated key sections of the childhood books, or he was not happy with the Duff version. Ransome, who can be trusted in such a matter, quite often translates the names of fishes differently from Duff, and in places keeps details from the Russian text that Duff glosses over. Aksakov's own excitement comes across very directly from Ransome, as could be expected of a fisherman. He also translated parts of Aksakov's fishing book, and put them and the childhood fishing memories, together with an explanatory and linking text, at the end of his own fishing book *Rod and Line* when it was published in 1929. This section is missing from current editions of the book, although Ransome insisted on keeping it in when his publishers wanted to remove it during his lifetime. He felt strongly about this. The Ransome Room at the Museum of Lakeland Life and Industry at Abbot Hall in Kendal, has his own copy of the 1947 edition of *Rod and Line*, with the original sub-title 'With Aksakov on Fishing' left out; there is an indignant manuscript note by Ransome restoring the sub-title, and adding 'omitted by some half wit at Cape's, restored that same year.'

Aksakov's account is vivid and full of the childish enthusiasm that was so appealing to Ransome. He describes how, as a small boy in 1794, he first fished the Dema river on a journey between the town of Ufa and his grandfather's country estate. He was helped by the local Bashkir nomads and by his own servant Evseyitch.

I began to beg my father to show me the fishing. At last we set out and Evseyitch with us. He had already cut some elm rods. They made floats of thick green reed, fastened the lines on and began to fish from the ferry-raft, trusting the Bashkirs, who said, 'Ai, Ai, fish bite very well.' Evseyitch made the lightest of the rods ready for me and fastened to it a thin line with a small hook. He baited it with a scrap of kneaded up bread, cast out the tackle and put the rod into my right hand. My left was firmly held by my father. On the instant the float stood on end and then sank down into the water. 'Pull! pull!' cried Evseyitch and with a great struggle I pulled out a fair-sized roach. I trembled all over as if in a fever and was beside myself with joy. I seized my prey with both hands and ran to show it to mother.

Descriptions of the Russian countryside and of the seasons are well conveyed in the translation by Ransome who was not at this time writing such things himself, but who was susceptible to elegant writing. Aksakov's description of the ice breaking up in spring on a big river is a classic:

> The river Bielaya could be seen from the steps of our house and I impatiently awaited its opening. Every time I asked father or Evseyitch, 'When will we be going to Sergeievka?' they answered, 'As soon as the river stirs.' At last came this longed-for day and hour. Evseyitch came hurriedly into my nursery and said, with a voice full of joy and excitement, 'The Bieleya has stirred!' Mother gave me permission and, in a moment, warmly dressed, I was standing on the steps greedily following with my eyes the long strip of blue, dark and sometimes yellow ice moving between the motionless banks. Already the road across the frozen river had floated far away and an unlucky black cow was running to and fro on it, as if mad, from one bank to the other. The women and girls standing round me accompanied with exclamations of pity each unsuccessful movement of the hurrying animal. I could hear its lowing and was very sorry for it. A bend in the river took it round a high cliff behind which it disappeared the road and the black cow running upon it. Suddenly two dogs were seen on the moving ice, but their anxious scurrying aroused not pity but laughter in the people standing about me, for all were sure that the dogs would not drown but would leap or swim ashore. I could easily believe this, and, forgetting the poor cow, laughed with the rest. The dogs were not long in justifying the general expectation and soon got across to the bank. The ice still moved in a powerful, solid, unbroken, endless mass.

Evseyitch, fearing the hard cold wind, said to me, 'Let's go indoors, little hawk, the river won't break up for some time yet and you will catch a chill. Better if I come and tell you when the ice begins to crack.' Very unwillingly I obeyed, but mother was very pleased and praised both Evseyitch and me. And indeed it was not until an hour later that Evseyitch came to tell me that the ice on the river was breaking up. Once more mother let me go for a short time and, dressing up still more warmly, I went out and saw yet another new picture I had never seen before. The ice split and broke into separate blocks. Water splashed between them. They collided with one another. The bigger and stronger submerged the weaker, but, if it met with much resistance, it rose with one edge on high. Sometimes it floated for a long time in that position. Sometimes both blocks broke up into fragments with a crash and sank in the water. A dull roar, sometimes with noises in it like a creaking or a distant groaning, came distinctly to our ears. After watching for some time this tremendous and terrible spectacle I went back to mother and told her feverishly and at length all that I had seen.

These childhood memoirs are especially interesting for the light they throw on the complex relationship between the small boy and his mother. She hated and feared his fishing (she was a sophisticated town lady who loathed life in the country), and used it as a weapon to control the child. Mother and son maintained a passionate but fraught relationship until the boy grew up. It may be that part of Ransome's interest in Aksakov is in the way his tortured relationship with his mother mirrored Ransome's with his own mother, with Ivy his first wife, and later even with Evgenia, of whom he was more than a little afraid. When, three decades later, Evgenia condemned the first chapters of the manuscript of Ransome's great historical novel *The River Comes First*, she might have been Aksakov's mother refusing to let him go fishing. Ransome accepted the judgement as dutifully as Aksakov would have done, and never went back to the book; the difference was that Aksakov was a small child and Ransome was aged 58.

The vehemence with which Ransome condemns Aksakov's mother when she stopped him fishing, so unlike Ransome's normal calm, perhaps betrays these feelings. This is Ransome summarising Aksakov's story in *Rod and Line*:

His father had told him that [the Ika] was as good as the Dema and promised that they should camp for the night on its banks and fish. However, when they were still some way from the river, his mother announced that she would prefer to stop in a Chuvash village, from which there was a fine view. 'What were fine views to me?' says Aksakov bitterly. 'All my dreams of fishing in the evening, when, as my father had told me, the fish bit so well, in a river as good as the Dema, dissolved like smoke and I stood as if sentenced to some kind of punishment.' However, his father borrowed a spare horse and drove on to the river. The wretched woman, who deserves for all ages the reprobation of all true fishermen, gave the little boy leave to go with his father so unwillingly and with such conditions that she took away the whole of his pleasure. He went with his father, caught a perch, but was unable to forget his mother's disapproval, fished as if in disgrace and in the end wept and returned to their stopping-place.

*

IN EARLY August 1918, Ransome retreated from Moscow to Stockholm, having arranged for Evgenia to join the Russian Legation there. They found rooms in a house close to the water on the sea approaches to the city, and Ransome fished for pike and observed and reported events in Russia. But he was not happy. He was with Evgenia, although still married to Ivy, who would not give him a divorce. In these circumstances he felt he could not live in England, which was where he wanted to be. He feared that his writing was deteriorating, and wrote gloomily to his mother from Stockholm:

I doubt if I shall ever write again . . . as for English prose, on which once I rather fancied myself, its gone for good. I am more than ever convinced that I am finished *qua* writer, and as I have no intention of setting up as a politician, my ambitions are getting smaller every day, and are practically circumscribed by a cottage in the country, a trout stream, and some winter pike fishing. Russia has broken stouter hearts than mine.

A quick trip to Russia with Evgenia in early 1919, as a result of which he wrote a short book entitled *Six Weeks in Russia in 1919*, still an excellent source for the personalities and atmosphere of that time, did not improve his mood. He was still dogged by allegations of being a red agent. Leaving Evgenia in Moscow, he returned to Britain through Finland in the company of Lincoln Steffens, a prominent left-wing American journalist, and William Bullitt, later United States Ambassador in both Moscow and Paris.

Twenty years afterwards Bullitt told Ransome what had happened during that journey. The Americans had come to Russia with a third person, who had stayed behind on the return. British officials had asked the Finnish police to arrest Ransome at the frontier, to put him in prison, and in no circumstances to let him contact the British Consulate. When Ransome crossed the frontier with the two Americans, the Finns assumed he was the third, absent, member of the party, and took little notice. A day or two later, a member of the British Secret Service presented himself at the frontier. The Finns assumed he was Ransome, and arrested him immediately; the more he insisted he should be allowed to see the British Consul, the more the Finns were convinced they had the right person. By the time the mistake was discovered, Ransome was safely on his way back across the North Sea. But this was not the end; on his return to London he was pursued by the same rumours.

Ransome records the episode in his *Autobiography*. He was met off the train at King's Cross by a tall man in dark clothes and a bowler hat, who took him to Scotland Yard to be interviewed by Sir Basil Thomson, the head of the Yard.

I was shown into Sir Basil Thomson's room and asked to sit down in the famous chair where so many criminals had sat before me. Sir Basil, extremely grim, looked hard at me. After a moment's silence, he said, 'Now, I want to know just what your politics are.'

'Fishing,' I replied.

He stared. 'Just what do you mean by that?'

I told him the exact truth, that in England I had never had any political views whatever, that in Russia I believed that this very fact had let me get a clearer view of the revolution than I could otherwise have got, that I now had one clear political opinion, which was that Intervention was a disastrous mistake, and that I hoped it would come to an end and so release me to turn to my ordinary interests.

'Fishing?' he said.

'We are very near the beginning of the season,' I replied.

From then on, Sir Basil was a friend and supporter.

In England, his priority was to agree a divorce with Ivy. He visited her and Tabitha (now almost nine years old) at Hatch, where he gave Tabitha her first fishing rod. In her account written for Hugh Brogan, Tabitha recalls how on this trip Ransome tried to teach her to fish on the Little Nadder and at Slapton Sands. He showed her how to avoid letting her shadow fall on the water which would alert the fish, and to be silent; she had to thread her own worms. But she caught little, and unlike the young Aksakov, was not convinced. At Slapton Ransome caught a very large pike, which must have pleased him, although the boatman was not very competent and took a long time to beat it to death. Ivy did not agree to a divorce. Ransome left for London, then went to Leeds, where his mother had a house, and dictated his book *Six Weeks in Russia* to a shorthand typist in nineteen days.

Evgenia was still in Moscow, and was now in some danger following the White Russian advances which threatened the city. Ransome tried desperately to get to Moscow, but could find nobody ready to employ him. In an attempt to keep calm, he fished for trout with the Collingwoods on Coniston and with Francis Hirst on the Meon, and for pike in Norfolk and on the Medway.

Eventually his luck improved. C. P. Scott, the legendary editor of the *Manchester Guardian*, had liked *Six Weeks in Russia*, and needed a Russia correspondent. He hired Ransome, who set off for Moscow as soon as he could get a passport and visas. The war between the Bolsheviks and the Whites was in full swing, and Ransome had great difficulty in crossing the lines. At last, with considerable courage, he walked across the front from Reval in Estonia carrying a diplomatic message from the Estonian government to the Bolsheviks, returning the same way a few weeks later with a reply, and Evgenia.

They settled in Reval (later renamed Tallinn) on the Baltic coast of Estonia, from where he reported for the *Guardian* on events in Russia, and they bought their first boat. There was a small lake near the house where he caught perch and pike for his landlady, and he fished the little river Joesuu in a nearby bay. He and Evgenia were given a tame hedgehog which ate ants, woodlice, bread-and-milk and scraps of meat.

On one visit to Russia he was able to visit his old lodgings, where he found that although his rooms had been sacked by the political police, his landlady had managed to save his fishing rod as one of his 'two most important things' (the other was a coffee mill he had acquired in Romania during a bombing raid).

Although Ransome fished regularly during this time, he had conceived a passion for boats which was to stay with him for most of the rest of his life. The first small boat soon gave way to a larger one, *Racundra*, able to undertake long Baltic explorations. Things began to improve. In the summer of 1921 they moved to Kaiserwald, a small town outside Riga, capital of Latvia, where they had a small house beside a lake in a wood, and a Lettish boat builder made him a small and very simple boat for fishing and sailing. They moved between Riga and Reval for the next two or three years. There was excellent fishing in both places, at sea and on neighbouring lakes at Reval, and on two delightful hill rivers near Riga, the Amat and the Brasle, both packed with trout and grayling. Ransome and a fishing companion stayed in a peasant's hut, where the fleas were so hungry that the fishermen had no difficulty in being on the river by 4.30 in the morning.

On a trip to England during this period he renewed his friendship with Ted Scott, son of the *Manchester Guardian*'s editor, and taught his eldest son to fish with a worm, with surprising results, as he records in his *Autobiography*:

> He was still a small boy when I came to Bosley one summer day and found them all at lunch. I put my car in the yard and noticed a fishing rod leaning against the wall. From the rod a long line hung and trailed along the ground. Thinking him a careless little brute to leave the line without winding it on his reel, I followed it and found that the end of it was buried in a tin of earth. In the earth, still on the hook, was a worm. Dick had kindly and thoughtfully made his worm comfortable while he ate his lunch.

Ransome's life had improved. He was able to fish and sail whenever he wanted (Evgenia preferred sailing to fishing), and was now undertaking adventurous expeditions. He records how on a voyage to Helsinki and through the Finnish islands they lived on eggs that tasted of seaweed, milk that also tasted of seaweed, and perch and pike they caught; the fish from the gulf were very much tastier than the same fish caught in fresh water. The pike behaved like salmon, spending the winter at sea and running up the streams to spawn in spring, when they had to avoid people lining the banks to catch them with spears, traps and nets. By 1923 he had written a very successful book, *Racundra's First Cruise*, about these trips.

On a trip to Moscow at this time to arrange for Russian contributors to an Economic Supplement to the *Manchester Guardian* he was taught to use a steel spinning rod and free-running reel by Colonel Mackie on the tennis court at the British Mission. Mackie, a giant of a man, cast so accurately that he could land his spinner in a bucket at the other end of the tennis court.

In 1924 Ivy finally agreed to a divorce. Within a month

Arthur and Evgenia were married at the British Consulate in Reval, and six months later they returned to live in England. The exile was over.

★

R ANSOME was now no longer just a knowledgeable Russian reporter but one of the *Manchester Guardian*'s star foreign correspondents. Shortly after his arrival back in England he was dispatched to Egypt and Sudan, where he approved of the colonial government, 'a team of Old Blues, carrying out a semi-Bolshevik policy, running a dictatorship on behalf of the native proletariat.' A few months later he was off again to China. He went by boat through the Indian Ocean, taking a small travelling rod made for him by Farlows, and fished in the sea on the way out, missing a shark at Aden, but doing better at Penang, where he caught catfish and a poisonous sea serpent. He was disappointed by the fishing he saw in China, which included men spearing fish in the lake at the Summer Palace; his own fishing was a single cold afternoon unsuccess-fully pursuing carp in a Shanghai park. He returned across Siberia and central Asia by train, thinking only of getting home to fish.

> It takes fourteen days in the train to crawl home from Peking . . . But the fourteen days go fast if the ice has broken in the Siberian rivers, and the rod in the rack is promising fishing in England . . . The last couple of days of that journey are hardly noticeable at all, so eagerly is the fisherman's mind casting ahead of him, and watching already for a rising trout in a pool nearly three hundred miles the other side of London.

Early in 1925 the Ransomes found the house they had been looking for, a small cottage in the hills east of Windermere, with a large barn that he eventually turned into a study. Low Ludderburn was high above the valley of the little Winster, and soon Ransome had permission to fish the upper part of the stream. When he bought a car, he was within reach of the rivers he had fished as a child with his father, especially the Crake where his father had had his fatal accident.

A fishing friend, Colonel Kelsall, had recently moved into a house across the valley and, having no telephone, together they devised a signalling system using a combination of diamonds, squares, triangles (each denoting a letter of the alphabet) and a cross, hung against the walls of their respective houses. The signals play an important part in *Winter Holiday*, though in real life they were to enable them to plan fishing expeditions. The largest set of signal combinations in the revised code ('February 1933. Cancels previous code.') – now in the possession of Dick Kelsall – concerned fishing:

D+	Shall we fish today?
DX	Shall we fish tomorrow?
+A	Shall we fish on . . . (day of week)?
+B	When shall we start?
+D	Shall we start at . . . from here?
XA	Shall we start at . . . from your house?
XB	Have you got any minnows?
XC	Have you got any worms?
XD	Have you got any maggots?
AC+	Salmon
ACX	White trout
AD+	Brown trout
ADX	Grayling
A+C	Eels
A+D	Perch
AXC	How many?

Other combinations dealt with the weather, places, days of the week and times, as well as messages about visits to each other and shared rides into town. Colonel Kelsall, who had recently retired from the Royal Engineers, took his code very seriously, keeping the code book padlocked when not in use. As Ransome remarks in his *Autobiography*, 'the fish never had a chance of learning beforehand what was planned for them.' Colonel Kelsall's diary records several expeditions farther afield with Ransome, especially to fish for grayling on the

frozen Eden at Great Ormside and Appelby, where they had
to break the ice at the edge of the river before fishing.

The two young Kelsall boys seem to have been among the
first children that Ransome got to know well, immediately
developing the easy and encouraging manner that was later
to characterise both his own relationships with children
and those of his surrogate self (especially Captain Flint and
the Fisherman in *The Big Six*) with children in the Swallows
and Amazons books.

Ransome and their father took the two boys fishing in the
Winster just below their house. Desmond was a keen fisherman, but Dick wasn't interested. However his mother
persuaded him to have a go on his own and he set off with a
thin ash plant, black thread instead of line, and a bent pin, with
a small tin of worms in damp moss. He fished a stretch of
the beck well away from the others, and caught a fair sized
trout, the largest caught by the party that day. Dick Kelsall
remembers the postcard Ransome sent him the next day:

> Congratulations on catching the best fish of the season. My
> best was only 7 inches. Perhaps they like thread. Anyhow
> now you have started on them, I suppose the trout in the
> Winster are in for a hard time.

At the bottom of the card was a sketch of a boy with a bent rod
catching a whopper with the caption 'RK catching the Winster
Whale.' This incident – the small boy catching the largest fish
while his elders and betters fish unsuccessfully elsewhere –
later turns up scarcely disguised in *Swallowdale*.

Desmond Kelsall, then aged about nine, was already keen,
and Ransome seems to have taken a special interest in his
development as a fisherman. He remembers Ransome sharing
his great enthusiasm at his first sea trout in the Winster,
although it weighed only half a pound. He also remembers
Ransome catching a 3lb pike on Windermere, using a perch
they had caught as live bait; Ransome talked to the pike as he
played it, and it was the largest fish Desmond had seen at that
time. Ransome went to endless trouble to teach Dick river-
craft, how to fish a worm effectively in a flood, where the

ANOTHER ONE TO PUT BACK
(from *The Big Six*)

trout were likely to be lying, how to present the bait, and
especially how to hook them. The fact that few fish were as
much as half a pound made no difference to Ransome's
enthusiasm as a teacher. Ransome also used to show the

Kelsalls his new equipment, including one of the early
Illingworth spinning reels, persuading Colonel Kelsall to buy
one himself, which Desmond Kelsall still has.

★

THE LIFE of a foreign correspondent no longer suited
Ransome. He was 41. He had found a perfect house, had
new and old friends, could fish every week, and was settling
down at last with Evgenia. Travel abroad was no longer
welcome. In 1925, an entirely new opportunity arose. On a
visit to Manchester, he complained to Ted Scott that the
Guardian was not doing what it might for fishermen. Scott
immediately said 'You had better show us what you think we
ought to do for them', and gave him a column a week with
which to do as he liked. Ransome was delighted, and
immediately started researching for the column, leaving
Evgenia to finish the house at Low Ludderburn.

> This gave me an excuse for fishing, and for several years I
> wrote a fishing essay a week. While Evgenia supervised a
> local jobbing builder and his mate turning the upper floor of
> the old barn into the finest workroom I have had in all my
> life, I managed to fish all the local rivers I had known as a
> boy: besides the Cumberland Derwent, the Hodder, the
> Ribble, the Dove, the Eden, the Eck at Inverchapel, and so
> on, a perfect orgy.

This was the start of his 'Rod and Line' column in the
Manchester Guardian, which ran most weeks, except when he
was out of the country, from mid-August 1925 to mid-
September 1929.

The column was a high point in Ransome's writing. He
demonstrated a sustained ability to engage the reader. His
style had matured; fined down by more than a decade of
critical books, political reporting and comment, it was now
sparse, ironic, transparent, quick and practical, full of the
small surprises and illuminating phrases of a writer who is
utterly confident of his material. And Ransome knew this
material very well indeed.

8 *Peter Duck* and *Beetle II* on Amouk Lake near Aleppo,
Syria, where the Ransomes visited the Altounyans in 1932

9 Ransome with a large salmon at Low Ludderburn

10 Ransome tying an elver fly

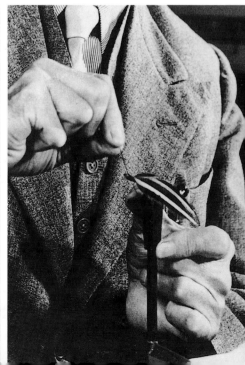

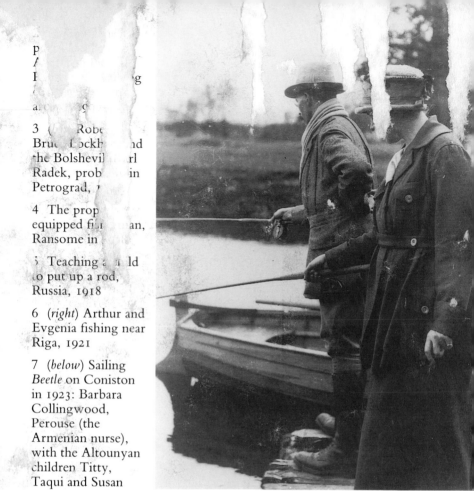

1 Arthur Ransome, fishing for bream in Russia, 1918

The column brought him into direct contact with many fishermen, a contact which he enjoyed and which stimulated him. With characteristic modesty, he later credited his readers with much of the merit of the column.

For many years now I have been writing a weekly article on fishing, a subject on which one would imagine there was really very little to say. I still remember how difficult were the first few weeks, and how, as time went on, I came to find myself merely an amanuensis for my fellow-fishermen. They wrote the articles, not I. I only held the pen.

His subjects ranged widely. In typical Ransome manner, he wrote in his notebook from time to time a list of potential future titles – 'watching fish', 'beetles and spiders', 'a hatchery' – many of which were later written. Their geographic scope was often limited to northern English waters – the Ribble, Lune, Hodder and Eden – but then suddenly jumped to Hampshire, Estonia or China. Although he himself had mainly been a game and pike fisherman since his return from Russia, Ransome wrote knowledgeably about coarse fishing, and occasionally sea fishing. He informed his readers about new and different techniques – the first column was about the new American barbless hooks being introduced to Britain – and regularly wrote about equipment or favourite flies. He contributed occasional obituaries of well-known fishermen, most of whom had been personal friends. He described fishing competitions with enthusiasm, and regularly reviewed fishing books. Some of the pieces were more personal, concerning Ransome's own feelings about bulls, or fish kettles, or sportsmanship, or simply about what it was about fishing that he enjoyed, and these are among those which read best today.

Because they are more often in the countryside than most people, fishermen are particularly aware of pollution and environmental destruction, and there is a long history of fishermen writing passionately in defence of the countryside. Ransome was not especially interested in nature or ecology as such, but he had a strong sense of place, and loved the countryside. He felt strongly about the environmental threats of his day. He wrote with feeling about river and lake pollution by industrial waste. 'With the river low it should be possible to trace the poison to its source. There can be no excuse for letting filth into the river in such a place, and none for allowing the practice to continue.' He was worried about tar from the roads poisoning neighbouring waters, and the dangers of deforestation and land clearance. Unlike many fishermen of the time, he wrote in defence of kingfishers and herons, not grudging them a share of the fish. This was an important advance on F. M. Halford's position, only twenty years earlier, that kingfishers 'are the most deadly foes of the fry and smaller yearlings . . . all and every means should be used to get rid of them.' Ransome was particularly incensed by poachers using dynamite to kill fish: 'even illegal netting is less destructive than this form of scoundrelism'. In one column he made a thoroughly modern economic analysis of the cost of river pollution by estimating the replacement cost of the dead trout.

At times the column took on a campaigning tone. On 17 September 1926 he drew the attention of his readers to the report of the Standing Committee on River Pollution, and the hopes that gave rise to:

> Something is at last being done to save rivers as yet not ruined. Something may some day be done to restore dead, murdered rivers like the Irwell to the life that man has taken from them. One factory after another will consume its own refuse. The river will cease to be a sewer, and the day will come when men stop in crossing a bridge in Man chester to see the trout feeding below it. A writer in 'The Fishing Gazette' mentions that sea-trout have gone up the Wear, thanks to the cleanness of that river on account of the coal strike. After the revolution in Russia, when for a long time almost all factories were at a standstill, a man who had lost most of his possessions comforted himself with the thought that at least there was now fine fishing in the Fontanka, the canal that runs through the middle of

Leningrad. We do not want to prolong the coal strike, nor to bring our factories to a standstill, but sooner or later they will have not only to stop poisoning the air with smoke but also to find a better way of dealing with their refuse than the poisoning of the rivers.

He had a particular aversion to the fast motorboats which had since his childhood taken over Windermere and other lakes. The Hullabaloos who figure prominently in *Coot Club*, the *nouveaux riche* landlubbers racing in large noisy motorboats along the Norfolk Broads, with their radios at full blast, disturbing birds and sailing boats alike, are already singled out for attack in *Rod and Line* in 1927:

> The Board of Trade has, it appears, handed over Windermere to the small group of rich men who find pleasure in moving on it at very high speeds . . . these few people are to be allowed to drive their boats as fast as they can. This is a serious blow to those who look to the lake for their fishing. The question of whether there is any pleasure in moving at frantic speed through beautiful scenery is altogether irrelevant. The question which ought to have been considered [at the enquiry], but was apparently not, is how far any man is justified in spoiling the pleasure of great numbers of other people for the sake of his own. By the decision of the Board of Trade it is clear that in this matter Windermere is to be in a worse position than a public highway. There at least there are some restrictions. Here there are to be none.

Altogether, Ransome wrote a hundred and fifty *Rod and Line* columns, and chose fifty to be collected in book form, together with a long essay about Aksakov, and translations of Aksakov's fishing writings. (The best of the *Rod and Line* columns not included in Ransome's book, which took its title from his column, are to be found later in this book.) Published in 1929, it has been in print ever since, with editions in 1932, 1935, 1940, 1947 and 1980. First and later editions command high prices in antiquarian book catalogues, and a collector's edition was published in 1993. It will probably be Ransome's most enduring book: the writing is timeless, and it is already part of the canon of fishing writing which starts with Dame Juliana Berners and Izaak Walton.

In 1927 Evgenia broke her ankle and Ransome took her to recover to an inn on the Thames at Newbridge where the inn-keeper said she could fish from her bedroom window. Although this proved impossible, the fishing was excellent, and friends such as the Hirsts and Hugh Sheringham, angling editor of the *Field* and prolific fishing writer, came to stay. Ransome wrote several columns about Thames fishing, being particularly excited by the capture of a large barbel, the only one he was ever to catch. He was typically downbeat about the achievement and the difficulty in fishing for barbel in general.

I have never fished for barbel. Fishing for barbel needs a greater expenditure of worms and faith than I have ever been in a position to afford. You enrich a river with a thousand lob-worms daily for a week to induce the barbel to look at worms favourably. Then you fish for him. His choice of feeding-places is such that you lose great quantities of tackle in the bottom of the river. But you hardly ever catch a barbel.

In September the following year the Ransomes visited his old friend Morgan Philips Price who had been the *Manchester Guardian* correspondent in Petrograd at the time of the Russian Revolution. After his return to Britain he had gone to live at the family home at Tibberton, a house where Cromwell was reputed to have spent the night. Price was no great fisherman himself, but the house had a large pond, which had perhaps once been an ornamental lake or fish pond, with an island and a boat on it. The water was very weedy, and ideal for tench. Here, in May 1928, Price had seen tench wallowing in the shallows and, ignoring the closed season, had caught a large basket of them. He wrote to Ransome in June, telling him of this exploit and inviting him down. Ransome waited until the trout season was over, looked out some floats with red tops, and travelled with Evgenia down to Tibberton. He described the result in a *Rod and Line* piece entitled 'Failing to Catch Tench'.

Ransome had been failing to catch tench for years. This time in Gloucestershire, wild ducks were the problem. Philips Price's pond had attracted first a pair of wild ducks, then several pairs, and by the time Ransome got there in September there were forty or fifty, disturbing the pond, destroying the weed which the tench loved, and scaring the tench into hiding. After fishing for two days and an evening with every sort of worm and maggot, and catching only eels, he wrote a lament in Price's visitors' book, which reads in part:

> O Philips Price! Did you not blench
> To catch and eat a Maytime tench?
> What wonder that a spell was thrown
> When such a monstrous deed was done?
> The affronted tench have gone for good.
> Ducks undisturbed eat all the food.
> The angler watching by the shore
> Shall see the great fish roll no more
> And Price's guests come late to meals
> Bringing no tench but wriggling EELS!

The next year, Ransome abandoned hope of tench and visited Price during the trout season to fish on the River Leadon, a tributary of the Severn which passed about a mile from Price's house. Price's nine-year-old daughter, Tania, was taken out of school for the day to accompany Ransome, and they were dropped off at the bridge together with a picnic. Ransome fished all day, up and down the beat. In his usual taciturn manner, he never said a word to Tania, who assumed she had done something wrong and was sick all the following night with worry. Although she said nothing to her parents, Ransome may have realised that he had been neglectful because the next day he went to Gloucester and bought children's fishing rods for Tania and her brother. He taught them to fish for eels on the tench pond, and how to kill the eels; and soon they brought back eels for breakfast.

Tania, now Tania Rose, remembers on a visit around this

time that Ransome announced he was thinking of writing a book for children, and that this was greeted by everyone present as a huge joke. Much later, when his reputation as a children's author was made, she was present at a discussion between him and her father when he insisted that it was essential to have one child in each story aged within a year or two of each intended reader if the readers were to identify with the characters in the story.

By 1929, Ransome was beginning to run out of ideas for fishing columns, and to tire of journalism. He found that the pressure of weekly fishing became just a preparation for writing, a dull duty which no longer gave him much pleasure. (Shortly after he stopped writing the column, he found he was enjoying fishing again.) It was agreed that he would end the column, and C. P. Scott offered to make him literary editor of the *Guardian* if he would serve a stint as Berlin correspondent first. He realised he had no desire to return to the life of a foreign correspondent and, aged 45, was determined to escape from journalism before it was too late. The way out was a children's adventure story he had been constructing in his mind for some time. In March 1929 he gave the *Guardian* three months notice, and started writing.

By April 1929 he had fifty pages of typescript of *Swallows and Amazons*. Jonathan Cape had invited him to write a series

CLIFFORD WEBB'S DRAWING
OF *SWALLOW* AND *AMAZON* FROM *SWALLOWDALE*

of books of essays on different topics to provide him with a regular income. In April Ransome went to London to see Cape, carrying the typescript of *Rod and Line* which Ransome proposed to make the first volume of essays, and also a sheet of notepaper with the title and chapter headings of *Swallows and Amazons*. Cape agreed at once to publish *Rod and Line*, although he said that he really wanted more general subjects. Ransome then broached the subject he cared more about.

With some diffidence I told him about *Swallows and Amazons* and showed him my half-sheet of paper. He glanced at it. 'That's all right,' said Napoleon Cape. 'We'll publish it and pay one hundred pounds in advance on account of royalities. But it's the essays we want.'

Ransome was launched on the enterprise that was to make his name a household word.

★

HUGH BROGAN was the first to reveal, in *The Life of Arthur Ransome*, the extent to which Ransome based his characters in the Swallows and Amazons stories on real people, and Christina Hardyment followed up by mapping the real geography behind his fictional settings and talking to those who were his models and knew the incidents in Ransome's own life that turned up lightly disguised in the books. Her search for answers to the question generations of readers have asked – 'Are the stories true?' – is recounted in her book *Arthur Ransome and Captain Flint's Trunk*. Further details were added when Roger Wardale called his book *Nancy Blackett* after Ransome's favourite yacht, which in turn took its name from the undisputed leader of the Amazons.

The names and to a large extent the characters of four of the five Altounyan children – Susan, Titty, Roger and Bridget – were taken wholesale into the Swallows' camp, while the eldest daughter, Taqui, provides at least some of the features of the Amazon pirate, Captain Nancy. Their father, Ernest Altounyan, an Armenian-Syrian doctor, had been at school in England where he became a friend of Robin Collingwood and was taken in the holidays to visit the Collingwood home near Coniston. Ransome had first met the family at the age of twelve when he found them picnicing on Peel Island in Coniston Water. Later, as a young man, he was adopted by the Collingwoods and often stayed with them at Lanehead overlooking the lake. There Arthur thought of marriage to Barbara, one of the two Collingwood daughters, but it was her sister Dora and her husband, Ernest Altounyan, who were to play a significant part in his life and his fame as a writer.

Together Ransome and Altounyan bought two old sea-going dinghies for the young Altounyans, and for the next few years a part of each summer was spent sailing and fishing on Coniston Water and the neighbouring becks and tarns. Sometimes Ransome fished alone from one of the little boats, which were later to play a central part in the children's stories. Taqui Altounyan recalls Ransome and Evgenia catching 150 perch in a day on Coniston and making them into soup. He had finally created for himself the life he dreamed of as a child, and it provided him with the raw material for a compelling mixture of fact and fiction that filled twelve longish books which have been read by millions in several languages round the world.

Fishing plays a small but important role in most of the books. Ransome appears in various disguises in several of them, most often as Captain Flint who teaches the Swallows to fish, but also as the anonymous fisherman in *The Big Six*, who makes it possible for the Coot Club to catch an enormous pike, and then behaves generously about a gang of children catching the monster fish he had marked down for himself.

Early in the first book, *Swallows and Amazons*, the Swallows fish for perch in the lake, using minnows for bait. This allowed a typical Ransome fantasy.

'Where's your float, Roger?' said the mate.
'And look at your rod,' said Titty.
Roger jumped up and caught hold of his jerking rod, which he had put down as he was counting the catch. He felt a fish at the end of his line. Just as he was bringing it to the

top there was a great swirl in the water, and his rod was suddenly pulled down again. Roger hung on as hard as he could, and his rod was bent almost into a circle.

'It's a shark! It's a shark!' he shouted.

'IT'S A SHARK'

(Clifford Webb's drawing for the second edition of *Swallows and Amazons*)

Something huge was moving about in the water, deep down, pulling the rod this way and that.

'Let him have line off the reel,' said John, but Roger held on. Suddenly a mottled green fish, a yard long, with a dark back and white underneath, came to the top. It lifted an enormous head right out of the water, opened a great white mouth, and shook itself. A little perch flew high into the air. Roger's rod straightened. For a moment the great fish lay close to the top of the water, looking wickedly at the crew of the *Swallow* as they looked at it. Then, with a twist of its tail that made a great twirling splash in the water, it was gone. Roger brought in the little perch. It was dead, and its sides were marked with deep gashes from the great teeth of the pike.

'I say,' said Roger, 'do you think it's really safe to bathe in this place?'

ROGER AND THE PIKE

(Steven Spurrier's drawing for *Swallows and Amazons* which Ransome rejected.
The first edition appeared with only Spurrier's map.)

Steven Spurrier was originally commissioned to do drawings for *Swallows and Amazons*, and produced one showing Roger apprehensively admiring a dead pike and another of the children cleaning a basket of perch. Ransome didn't like these drawings, feeling they did not contribute directly enough to the story. Clifford Webb was then asked to produce some and these appeared in the second edition of *Swallows and Amazons* and the first of *Swallowdale*. Ransome then took over with his own characteristically flat sketches that contribute so strongly to the feel of the books. Eventually he even replaced Webb's drawings in the first two books with his own.

The fishing theme is developed in *Swallowdale*, in which trout make their first appearance, in the small Lakeland becks and in the tarn above the dale itself. Captain Flint, in this book unmistakably Ransome himself, teaches the Swallows to fish with a fly, and which flies to use: woodcock and orange, snipe and purple, and a black spider for a hot day. Nowhere in his fishing reportage does Ransome write for the beginner, on how you actually fish with a fly or a float. But there is almost everything you need to know about the mechanics of fly fishing in the short description of Captain Flint teaching John on Trout Tarn.

He began moving slowly up the southern side of the tarn, the side from which the wind was coming, swishing his rod backwards and forwards, letting out line, and then letting the flies drop on the water far out along the edge of the ripples, waiting a moment, and then slowly, inch by inch, lifting the point of the rod, bringing the flies in again until with a steady upward lift he picked the line from the water, sent it flying up in the air behind him, paused a half-second for it to straighten and then, switching the point of the rod forward again, sent the flies out to fall light as scraps of down one behind the other, a yard farther up the tarn. The third or fourth time his flies dropped on the water there was a splash at the woodcock and orange, the rod bent, and a moment later a fat little trout was being drawn over the net

ROGER FELL ON IT
(Ransome's drawing from *Swallowdale*)

that John was holding ready for him quite still and well below the surface . . . Then Captain Flint gave John the rod, and for a moment or two John tried to make the line straighten high in the air behind him and then shoot forward, unrolling itself until once more it straightened out, this time in front of him and well above the water, so that the flies should drop like snowflakes.

'Up, now . . . Pause . . . Forward again,' Captain Flint was saying. 'Aim about two feet above the water . . . Don't take the rod too far back . . . No need to force . . . Make the tip of the rod do the work . . . Look here. Let me hold your hand and show you the way to do it. Now then.'

It was not a very good cast, for two hands on a rod are not better than one if they belong to different people. Still, the flies did, at last, go out instead of landing in a mess only a yard or two from the shore. There was a splash, John struck, the flies flew back over his head and caught in the heather behind him. Captain Flint crawled back and freed them.

'I say, that *was* a trout, wasn't it?' said John.

In an episode inspired by Dick Kelsall's success on the Winster a few years earlier, Roger and Titty tire of waiting their turn with the fly rod, wander up the tarn and catch a two pound trout, a real whopper for such a water, on a worm. The Swallows' enigmatic mother has it for supper, although she spoils the effect by declaring she has seen much larger trout in New Zealand.

During the interval before the next book, the Ransomes visited the Altounyans in Aleppo, where Ernest was in charge of a hospital, taking a sailing dinghy with them as a present. Ransome went after cat fish, and Brigit Altounyan, now Brigit Sanders, who was five at the time, remembers him fishing at night and catching 'monsters'. The local fishermen decapitated their catch before taking it to market because the fish were so extraordinarily ugly that customers would be frightened; Ransome was when a cat-fish put its head out of the water, large as a water-buffalo, near where he was fishing and snorted like a bullock before disappearing.

The next books in the series – now at last beginning to be successful – have only brief fishing episodes. In *Peter Duck*, which takes place on an imaginary tropical island, an old sailor fishes for big-mouth using bait. There is a brief description of tropical fish, which Ransome must have remembered from his sea voyage to China. In *Winter Holiday*, the perch Ransome saw during his schooldays frozen into the ice of Windermere makes an appearance, 'as if it were swimming in glass.' In *Coot Club* Dr Dudgeon, father of Tom, the hero of the story, is a keen fisherman who listened to the big bream coming up in the evening and turning over on the top of the water, and had a weathercock with a bream on it. The twins nicknamed Port and Starboard appear in this book, a name Ransome was later to give to a green and red fly he invented. An eel fisherman, babbing for eels with a ball of worms, makes his first appearance.

At the time that these books were written the Ransomes continued to live at Low Ludderburn. The house was small, which helped one child at least to confuse Ransome with Jeremy Fisher, but suited Ransome perfectly, particularly for the associations it had for him with his childhood, and the nearby fishing. He had filled his study in the barn with books and papers, as well as a jar of parrot feathers his mother had given him to tie flies with, and a large mounted pike in a glass case. In a short autobiographical piece published in 1934 in *The Junior Book of Authors*, he describes the house in pastoral terms:

> I live in a cottage more than three hundred years old high up on a hillside. I can see forty miles from my cottage door. The lakes I knew best as a boy are close at hand, and, on the nearest of them, a little boat, *Swallow*, lies at her moorings and sails as well as ever she did. There is a long row of fishing rods hanging in the cottage, like the pipes of an organ, people say.
>
> When there is news that the rivers are in good trim, I usually manage to take a rod and go down the hill to one or another of them. This very day, the moment I have put this paper into its envelope, I shall be off to fish a river that was fished by my father long before I was born, and by my grandfather before him.

At Ludderburn they had excellent neighbours in the Kelsalls, who played an important part in Ransome's life at this time in addition to the fishing parties and the signalling system between the two houses. Ransome used to read the early parts of *Swallows and Amazons* to the two Kelsall children, Desmond and Dick, as he wrote them, to get their reactions; their father also listened. A west African grey parrot given to the Kelsalls by a doctor cousin made the foot print used as a signature on the 'ship's papers' at the start of *Swallowdale*, by being induced to grip in turn pieces of paper wrapped round a broomstick, one coated with a mixture of soot and oil.

In the following year they decided to sell the house: they

wanted a larger, sea-going boat and, perhaps most important, Evgenia found the house damp and primitive. After a long search, they found a new house near Pin Mill on the River Orwell in Suffolk, and shortly after moving in they commissioned a seven-ton cutter, *Selina King*, to replace his favourite yacht, *Nancy Blackett*, whose galley Evgenia always complained was far too cramped.

In all, six large yachts – most of them built to his own specifications – and many sailing dinghies kept Ransome afloat until he had turned seventy. With Evgenia, he made his last sea voyage across the Channel to Cherbourg in 1954, when he settled on making the return crossing by night. Having cleared the harbour entrance, the engine stopped and continued to give trouble until they returned to their mooring at Chichester, so forcing Ransome often to rely upon sail alone as he crossed the main shipping lanes. Once in the night he had to alter course to avoid a steamer, a manoeuvre he had negotiated before in his imagination while writing his master-piece *We Didn't Mean to Go to Sea*.

In this book the Amazons make no appearance and the Swallows alone face the hazards of accidentally drifting out to sea in a yacht, The *Goblin*, that does not belong to them. To ensure the authenticity of the North Sea crossing that the Swallows never intended, Ransome had first taken *Nancy Blackett* on a voyage with an inexperienced sailor (who slept for most of the rough 25-hour crossing) from Harwich to Flushing in Holland. *Nancy*, the model for *Goblin*, was sailed for a total of more than 800 miles before Ransome parted with her. Roger Wardale, who in 1991 published an entertaining account of Ransome's sailing life, records how he caught eels from *Nancy* while she had a mooring at Pin Mill. Ransome bartered the eels with Mr Gee, the self-styled mayor of Pin Mill, for fruit from his little greengrocer's shop known as the Mayor's parlour.

He would often fish for eels while he was at work in *Nancy*'s cabin. He rigged up an arrangement whereby if an eel took his bait the butt end of the rod in the cockpit knocked on the cabin door and brought him up on deck to deal with it.

Another of Ransome's favourite East Coast haunts was Kirby Creek in Hamford Water, where he often took his young friends, George and Josephine Russell as crew aboard *Nancy*. This was the setting for *Secret Water*, in which a local fishing boy – the Mastodon – who keeps rods and gear in his cabin in a wrecked boat teaches Roger to catch eels. This device of a local fisherman was becoming a feature of the books, useful because it allowed Ransome to explain local fishing techniques.

Although several of the earlier children's books have fishing episodes as part of the background to life in the country, in *The Big Six* fishing becomes an important part of the plot itself. Following on from *Coot Club*, a group of Norfolk boys, the Death and Glories (named after the converted ship's dingy on which they live), is unjustly accused of casting boats adrift in a feud with a group of local thugs.

The book is densely packed with descriptions of the life of the Broads. Ransome had spent a childhood holiday on a wherry on the Broads, fishing for pike, and since moving to Pin Mill had immersed himself in local fishing methods. He uses a detailed description of eel fishing to create the Broads landscape, and the eelman – 'an old man with a mane of grey hair that hung down on his shoulders from under an old black hat' – is one of his best adult characters. The Death and Glories spend the night on the eelman's boat and help him raise the eel sett, a net across the river with pods of osier woven into it into which the eels are gathered. He shows them how to kill the eels, a messy and difficult procedure. The boys take home a bucket of eels, and smoke them on the stove of their own boat.

Pike fishing provides an important secondary theme to the book as a whole. Ransome writes himself into the book, as a dedicated pike fisherman, much more single-minded and able to cope than Captain Flint. He lives on a specially-designed fishing motor boat, called the *Cachalot* after a type of whale; it would be unworthy to think Ransome intended a fisherman's pun. Ransome probably designed boats like this for himself in his mind when he was not actually building his next sailing boat. Unlike the Hullabaloos' motor-boats, this one is handled considerately.

> The cruiser was coming very slowly and the man at the wheel slowed her down even more when he saw that Pete was fishing. He even put his engine out of gear and the little cruiser slipped along almost silently. Pete had a good look at her and saw that she was not an ordinary cruiser but a boat specially built for fishing. He saw rods lying in rests along the cabin top, and other rod-rests fixed to cockpit coamings.

The fisherman commissions Pete to catch him some roach as pike bait, and gives the *Death and Glory* a tow down river. The

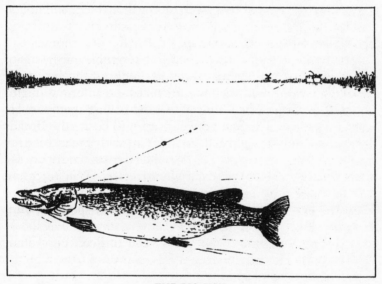

THE BIG FISH
(Ransome's drawing for *The Big Six*)

following morning the boys are keeping an eye on the fisherman's pike rod while he goes to the pub for milk when a pike takes the bait. Ransome describes the drama in a passage unusual in that in his fishing writing he rarely describes the actual catching of a fish. The fictional account allows him to include some of the emotion he clearly felt at such times.

Twenty yards down the river it was as if there had been an explosion under water. Just for a moment they saw an enormous head, a broad dark back and a wide threshing tail, as the big fish broke the surface and dived again.

Bill was blowing the horn. Joe, holding up the rod and feeling the heavy tugs of the fish, was shouting at the top of his voice. But there was still no sign of the owner of the *Cachalot*. The big fish turned and came upstream again. Joe, desperately winding in, saw the line cutting the water only a few yards from the boat. Again the pike rushed away upstream. The reel screamed. Joe tried to brake it with his thumb and nearly had the skin taken off.

'Hang on to him,' said Pete.

'Ain't I?' panted Joe. 'Why don't that chap come. Hey! Hey! Hey!'

The reel stopped spinning. Joe began winding in again, getting a few yards, and then having to get his fingers out of the way of the spinning handles when the pike made another rush. And then the great fish came downstream, this time deep in the water, so that they did not see the floats as he passed. The line tautened again. There was another sudden, long rush, on and on, as if the pike were making for Yarmouth. It stopped. The floats showed on the surface far downstream opposite a big clump of reeds, in the place where they had been lying before the pike had taken the bait. They rested there a moment, bobbed, and came up again close to the reeds.

'He's going back to his holt,' shouted Pete. 'Stop him! Stop him! There he go . . .'

The floats shot suddenly sideways into the reeds.

The boys chase the pike out of the reeds and, with the help of the fisherman, who returns in the nick of time but honourably refuses to take over the rod, land the record fish.

At the *Roaring Donkey* pub the 'world's whopper' pike is weighed at just over thirty pounds and the boys are paid ten shillings and sixpence each by the landlord. They are told to keep it secret until the fish is mounted and displayed in the pub, where the landlord is sure it will make his fortune. This secret money is important later in the story when it is used against the boys to suggest that they have stolen some shackles. The Ransome/pike-fisherman character is the first to believe in the boys, but in the end their innocence is proved by some fancy detective work led by Dick and Dorothea. The book ends with the world's whopper being set up in the *Roaring Donkey* in front of an admiring crowd.

The old fisherman with the white beard turned from looking at the pike to look at the Death and Glories.
'Are you the boys who caught that fish?' he asked.
'We didn't exactly . . .' began Joe.
'Poor lads,' said the old man. 'Poor lads . . . So young and with nothing left to live for.'
'Let's go and catch another,' said Pete.

Ransome's most evocative picture of Lakeland life as he had known it in childhood is to be found in *The Picts and the Martyrs*, which contains more lessons from a local fishing child. In this case Jacky teaches Dick and Dorothea to tickle – 'guddling' Ransome calls it in Lake dialect – trout for supper while they are living in a deserted hut in the woods.

With his head close to the ground, Jacky was dipping his arm under water. He wriggled a little nearer. His arm went in to the elbow. They saw one of his feet that had been moving stop as if it had been suddenly frozen. Half a minute went by like half an hour. Suddenly Jacky rolled sideways. His arm shot up out of the water and something flew through the air over the heads of the watchers. The next moment Jacky was on his feet searching the brambles where it had fallen. They saw his white arm plunge. They saw him bang something on a stone. He came back to them grinning with a small trout in his hand . . .
'But why doesn't the trout just bolt?' said Dick.
'It's the guddling,' said Jacky. 'If you go for to take him he's gone. You mun keep guddling and guddling till you've your fingers round the middle of him. He'll lig quiet. But

you mun keep guddling. And you mun keep clear of his tail or he's off. Let's see you get yin. There's aye a good yin under yon stone.'

Some see the book as the funniest of the Swallows and Amazons series, though the Lakeland accent tends to get in the way of the story. Evgenia was especially harsh in her judgement and told Arthur he had 'missed the bus on all counts'. The script lay unpublished for months while Ransome tried to regain confidence, and she continued to disapprove when it was finally published and well received in a form little changed from the original draft.

★

WHILE Ransome was busy with his children's books during the 1930s he continued to write occasional fishing pieces for the *Guardian*. He was also putting together a book on salmon flies and at the same time wrote reviews of detective stories – sometimes as many as five or six a week – for the *Observer* under the pseudonym William Blunt. Once he got into trouble with readers for revealing the outcome of the plot. In addition he was reviewing books on travel and sailing for the same paper.

He reviewed Robert Bruce Lockhart's book *Memoirs of a British Agent* not once but twice when it appeared in 1932. Lockhart and Ransome had drifted apart after their time in Russia and their political views diverged, but nevertheless Lockhart showed his draft of the book to Evgenia, who told him to make it more personal and dramatic. Ransome found the final work 'excellent' in the *Manchester Guardian*, but a few days later only 'quite good' in the *Observer*. In his diaries, Lockhart describes dining with Ransome in 1932 – 'very fat, has lived on milk for the past three years on account of a duodenal ulcer'. Ransome was upset by Lockhart's account in the book of giving Evgenia a passport, although presumably she had read this herself in the draft.

Ransome and Lockhart had many things in common besides their knowledgeable and sympathetic interest in

Russia, and Lockhart's career in several important ways mirrored Ransome's. Like Ransome, Lockhart was interested in folk stories, and proposed a book of fairy tales to the publishers Longman, who turned it down. He had more success as a journalist: he started Londoner's Diary on the *Evening Standard* in 1928 and wrote intermittent articles for newspapers all his life. Lockhart shared Ransome's admiration for Sergei Aksakov, and fell in love with a Russian woman, Moura Budberg. Although he never married her, she remained a friend all his life.

Above all, Lockhart wrote entertainingly about fishing. In fact he fished much more widely than Ransome, starting during childhood holidays on the Spey, where he had been given a rod almost as soon as he could walk. After the Russian adventure, Lockhart worked for a British bank in central Europe, but spent much of his time fishing for trout in Slovenia, Croatia, Bosnia, Austria, Moravia and Bavaria; he also fished unsuccessfully for huchen in the Danube.

Although Lockhart never had a regular fishing column, he wrote fishing sketches from central Europe for *The Times* in the mid-1920s, at around the time Ransome's *Rod and Line* column was appearing in the *Manchester Guardian*. Lockhart's fishing book *My Rod My Comfort*, first published in 1948 in a limited and very expensive edition and republished in a normal edition in 1957, is a charming account of a fishing life. It gives a vivid picture of a fisherman's Europe between the wars, when an experienced traveller like Lockhart, with good languages and some easily packed tackle, could combine a few days banking or diplomacy with a few days on excellent trout streams, if he was wise enough to do his banking in Slovenia and Bohemia rather than Paris or Brussels.

At the time, Ransome was stuck with the *Rod and Line* columns and never able to move far from Manchester. He must have envied Lockhart when they occasionally met in London. In the end, however, *My Rod My Comfort*, written late in Lockhart's life as an old man's memoirs, has little of the pace and breadth, the surprise and delicate touch, of the *Rod and Line* columns. Although his favourite among his own books, it does not measure up to his *Memoirs of a British Agent*, which remains one of the most important of early twentieth century autobiographies.

Negley Farson was a fisherman with a similar background, who used to drink with Lockhart in London in the 1930s, and although there is no record that he met Ransome, it is not unlikely. He was an American foreign correspondent and writer who had been in St Petersburg selling munitions at the time of the revolution. In addition to political journalism, Farson wrote one of the best books of fishing essays, very much in the Ransome and Lockhart style. *Going Fishing*, first published in 1942 in a Country Life edition with striking woodcut illustrations by Charles Tunnicliffe, describes the adventures of a nomadic fisherman in America, Europe and Asia. In his case, journalism proved as good a way to get to the best rivers and streams as banking had for Lockhart, although his repertoire was even wider. Farson had fished in the Gulf of Finland in the spring of 1917, listening to the guns firing at Kronstadt across the water, and had fished in the Soviet Caucasus in 1929. His drinking impressed even Lockhart, who was no mean judge. Oddly enough, the book is not mentioned in Ransome's list of indispensable fishing books published in 1955, suggesting that Ransome disliked either the book or its author. It is perhaps the most notable omission from the list. However, when Ransome was trying, unsuccessfully, to put together an anthology of fishing stories in the 1950s, he lists Negley Farson's description of fishing for rainbow trout in Chile as a potential chapter.

At this time Ransome fished regularly on the Meon in Hampshire with Francis Hirst. Hirst was congenial to Ransome not only because of his passion for fishing but because he was a chess player of exactly Ransome's standard. They had both dissented from conventional wisdom about the Russian revolution and had made themselves unpopular as a result, Hirst losing his job as editor of *The Economist*. Hirst's water on the Meon was at Droxford, where Izaak Walton had once lived. They would lodge at the inn at Droxford and take the beats in turn, meeting for lunch at the inn. The Meon at this point is a tiny stream, now further reduced in flow by water abstraction, but in Hirst's time it had some good small trout, 'plump and valiant' according to Ransome.

The most skilful of Hirst's fishing friends to be invited to the Meon, was the all-round sportsman C. B. Fry. In fishing as in everything else, Fry excelled. He was a skilled caster, effortlessly throwing a longer, straighter line than anyone else. The problem was that his line was so straight that the fly, pulled by the current, dragged across the surface the moment it touched the water, making an unnatural movement and scaring the fish, while Hirst's (and perhaps Ransome's) messy casts didn't drag at all because there was so much slack line on the water.

Hirst was famous for the simplicity of his equipment and his inability to tie knots. Surprisingly, in a company where most fishermen tied their flies, Hirst did not tie his own, but this did not prevent him from designing a very successful fly – 'Hirst's Fancy' – which Ransome often used. It had pale grey wings, a bluey-grey hackle and a silver body, and Hirst fished it both wet and dry, using it most of the time. Ransome describes him at the riverside in *Mainly About Fishing*:

> His most remarkable gift as a fisherman was his invisibility to fish. This was a never-ending wonder to his friends, for he was a tall, broad-shouldered man. They, kneeling sodden in the water-meadows, watched the bow-waves of departing trout before ever they had dared to cast. They would look up or down stream to see Hirst, most unsuitably dressed, with a dark, even a black, jacket, a cap or a linen hat, flannel trousers, a figure noticeable as a windmill, one would have thought, approach the stream scarcely troubling to stoop. If one of them had done as much every trout in the pool would have fled to cover. FWH would stand and watch the water and presently make an unhurried cast and be battling with a Meon trout.

During this period also, Charles and Margaret Renold became close friends. Ransome had turned Charles Renold into a keen fisherman, 'not a mere fly fisher, but one who

MARGARET LOOKS AT HER WATCH

Ransome's drawing of fishing with the Renolds on the Norfolk Broads

shared my pleasure in the sort of fishing I had had in Russia, float-fishing for coarse fish.'

Renold's daughter, Penelope, recalls that her father rarely caught a salmon when he went out with Ransome, but was more successful with trout. Ransome tried to interest Renold in sailing as well, going so far as to commission a small sailing boat for him from the builders of the original *Swallow*; the boat was called *Coch-y-bonddhu*, the name of a Welsh fly made from herl, the soft iridescent green fibre from peacock feathers. But Renold did not take to sailing and the boat stayed with Ransome in Norfolk and in the Lakes.

★

WITH THE END of the *Manchester Guardian* fishing column, Ransome felt free to enjoy fishing once more. He was an innovative fly-tier, with several new flies to his credit. These included the Port and Starboard, a sea-trout fly tied with red and green fluorescent wool, and the Glowworm with a bright green tail which glowed in the dark. He also tied a fantasy salmon fly, which turned out to be very effective. In *Mainly About Fishing* he wrote:

> Five years ago a little girl came to tea at my house. She was thirteen and from her babyhood had never been known by any other name than Copp, which name was given to her because of her magnificent mane of burnished copper hair.

At that tea party I happened to see the sunlight on it, and was startled into exclaiming, 'Copp! That hair of yours is wasted on you. It ought to be made into salmon-flies.' Last summer, five years later, I met her again, now a grown-up young woman, and she said, 'Once upon a time, long ago, you said something about using my hair for salmon-flies.

'THE 3LB GRAYLING YOU ARE GOING TO CATCH'
Christmas card, 1938, to Charles and Margaret Renold

Well, my plaits were cut off that winter and I kept them for you in case you really wanted them.' I said I really wanted them and Copp, that noble girl, brought me her plaits, resplendent plaits of burnished copper, preserved, for the best of all purposes, in a shoe-box.

The fly, inevitably, was named Fair Cop, and Ransome's fishing diary mentions that Copp's father caught several large salmon with it.

Busy with flies like these, Ransome conceived the idea in 1944 of a book, to be produced jointly with Charles Renold, on the history of flies. It would be called *A Plague of Flies*, and would be illustrated with coloured pictures of ancient and modern flies made from colour photographs of actual flies tied for the purpose. His publishers, Jonathan Cape, were enthusiastic. Ransome wrote to his fishing friends asking them to send examples of their favourite flies. In the end the book never appeared, colour printing technology not being sufficiently developed for what Ransome had in mind, but much of the material found a place in his second fishing book, *Mainly About Fishing*, fifteen years later.

★

THE RANSOMES moved back to Coniston in 1940, and bought a house on the eastern shore where they had half a mile of lake frontage with good trout fishing. Because of wartime restrictions, there was only enough petrol for a weekly shopping trip into Ulverston, but now and then he was able to go by train to Cockermouth on the River Derwent to fish for salmon. In 1941, after two hernias, his doctor forbade Ransome to sail but allowed him to fish as much as he liked as long as he didn't slip or wade in fast water. He wrote two more Swallows and Amazons books at the house at Coniston, but was tiring of the format, just as he had tired of the *Rod and Line* columns ten years earlier. He was thinking of something quite new, a major historical novel with a fishing theme.

As early as 1930 he had toyed with an idea of a book set in

the mid nineteenth-century, about 'an old schoolmaster and a fisherman and a boy and a river.' He thought about the story in 1938 but was strongly discouraged by Evgenia. In 1942, with inspiration for Swallows' adventures running low, he took out his notes again. He very much wanted to build a story around a river and an old gamekeeper he had known in childhood. The book was to be called *The River Comes First*, an accurate statement of Ransome's own priorities.

The river was the Bela, where his grandfather and father had both fished before him. The book would sum up Ransome's feelings about the proper relationship between man and the natural environment, and would be centred on the life story of the old Bela gamekeeper Tom Stainton, scarcely disguised as Tom Staunton in the book. Ransome used a story about his grandfather as his inspiration. In his *Autobiography* he records that when, in 1930, he first came to fish the Bela,

> the old keeper, Tom Stainton, told me of a remark of my grandfather's sixty years before. Tom was appointed keeper on the Beela by the little club that controlled the water, and one of the committee raised the question as to what was to be done about a superannuation fund. 'Superannuation!' exclaimed my grandfather. 'No man appointed beck-watcher on the Beela will ever want to be superannuated.' 'And by gum,' said old Tom to me, 'I never have and never will.'

This dedication to a river was to be the big idea behind the new book. In the unpublished part of his *Autobiography*, Ransome recalls another story about Tom Stainton, clearly a legendary figure. 'On the opening day of the season,' he wrote, 'there was always a gathering of members on the Bela, by Tom's cottage, and Tom, once a famous wrestler, now a very old man, used to walk around with a matchbox full of his favourite flies (Waterhen and Crimson) to make sure that every member had one on his cast.'

Moving back to Coniston reminded him of this plan. He drew up a synopsis and was soon in trouble over the mechanics of writing a historical novel – whether it should be

in first or third person, in dialect or not. He wrote several
fragments, the most substantial of which are reproduced by
Hugh Brogan in *Coots in the North*, a collection of Ransome
stories first published in 1988.

Ransome drew a detailed ink and watercolour map of the
river, with the locations which were going to feature in the
story marked on it; this map is preserved in the Ransome
archives in Leeds University. The two pieces in *Coots in the
North* are taken from the early part of the book. In one of them,
entitled *Cloudburst*, the young Tom and Jenny are marooned
on a small island in the river by a flash flood, and threatened by
the rising water. Tom manages to rescue them by applying the
principle of the wet fly 'across-and-down' method: he swims
the swollen river, attaches a rope to a tree on the other side,
returns with it, and allows the force of the current to swing
him and Jenny back to safety. It is an exciting incident, with
Ransome's narrative powers at full stretch. The second
fragment is a vignette of Ransome's best fishing writing. The
young Tom Staunton skips school to watch the salmon which
are running the river. His teacher, Canon John Williams, is a
keen salmon fisherman. By the time the Canon gets down to
the river after school with his rod, Tom is hidden in a large oak
tree just above a 20lb salmon, and he watches the Canon fish
down towards him.

Slowly, two yards at a time, Canon John Williams fished
down the Oaks Pool. A glance over his shoulder, a lift of the
long rod and away the line would go straight up the river,
clear of the trees along the bank, and then, out, down and
across, and the line doubled back on itself, unrolling as it
came till it laid the big salmon fly with hardly a splash close
to the opposite bank and well below the fisherman. Then
the fisherman would wait, his rod pointing straight across,
the end of it perhaps two feet above the water, one hand
three feet up the rod, the other at the but of it, while the pull
of the stream brought the fly slowly round, deep under
water till the line pointed straight down river from the
fisherman. A pause, two quiet steps down the shallows, and

SALMON TAKING A FLY
The likely model for Ransome's drawing on page 77,
– a woodcut by Eric Fitch Daglish for Viscount Grey's *Fly Fishing*

then the glance over the right shoulder, the lift, the line
straightening in the air upstream and then, once more, the
cast forward and down towards the opposite bank, where
Tom, high over the water among the oak leaves, watched
and waited to see the old Canon tighten in a fish.

The Canon gets his fly caught in the tree where Tom is hiding.
Tom reveals himself, frees the fly which is taken by the salmon
and, after a longish fight, Tom lands the fish. The Canon
reconciles duty with instinct by punishing Tom on the spot for
not going to school, gives him the Latin lesson he had missed,
and with his help catches another salmon. The character of
Tom is firmly established as a boy for whom 'the river comes
first.'

The fragments of *The River Comes First* in the Ransome
Archive in Leeds show this to have been an important new
enterprise for him. The book was to be set in the Lakeland
country he knew so well, on a river he and his family had
fished for three generations. The quality of the writing is
superior to that of Ransome's other fiction, and it may be that
writing for a more adult audience peculiarly suited Ransome at

this time. Had it been finished, it might perhaps have moved him into a whole new genre of fiction. The passages that were completed read easily, and would have fitted smoothly into a final manuscript; it is as though Ransome had found a pace and form in fiction which he could sustain easily. He is after all writing about things he had done, thought about and written all his life. Making fishing, on which his writing skills had been sharpened by five years of the *Rod and Line* column, a major theme of a fictional work – using skills developed over a decade of the Swallows books – brought together two of the main threads of his career as a writer.

Several important innovations are revealed in what remains of *The River Comes First*. Hugh Brogan and others have pointed out that the relationship between the adolescent Tom and Jenny has a hint of the sexuality oddly absent from the Swallows books. Here Ransome reveals his complex feelings about class and his instinctive but romantic position on the side of honest rural working class people against the gentry and the new rich. At the same time, he is against poachers and other working class villains; he constructs a fragment of the plot around the emotional appeal that poachers make against gamekeepers to unite against the gentry, and why this shouldn't happen. Elsewhere the manuscript shows him being decidedly romantic about the established order. The young boy is getting a lesson from his parents about how to address the gentry. His mother is in favour of respect, but his father has more complex notions. ' "Sir" mostly means "gummock" ' the father tells the boy.

> 'You needn't be ashamed to say it if you know what you mean by it. It means one thing when you say it to the Dominy, for he can fish with any man on the river, and another thing altogether when you say it to the folk with their new rods and their new flies and their new brogues, folk who can't catch a fish if you were to hang it on their damned hooks.' 'And to the Doctor. Will I say it to him?' 'He's a good caster the doctor, and you can say it to him for a good cast, but he's over hard on the strike . . .'

This is the same Ransome who in a later book quotes, with implicit approval, the cobbler John Younger's phrase about 'fox-hunting, man-hunting dukes and squires, who would also hunt cobblers if cobblers could run fast enough.'

None the less, the book was doomed. Evgenia, always his severest critic at least until the books were successful, disliked the idea from the start. After working hard on it in early 1943, he broke off in the middle of the year, and it is highly likely that Evgenia's disapproval was the reason. It was more than the end of a book. As Hugh Brogan says, 'from that moment the end of his creative career was in sight'.

In the Ransome room at Abbot Hall Museum in Kendal is a typed sheet of paper among Ransome's things left to the museum. Although it has no date, it may have been written around this time. It reads:

> It is very good for geese to be thought swans. They are likely to be better geese through trying to live up to their reputations. It is still more important for cygnets. Swans they will be, some day, but they will be poor swans if their confidence in themselves has been destroyed. Destruction of a writer's hope that he can write is an easy, cruel form of murder. It can kill an old writer as well as a young one. The confidence built up by the friends of one's youth should be stored against a rainy day and may help a man to weather much discouragement later on.

The sadness and bitterness of a writer who had abandoned what would almost certainly have been his most important work shines through.

*

IF 1943 was a disaster for Ransome the writer, it was an important year for Ransome the fisherman. As the book headed for rejection, two inventions show him hard at work experimenting with fishing.

Coniston and Windermere have a population of char left behind after the last Ice Age, and there is a long local tradition of trolling for these fish from a slowly moving boat at depths of a hundred feet or more with a heavily weighted plumb line attached to a rod eighteen or twenty feet long. Ransome had fished on both lakes since childhood, but because of his hernias he was now unable to row and so could no longer fish for char. He thought about this, and in mid-September, as the char season was opening, reported his happy conclusion to his mother.

> though I can no longer row a boat at all, I can catch char by sailing. The method is that of the Bay of Biscay tunny-fishers, you must have seen them, with mast-high rods, trolling under an easy sail. The whole difficulty is to sail slow enough. Finally, after a lot of experiment, I have got the thing to work, and last night we had a most luxurious supper on a brace of char.

His second invention concerned salmon flies. He had, like fishermen before and since, long puzzled over the question of why salmon take flies. When salmon return to the river to breed, they stop eating, their stomach atrophies, and they live off fat. Many die after breeding. Fishermen have theories about why salmon which do not feed in fresh water nevertheless take the lures offered them. Some think it is the memory of their time in the river as young parr when they feed voraciously, or of the most recent food they have fed on at sea; others believe that they attack the bait from instinctive aggression, or as a reflex, or to defend a small territory. Ransome, an experienced salmon fisherman, had worried about this question from time to time. In his fishing notebook preserved in the Brotherton Collection there is a short passage in draft, not used in his later pieces on salmon flies, about this mystery. 'The trouble is that so often the salmon does not seem to know the rules of the game. It is as if we were to run a cricket match between two teams, one of which obeyed the rules of the MCC while the other believed it had been invited to play football.'

Then, perhaps while he was thinking about salmon for *The River Comes First*, inspiration came to him, in unusual form.

11 Portrait of Ransome by J. Gilroy in the Garrick Club, London

12 (*left*) Eel fishers on the Norfolk Broads

13 (*above*) A 21lb pike caught by a twelve-year-old boy near Horning, still displayed at the Swan Inn. It was the model for the pike caught by Coot Club members in *The Big Six*

14 Evgenia with Polly and Podge at Broke Farm near Pin Mill

15 Charles Renold fishing on Loweswater near Cockermouth, 1948

16, 17 Ransome with a large salmon he caught near Cockermouth
on the River Derwent, 1947

18 Writing on board the last of Ransome's six yachts, *Lottie Blossom*, in which he made his last Channel crossing when he was 70 in 1954

19 A wet day's fishing in 1954

20 Ransome fishing the river Derwent near Cockermouth for sea trout, 1956

Now, in 1943, it so happened that I had influenza while staying in London, at the Park Lane Hotel in Piccadilly. On my first day downstairs, light in the head and shaky on my feet, I was sitting in the lounge and trying to forget London by thinking, naturally, about salmon. Sitting there in that hotel, I was on the banks of a river far away, thinking about salmon and, as so often before, about salmon flies and the general, regrettable, unreasonable hitty-missiness of their design. Why on earth should the salmon, unable to eat in fresh water, be sometimes ready to take our flies? 'The salmon does not eat in fresh water', I was saying, sleepily, to myself. . . 'His digestion is out of gear . . .' 'The salmon does not eat . . .' And suddenly I sat up with a start and looked about me. Now the Park Lane Hotel, in 1943, was much used by American officers and men. The lounge was full of them. They were passing by, sitting reading papers, waiting for expected guests, busy with this or that. The salmon does not feed in fresh water. Neither does the American military man feed in the middle of the morning. It is not a meal time. These Americans were not eating. Only a few were talking. But the jaws of every man were going like a machine. Two and two made five at once. I jumped like Archimedes in his bath. A flash of revelation had lit up the whole problem of the salmon and the salmon-fly. In the north, when a new idea hits our hard heads, we are apt to say 'By gum!' 'By gum!' I exclaimed, and indeed gum was the answer. The salmon does not feed in fresh water. No, but HE DOES CHEW GUM.

Thinking that the salmon might be doing something similar to the American soldiers he saw around him in the hotel, Ransome immediately asked several of them why they were chewing. He learnt that gum is not chewed merely for exercise or to strengthen the jaw muscles, but also for its own taste. He reasoned that perhaps the salmon was doing something similar with the fly, chewing in order to recapture the flavour of its recent food, most likely sand-eels and especially elvers. The task, Ransome thought, was to produce a fly so like an elver that it would induce in the salmon the memory of a flavour it had recently enjoyed and a wish to take the fly in its mouth in the hope of enjoying that flavour again.

When the elver comes into the river, (the time it is most likely to be taken by a salmon), it is three inches long and looks like a semi-translucent white strip. The problem was how to produce a lifelike version of this.

White hackle feathers, the standard fly-tyer's answer, were lifeless in the water. Then Ransome had a stroke of luck. He had corresponded with Major H. E. Morritt a decade earlier about the proposed book on salmon flies, and Morritt had sent him some flies tied with an exotic feather, long and narrow, with a sharply defined chalky white central ribbon on an intense dark blue background. The effect was extraordinarily like a white elver swimming in the dark sea. Morritt had taken the feathers from a bird he had shot on an African hunting trip some years earlier. Ransome recalled the incident in a letter to Morritt (not sent, but preserved in the Brotherton Collection) five years later.

I was mightily struck by that feather because it seemed to me to offer the most delightful opportunities of copying elvers and sand-eels. My notion was that these being probably the last edibles tasted by the salmon before coming up the river for his Lenten season, sight of something of the sort might make him say, 'Hullo! That's rather like those things I enjoyed only a week or so ago. Nice taste anyway, even if I don't want a five course dinner. Have at it . . .'

Ransome drew the feather in colour, and sent the drawing to Myles North, a friend who was working as an ornithologist for the Colonial Office in Africa. North identified the feather as the neck hackle of a vulturine guineafowl, a bird common in the dry scrub country of Uganda, Kenya, Ethiopia and Somalia. He sent Ransome a cape of feathers to try. They were perfect, not only for fly-tying, as he discovered when he sent some to Morritt, 'on whom, however, they were wasted because, by unfortunate chance, they were forwarded to him in America and he opened the packet at the breakfast table so that an hour or two later Vermont (I believe) had its first look at them, adorning his hostess's hat.'

After experimenting with the feathers in 1943 and 1944, in 1945 Ransome fixed on the pattern and tied a series of flies which had a body of black floss, ribbed in flat silver foil, and were adorned with one or two guineafowl feathers, with the white centre stripe about two and a half inches long. The fly might have small jungle cock feathers to represent the elver's eyes, although Ransome was not dogmatic about this ('these please the angler but I do not think the fish cares one way or another'). Ransome tied some of the flies in the sitting room at the Flyfishers' Club in London, where there are several sets

RANSOME'S DRAWING OF THE ELVER FLY

of vices and other equipment so that members can run up a few flies while waiting for lunch, and the success of these prompted other members to tie their own with a consignment of feathers sent from Africa. Soon Ransome and others, especially fellow members of the Flyfishers' and Garrick Clubs, were experimenting with the elver fly in different sizes and in wet and dry form.

Once the fish showed they liked the fly by taking it, Ransome gave it to several commercial dressers and passed as correct the copies made by them. The fly was stocked by Farlows in Haymarket, Westley Richards of Conduit Street and Messeena in Leamington, each of whom imported the guineafowl feathers directly from Africa. To Ransome's enormous pleasure, friends reported that the fly was very successful, often persuading salmon to be caught where other flies had failed. He later said that the invention of this fly was the only creative act of which he had ever boasted.

When the supply of vulturine guineafowl feathers ran out, Ransome was able to call on Desmond Kelsall, who was working then as a Fisheries Officer in Tanzania. Vulturine guineafowl were a very local species in that area, and strictly protected, and Kelsall was an Honorary Game Ranger. Recognising a crisis, Kelsall contacted a friend who was also a game ranger and explained the problem. A week later Kelsall received, without comment, a modest supply of the feathers, which he forwarded to Ransome. But he never dared to get any more. The supply of feathers continued to bother Ransome, and eventually he advertised in *The Times* personal column for 'sittings of vulturine Guinea fowls and Curassow eggs, or the birds themselves', the Curassow presumably for another fly he had in mind. His idea was to keep the guineafowl, like peacocks, with a supply of feathers to hand, but Myles North pointed out that they were tropical birds, unlikely to thrive during Lakeland winters.

The elver fly was widely taken up by salmon fishermen, but it also led Ransome into a dispute with Richard Waddington, a distinguished fisherman and fly-tier. Waddington had been thinking about salmon flies in 1942 as a distraction from the war in North Africa, and he had come to similar conclusions as Ransome, particularly about the role of elvers. Waddington also altered hook design by rejecting the large salmon hooks, then universally used, in favour of much smaller treble hooks attached to a steel shank body, with a fly tied without wings but with plenty of hackle. These are the flies known today as Waddingtons.

There is no dispute about Waddington's claim to have invented a revolutionary type of salmon fly. However, in his book *Salmon Fishing: A New Philosophy*, published in 1947 when Ransome's theories were well known and his flies had been on the market for two years, Waddington stressed the importance of elvers in the salmon diet without mentioning Ransome. Worse, in his 1951 book *Fly Fishing for Salmon: A*

Modern Technique, he specifically praised the elver fly and implied that it was first tied by a friend prompted by his own earlier book. Ransome felt strongly that this was unethical. A correction slip was inserted into the book, pointing out that this was in error, and that the elver fly had first been tied by Ransome. His friends consoled him with stories of the success of his elver flies compared to Waddington's. Morritt wrote to him the following year:

> For myself I reserved the Elver for a suitable occasion, which arose when I had failed twice fishing over a salmon I had seen break the surface. I destroyed him with the Elver (21 lbs). I then lost the fly in a tree. The second Elver I presented to my hostess who did very well with it. Incidentally, she fished a pool down after a friend who would fish with nothing else but Mr Waddington's Efforts and shook him considerably by catching 3 fish after he had entirely failed to interest anything.

The elver fly is still widely used by salmon fishermen, especially on the Grimersta river system on Lewis in the Hebrides, near where Ransome fished at Uig in the 1940s, although it is now sometimes tied with a heron feather. But vulturine guineafowl are raised in Britain for this purpose in small numbers by a few specialised commercial fly-tiers.

★

As a writer, Ransome never really recovered from Evgenia's condemnation and the putting aside of *The River Comes First*. He continued to write of course. *Great Northern?*, the last of the Swallows books, came out in 1947. It is an exciting story although not a very good book; Ransome's heart had gone out of fiction, especially the adventures of the Swallows and Amazons. The story was suggested to him by Myles North, the man who had sent him the first consignment of vulturine guinea fowl feathers. It was set on the island of Lewis in the Outer Hebrides, which Ransome may have visited before the war, and where he certainly fished regularly afterwards. He and Evgenia went to Lewis in 1945 to get local colour for the book, and again in 1946 and later years.

On one of these trips, his stomach ulcer was causing him such pain that all he was allowed for his picnic lunch were biscuits and a bottle of milk. The hotel made a mistake one day and gave him the packed lunch of a visiting Air Vice Marshal; this was even simpler, consisting only of a bottle of whisky.

During that trip a tiny motor launch put into Stornoway harbour packed with Estonian refugees escaping across the Atlantic from Stalin. Ransome went down to the harbour and started to talk to one of the women in the little Estonian he remembered. She was overjoyed to hear her native language, but he was soon out of his depth, and switched to Russian. Fearing the worst, she fled.

BOILING WITH GRAYLING
Ransome's sketch

Ransome fished a great deal through the 1940s and 1950s whenever he could get away from writing and domestic crises. He kept a notebook of places fished, hotels to stay in, flies which caught fish. This lists 31 rivers and twelve lakes he had fished in England alone, including most well-known north of England and Lakeland rivers, but also some of the best trout streams in central England (such as the Dove and

Derbyshire Wye) and the south, where he fished the Itchen, Windrush, Wylye, Nadder and Avon, although not the Test. His fishing diaries are not very informative, listing mainly fish, the flies they were caught on, with the Port and Starboard very prominent, and occasional fishing gossip. Only rarely does his imagination take over, as in a 1956 entry: 'I saw an enormous cock fish . . . it looked like a red upholstered sofa.'

Despite ill-health, much of Ransome's fishing – particularly for salmon and sea trout – was demanding, needing long walks, and strenuous exertion when a fish was hooked. One of his fishing companions says of a day on the Cothi in Carmarthenshire in 1946, when Ransome, aged 62, caught a small salmon, 'a stout performance, as he had to climb up the bank, run the length of Jones Pool and climb down again to kill his fish.' On this occasion he returned to London carrying a sea trout for the hall porter's cat at his block of flats in Putney.

Anthony Wilson saw him in August 1956, fishing in the Leven between Windermere and Morecambe Bay. This is a rapid and powerful river, and Ransome, by then aged 72, was wading up to his chest and occasionally casting with a long salmon rod. Wilson asked the keeper about him.

> The dominant figure was a walrus moustache, hovering above the current much as a bull walrus would have borne it as he surveyed the scene while pausing for breath. 'Him?', said the keeper, a sturdy Lancashire yeoman, 'him? That's Arthur Ransome. He's a grumbly old bugger, and he hates children.'

He was no longer interested in fishing abroad. Although he had travelled all his life, and had fished in many foreign places, towards the end of his life he became increasingly parochial about both travel itself and fishing outside Britain. In this mood, he wrote that he felt fishing to be one of the consolations of travel, not its proper object. By then he was verging on xenophobia.

> All foreign fishing is but makeshift after all, owing much of its pleasure to memories of home. The fish may be bigger,

but what of that? The pride of catching a monster is shaded by the thought of how much greater that pride and that pleasure would have been if the big fish had been caught in home waters. These foreign leviathans do not count in the same way. They are somehow unreal. We may catch them and feel them tugging but, abroad, we can hardly be said to be ourselves, and as for the fish, at the bottom of our hearts we know them to be not much better than photographs, substitutes for English fish, with a flavour of artificiality about them, margarine instead of butter, more of them, perhaps, but not the same thing.

According to Evgenia, his favourite fishing place was on Lewis in the Outer Hebrides, where they stayed with James Dobson and his family who rented Uig Lodge on the Atlantic coast at the head of a small bay covered at low tide with dazzling white sand. It was an atmosphere which suited him, 'where the family, father, mother, three adult children (and later their spouses) were so completely absorbed in their salmon fishing that they had not time for any non-fishing guests.' Here he could fish for trout in mountain lochs, or more seriously for salmon and sea trout in the Red River or sea lochs like Sgailler and Stacsavat near Uig, which he had used as the setting for *Great Northern?*

In later life Ransome remained very interested in boats. He commissioned two, *Peter Duck* and *Lottie Blossom*, the former originally conceived as a fishing boat. He also suggested titles and wrote introductions for a series of books about sea voyages published by Rupert Hart-Davis. He gave a series of radio talks about fish, the elver fly and fishing books; these were reprinted in *The Listener*. In 1954 he was told by his doctor he had to give up boats because of his health, but he consoled himself with the thought that he could still fish. He continued to write book reviews for the *Spectator* and occasionally the *Sunday Times*.

Fishing, and reading and writing about fishing, remained his main consolations. There was a large job to be done to bring together his journalism and broadcasting in more

permanent form. In 1955 he wrote an excellent National
Book League Reader's Guide to fishing books, listing and discussing in 30 pages the fishing books he most enjoyed. The
booklet starts with a long introduction which reads like a *Rod
and Line* piece. Ransome is incapable of being dull or pom-
pous. Every now and then he slips in a story or a phrase which
surprises and delights the reader, such as a short account
of the embittered argument between W. C. Stewart and
Cholmondeley Pennell, the one supporting and the other
opposing upstream fishing for trout.

> Well, they have both been long dead and, I suppose, fish the
> Styx, one fishing up and one fishing down and pass each
> other without speaking.

The list of recommended titles, each accompanied by a short
synopsis, is arranged under such headings as 'The Indispen-
sables', or 'Trout Fishing', the whole list adding up to 'The
Fisherman's Library'. Compiled with Ransome's usual
erudition and flair, it remains the best starting point for a
fisherman wishing to build up a library today. He felt strongly
about fishing books:

> We do not think of them as books but as men. They are our
> companions and not only at the riverside. Summer and
> winter they are with us and what a pleasant company they
> are. Here is Walton the ironmonger and friend of bishops,
> Cotton the somewhat graceless cavalier, Plunket-Greene
> the singer, Younger the cobbler, Martin and Walbran who
> kept fishing tackle shops, Nelson the schoolmaster, Grey
> the politician, sundry journalists, many soldiers, a bench of
> lawyers, a synod of parsons, and Thomas Tod Stoddart
> who, when a contemporary who had risen high in the
> world asked him what he was doing replied almost with
> indignation, 'Doing? Doing? Man, I'm an angler.'

This feeling that books were alive lead him to collect
voraciously, and his own library was extensive and eclectic.
There were several series of English classics, Marx's *Das
Kapital*, a large number of detective stories from his reviewing

days, poetry, essays, travel books, 35 books on chess, 250 biographies and over 400 books on sailing and navigation, about 200 on Russia and China. There were more than 300 fishing titles in the list. Given that his earlier library had been sold, to his despair, by his daughter Tabitha in 1940, this was an extraordinary collection.

The library contained many fishing books of great value and historical interest. Several of the books had belonged to his father, others were gifts from fellow fishermen, including a copy of Dame Juliana Berners's *Treatise on Fishing with an Angle*, which had been given to Francis Hirst by Herbert Hoover, and then by Hirst to Ransome. Many of the books had review slips inside them, some with Ransome's notes for his reviews on the back.

There were some valuable books in the collection, including a partial manuscript of the draft of John Beever's *Practical Flyfishing*, seven editions of Walton and Cotton's *Complete Angler*, and a first edition of Robert Nobbes's *The Complete Troller* of 1682. There were only two of F. M. Halford's books, the standard fishing texts of Ransome's youth, although most of Halford's rival G. E. M. Skues's books were there. (As a northern fisherman, Ransome was bored by the extended quarrel between followers of Halford and Skues as to the merits of upstream and downstream fishing and the use of nymphs; he nowhere refers to it in his writing. Skues is quoted approvingly in *Mainly About Fishing* for a remark on acquiring fly tying materials cheaply.) The library also boasted six fishing books in Russian, although surprisingly not a copy of Aksakov.

After his death, Evgenia sold many of his books to California State University at Fullerton. Others are now in the Ransome room at Abbot Hall Museum in Kendal, along with part of his furniture and fishing equipment.

As he became less able to move around Ransome spent more time with his books. He was generous with advice to other fishermen who tried to write. In 1957 he took up the cause of his friend Harry Morritt, who had sent him the original vulturine guineafowl feathers with which the elver flies were made. Morritt had published a small book in 1929 called *Troutfishing: Ways and Wiles*, and it was republished with Ransome's help in 1950. For some years Morritt had been putting together a sequel, and Ransome suggested his own publisher, Jonathan Cape. The trouble was that Morritt had written only 26,000 words, and Cape doubted this would make a viable book, even if drawings were included as Ransome suggested. Ransome was by now acting as Morritt's agent and editor, encouraging him to write more and even suggesting how to do it.

> Books ought to be, or very well can be, like the deathless worm or the cooked whiting, their heads and tails closely connected. Now then, couldn't you expand, and enjoy expanding, on Harry Morritt as a little boy in relation to at least two earlier generations of fishermen. Father, grand-father, aged keepers (who were probably quite young but seemed Methusalahs). And, at the other end of the book take a hint from Abraham sacrificing Isaac, and make a burnt offering of your Robin, serving him up garnished with little trout from the Tees, telling how at a discreet distance you watched him paddling and catching fish where you had done the same once upon a time.

In response to Ransome's suggestions, Morritt added a chapter on teaching his son to fish. Cape was still unhappy, and Ransome contacted the publishers Adam and Charles Black, who agreed to publish the book which still had less than a hundred pages. As Ransome had suggested, it was illustrated with woodcuts by Raymond Sheppard. Ransome proposed the title *The Constant Fisherman*. The book was published in 1957 and quickly achieved a classic status it has never lost.

Ransome was putting together his own book at this time; in fact, he was thinking about two new fishing books. The first was provisionally named *Best Fishing Stories*, and he had been negotiating with Faber over it since at least 1952. The idea was to extract the best fishing stories from a large number of authors and bring them together in a single volume. Ransome made detailed preparations for the book, including a list of authors and episodes, and went so far as to count the exact number of words in each piece. The original list of authors had a strongly literary slant, including Hazlitt, Burton, Thoreau, Mark Twain and Bunyan, but this was pared down to a list which included the literary, such as Maupassant (*Deux Amis*), Kingsley (*Water Babies*), and Blake (*A Princess of Thule*), the popular, including Williamson (*Salar the Salmon*) and Buchan (*John Macnab*), as well as contemporary fishing authors such as Plunket Greene and Negley Farson.

In his notes, Ransome asked himself whether true accounts would be allowed, and concluded they should, as long as they were as good as the fictional ones; in the most complete list of titles, factual accounts outnumber fictional ones. The material Ransome gathered was even more varied than that, including a 1947 letter from the American professional angler and fly tier James Leisenring to G. E. M. Skues about using Skues's nymph patterns on American streams. The book was to be 85,000 words long, and was announced by Faber in the early 1950s.

Then something went wrong. Despite putting together a considerable file of material, Ransome eventually abandoned the book. In 1958, six years later, Faber wrote to him in desperation 'Do please try to finish off this collection before too long as we are most anxious to have the book, and it has been announced now for I hate to think how many years.' The plea was in vain, and the book never appeared. But many of the pieces on Ransome's list made their way into the fishing anthology *The Magic Wheel*, edited by David Profumo and Graham Swift in 1986.

The second book was to be all his own. The raw material was his radio talks and writings on fishing since the appearance of *Rod and Line*, and especially some of the pieces written for the book on flies which never appeared. His original idea seems to have been to do a revised edition of *Rod and Line*, because his own copy of that book, now in the Ransome room at Abbot Hall Museum, has a list of 'Possible additions' written by Ransome at the back, and this includes most of the broadcasts. But at some stage he decided a completely new book was needed.

The centre-piece was the story of the elver fly, but the collection, published in 1959 as *Mainly About Fishing* after alternative titles such as *Talking of Fish* – referring to the origin of several of the chapters as radio talks – and, more strangely, *Fishy Papers*, had been rejected. It is illustrated with several photographs in colour and black and white of exotic plankton and some of Ransome's own flies, including a frontispiece showing his Port and Starboard and elver flies.

The book has fewer but longer pieces than *Rod and Line*, and the subject matter is less eclectic, yet Ransome had lost none of his ability to write about complex subjects in an accessible way. He is less ironic in this book than in the earlier one, and his erudition and wide reading are more evident. There is a notable cast of fishermen and their books and diaries, including such nineteenth-century fishing diarists as Kilvert, Hawthorne and Dorothy Wordsworth, the Cromwellian trooper Richard Franck and his fly tying bag, an eighteenth-century Yorkshire poacher, and the painter Zoffany who put an accurate salmon fly into a portrait he painted of the Atholl family. There is also John Younger, an early nineteenth-century shoemaker, author and expert salmon fisherman in the Tweed, who had thought deeply about salmon flies and had anticipated some of Ransome's conclusions, a clutch of Victorian fly-dressers, and a tailpiece about a strange misprint in the first edition of Izaak Walton's *Compleat Angler*. A couple of pieces in the old style, one especially about the pleasures of a travelling fishing rod, display Ransome's writing at its best.

No man who has ever travelled with a fishing-rod finds himself able to travel happily without one. A rod marks the difference between travel and going to work, though, indeed, a rod in the rack is sometimes enough to make going to work a kind of holiday. It has a magic effect upon its owner, as he sits on the carriage beneath it, conscious of it. The sloth of the imagination is stirred by its mere presence. To have a rod in the rack over your head is to have the fishing faculties on the alert. The landscape swaying past is no meaningless phantasmagoria. The rivers are not sleeping beauties but awake and beckoning as on a fishing day . . . The presence of a rod in the rack above the traveller is enough to put mere land in its place, as something between rivers, as stepping-stones, or viaducts, as material for river banks or beds.

The title of the book got him into momentary trouble, as a short letter to Ransome from Robert Hartman, a fellow fisherman who had in 1935 published a book called, simply, *About Fishing*, pointed out.

Dear Sir

The three-word title of your latest book on fishing has absorbed the whole of the title of my own book on fishing! I feel that the least you can do in return is to send me some vulturine hackle feathers.

Yours truly
Robert Hartman

Ransome replied, full of contrition, three days later.

Dear Sir

Your letter horrifies me. What a dreadful thing to have done . . . Mr Black and I had a lot of trouble in finding a name for the book. Then, suddenly, we had it. I now know how we got it, and cannot sufficiently apologise for my unintentional, half-witted, kleptomaniac picking up of your title.

A row was averted large because Ransome had written approvingly of Hartman's book in the 1955 National Book League pamphlet ('Combines elementary instruction for the beginner with ripe wisdom to be pondered by all . . . it includes some good common sense on the tying of flies illustrated with beautiful clarity by the author'), and Hartman had, in his book, listed *Rod and Line* among his favourite eight fishing books. Ransome quickly sent off some vulturine guineafowl feathers, and in return Hartman recommended a chess problem book. A new friendship was made.

Mainly About Fishing was dedicated to one of Ransome's

fishing companions, Roland Pedder. They had both been in hospital in early 1958 while the book was going through the press, and had kept each others' spirits up by jointly translating a poem about a salmon by the seventeenth-century poet Henry Vaughan. The original was in Latin, and they put it into English in the metre of Longfellow's Hiawatha. Pedder did the first draft, and Ransome modified and improved it.

Henry Vaughan (1622–1696) sends a salmon

Pray receive this gift of salmon
From your old friend Henry Vaughan,
Caught on fly and honest fish-hook,
Not on minnow, worm or prawn.

From the lowest depths of ocean
To the rushing, rapid stream
Came this swift, strong, silly salmon
Crazed by love's compelling dream.

Salmo salar, tricked by feather
(False in fact though seeming fine)
Tricked by hackle, silk and tinsel,
Tugs in vain at rod and line.

Peace was his: he lay in secret,
Hid in swiftly swirling pool.
But he gave up ease and pleasure
When he took my fly – the fool.

Safe he was until he caught it,
That pretended shrimp or fish;
Now, being caught himself, the captor
Lies in state upon the dish.

Moral

Meditate and learn the lesson
Sport is ready here to teach;
Men no wiser are than salmon;
There's a fatal fly for each.

Ransome found fishing increasingly hard, although he continued with all the old enthusiasm for a few more years. In September 1960, at the age of 76, he caught a 7lb salmon at Cockermouth, but noted in his diary 'I expect this will be my last fish.' It was. By 1963 he was limited to his wheel chair, and confined to the top floor of his cottage. In 1965 he was moved into a hospital near Manchester where he died in 1967.

★

Ransome's own judgement of himself as a fisherman was characteristically modest. He records that he was over 60 before he caught a 20lb salmon; that his biggest brown trout, caught in 1955, was only 3¼lb; and his biggest sea trout, caught in 1956 in daylight on a very small (7/16″) Port and Starboard fly of his own design, was only 5½lbs.

I think I should say here that I have never claimed to be a good fisherman, but only one who thoroughly enjoys fishing. Going fishing I have never thought to catch more fish than anyone else, luckily, for I should seldom have succeeded. Then, too, in the matter of enjoyment I am fortunate in that no sort of class-consciousness affects my pleasure. I have had great pleasure fishing for salmon, sitting as it were on the strong supporting stream. But I have also had great pleasure sitting on a wicker basket, one of a row of fishermen on the tow-path beside a still canal, watching for the slight quiver of the float that should signal a roach mouthing my maggot. It is now too late for me to catch every kind of English fish . . . I have not caught a vendace or a shad or a sturgeon. Nor have I caught any very big fish. My most notable was a perch 3lbs. 2 oz., before which a plumber stood in a Hampstead lodging unable to tear himself away, muttering reverently 'The FISH of a LIFETIME!'

His importance as a fisherman was not that he caught record fish. Ransome's fishing writing, which occupies the rest of this book, together with his published works, gives a picture of him as a particular type of fisherman. He was an all-rounder, an unusual figure among fishermen who tend to specialise in coarse fish, game fish or sea fish. Although he had little sea fishing experience, Ransome was completely at home with coarse and game fishing. In later life he fished mainly for trout, sea trout, grayling and salmon, but his *Rod and Line* pieces show great familiarity with coarse fishing techniques and great affection and respect for coarse fishermen. And within the game fishing tradition, he was very much a northerner, not at all interested in the disputes which tore southern English fishermen apart during the early years of the century. For him, fishing was too important a part of everyday life to be treated as a rarefied pursuit set around with snobbish rules. 'We in the north . . .' he regularly writes, and he was proud to belong to two strong regional traditions, those of Yorkshire and of the Lakes, which fished in a down-to-earth way using any method which seemed appropriate.

Fishing was for him, as for many, a respite from the complexities and concerns of everyday life and relationships, an escape from confusion and from boredom. He thought of fishing as a link with his father's life, which he had not managed successfully while his father was alive. There was an element of almost pagan ritual in his approach to fishing and to the countryside. Whenever he visited Coniston he furtively dipped his hand in the lake to mark his return. The sense of participation in an ancient ritual larger than himself pervades his essay 'The First Day at the River' and several others in *Rod and Line*, like secret music he and a few fellow enthusiasts alone can hear. It is perhaps a sign of a self-sufficient person who has been disappointed by much in life, but who knows that fishing will not fail him.

His fishing writing mirrors these concerns. His approach was both scholarly – he was meticulous in researching historical sources and crediting previous writers with important insights – and direct: he wrote from his own experience about what happened to him and what he saw around him. His appeal is that he is a writer who fishes, and tells the reader about it, rather than a fisherman who writes. As a result, there

is an important difference between his approach and the way
in which most people write about fishing. In most fishing
writing only one of two things happens: the fisherman does or
does not catch the fish. The fisherman who writes in his spare
time tries endlessly to vary the way this is described, and
usually, desperate to say something new, ends by describing
the moment in increasingly extravagant terms.

Ransome, a professional writer of considerable skill, does
the contrary. He rarely describes catching a fish at all, and
when he does it is likely to contain unusual elements or
perspectives: the carp which has broken the line returns
the float to the fisherman; the fisherman, thinking himself
unobserved, talks to the fish; or the action is interrupted by
an apt reference to an eighteenth-century fishing writer who
had a similar experience.

Ransome's pieces contained in the rest of this book give us
material that has remained hidden for the last fifty years. They
confirm his reputation as one of the most important writers on
the countryside and fishing this century. He is the best guide
we have to fishing and to other fishing writers. Above all, he
conveys the excitement of fishing. This is the voice of a
humane man, an intelligent observer, and an exceptional
writer for whom fishing was a lifelong passion. Few people
are lucky enough to find their passion; fewer still convey its
essence to others with Arthur Ransome's skill.

*

Most of Ransome's fishing writing that follows has not
been reprinted since its first appearance in newspapers
and magazines between 1911 and the 1950s. A few pieces
printed here have not been previously published at all, and are
taken from Ransome's own manuscript copy; this includes a
fragment from his unfinished novel, *The River Comes First*,
which was not published with the others in Hugh Brogan's
collection, *Coots in the North*. One excerpt from the Swallows
and Amazons books (all still in print) has been included. All
the pieces that are not attributed to another source are taken
from the 'Rod and Line' column that appeared weekly in the

Manchester Guardian between 1925 and 1930. In a few cases, I have lightly edited his journalism, as Ransome did himself for his own book *Rod and Line* when it was first published in 1929. This consists mainly of correcting misprints and removing references to contemporary fishing events. I have also taken out other less relevant material and a few repetitions.

THE CATCHING OF THE GREAT TROUT
(Clifford Webb's drawing from *Swallowdale*)

ON
FISHING

by

1 • UNDILUTED PLEASURE

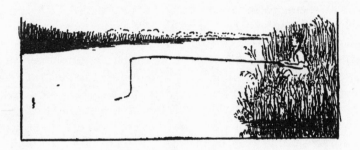

Fishing by the Way

WALKING THROUGH B—— at 12 o'clock on a Saturday morning, I noticed some fishing tackle in an iron-monger's window. There were stiff, four-jointed light rods, and sturdy, big-ringed rods for pike, spinning bait, floats of many colours, and little wooden frames wound with lines; all the materials for coarse fishing, which sport I had never tried. Time does not matter on the road. Adventures do. So I walked into the shop and asked, 'Is there fishing in these parts?'

'There is for members of our Association,' he replied. 'We fish in the river; jack, perch, roach and dace. There are trout, too, they say. Are you a Waltonian, sir?'

'I have never fished for anything but little trout,' I said, but I suppose he saw that a magic was in progress between a case of floats and my inquisitive eyes.

'I could put you up for a member,' he said. 'Are you staying here?'

I told him no, but asked him how much it would cost to fit me out with rod, line, hooks, and one of the magnificent floats.

'I could do it for a few shillings,' he said. 'We will make it as cheap as we can. But you will have to see the President.'

'And who is he?'

'Mr Martin. You will find him at the post office.'

In this way the adventure started. He wrote his name on a piece of the official ironmongery paper, and with this credential I went to the post office. Mr Martin was at lunch. The day being Saturday, he would not return till 6. 'Where did he live?' They told me, and I walked for a mile and a half up the hill behind B——, and found a curly-haired postman in a white little house. I told him of my ambition, my hopes, my eagerness, and the President became eloquent and instructive. He took my three-shilling subscription, and gave me a little orange card that lies on the table before me, setting forth the prize list, the list of private waters where I might fish, notices of competitions, a list of the officials of the B—— Angling Society, and, in the space for the member's name, my own, written in the official handwriting of the President. I took on a new dignity as I put it in my pocket. For a similar feeling of exaltation I had to look back to the day when in the little book-lined room in the big buildings in the rue de Richelieu, I had been handed the card that authorised my admission to the reading rooms of the Bibliothèque Nationale. That card was not signed by a President. This was.

He went on to talk of worms, and the use of the float. From a manure heap in his back garden he plucked out worms and put them in a tin box. In the scullery of his presidential house he held a hunk of bread under the running tap, and squeezed it to a sticky, white pulp in the fold of a towel, wrapped it up in newspaper, gave it me and told me it was better than the worms.

I left him with the feeling that I had already caught a creel of handsome fish. At the ironmongery there were spread on the counter a coil of line, a little reel, six hooks of huge size, gutted and ready for use, a little box of split shot, a length of fine gut, a bamboo fishing rod, and no float. I looked eagerly for one of these emerald and scarlet monsters.

'What about a float?' I asked, disguising my enthusiasm, but glancing in spite of myself at that shining case.

'You had better have a quill,' he said, and took a slim, mottled porcupine quill from a drawer behind the counter.

The original motive of the adventure had been snatched away from me. But I was a member of the B—— Angling Society, and had put away childish things.

'Are quills better?' I asked, weakly.

'Much better,' he replied, and I turned my back on the case of floats. I could not bear to look at them.

We wound the line on the reel, and fixed it on the rod with indiarubber rings. He rigged the tackle for me, even putting on the split shot, that I might lose no time by the waterside. 'You bait with bread,' he said, 'and if that doesn't answer try worms. Go to the left outside here, and then to the right and round the church, by Charing Yard. You cross the railway, and the bridge over the river, and then to the left over the meadows. You can't miss our waters. Good luck to you, sir, and I hope you will have a pleasant day.'

I went out bravely.

In the window were those mighty floats, like eggs in carnival. I looked at them, hesitated, and went back.

'I'll have one of those, just to put in my pocket,' I said.

He gave it me without a smile.

At an inn further up the street I ate bread and cheese and drank beer. The landlord talked fishing, and I sailed close-hauled to the wind and was not taken aback. Then down by the church and over the bridge. On the path across the meadows I met three small boys with sticks and threads, not members of the B—— Angling Society. I could not help asking them the way to the Society's waters, and they told me with respect. The Wey at B—— is a sluggish stream, flowing leisurely below the hills. The meadows lie flat beside it on one side. There are woods on the other. The river turns and twists, so that the angler has a rich choice of fishing ground. I passed one or two old men sitting on camp stools watching their quills. My float itched in my pocket. I chose a pleasant place between two willows, took my mackintosh from my knapsack, spread it on the ground, put the rod together, led the line through the rings, fastened on the gut and float and fixed bread on the hook, and, after sounding for the proper depth with a piece of string and a pipe-cleaner, swung the tackle out up-stream, lowered it till the quill rested in the water, and watched it float slowly down. This I repeated many times, crouching on the mackintosh.

A kingfisher, in his suit of azure mail, flew swiftly up and down before me in the sunshine. A water-rat, keeping his whiskers dry, swam past close under the bank, throwing a wash to either side of him, and looking up at me with a wide, wary eye.

Far down stream one of the old men landed something. I was watching him when my quill dived out of sight. I struck hard, and an empty hook leapt high into the air.

I rebaited and began again. The hours went on, and the sun shone, and the brown water flowed by, slowly carrying my quill until I lifted it gently out, and dropped it, splashless, above. I had always maintained that, of the pleasures of walking, few are comparable to that of sitting still, and here, on my way into London, with only one day's tramp to bring me to Hyde Park, I had fallen into the most delicious of sedentary adventures. Three centuries rolled back for me. Dimly, as I remembered, I heard Piscator and Venator discussing on the bank beside me, and, over the green meadows, 'The Milkmaid's Song.' I looked at my boots, expecting to find them buckled shoes.

And then – it seemed incredible at the time, and is so now – I caught a fish. The quill dipped, I struck, but not too hard, a violent excitement communicated itself to my wrist, and I lifted out of the water, lashing to and fro in shining, agitated curves, a very indignant little fish. Mine was the happiness; but the glory belongs to President Martin of the B—— Angling Society. He had made the bait, and told me exactly how to use it. In fact, with me as an unworthy instrument, he had caught this little, wriggling, silver-bellied roach. I could not climb the long mile to his house to take it to him. And, perhaps, he did not want it. I did not want it myself. So I unhooked that energetic little fish, felt him wet in my hand, observed his fins, his panting gills, and, being assured that the honour of the B—— Angling Society had been upheld, set him gently in the water. He wriggled and disappeared.

I rebaited and fished on, but caught no more. Only, as the afternoon failed, and the sun cooled, I watched the kingfisher shooting to and fro, and thought of Walton, and fishing, and of a tent by a little trout stream in the north, a little wooded stream whose trees are garnished with my hooks. I thought of these things and of the hospitality of the road, that had suddenly given me, a stranger, walking and alone, this afternoon of eighteenth century quiet. These other anglers, on their stools, had fished here every night. Yet, here was I among them who had never been in B—— before. And I praised the road and Mr Martin, and set the adventure among my memories. A mild adventure; yes, but what of that? We do not judge our memories by their violence.

At dusk I packed my rod and pushed it through the straps of my knapsack. I was to sleep in Guildford that night. I pulled the float from my pocket. It shone still glorious in the twilight. Half-angry with myself, half-sentimental, I flung it far up stream, an offering to the river. Before I left the bank I watched it swim majestically past me round the bend of brown water and out of sight, in all its panoply of red and emerald.   (from *The Tramp*, February 1911)

On Fishing Too Well

LET ME hasten to explain that I can write on this subject in a wholly disinterested manner. I am never likely to fish too well myself. At the same time I disagree with those who say at once that it is impossible to do it. All depends on the object of fishing. If the object is merely the rapid collection of corpses in a basket, then, I suppose, it is impossible to fish too well. But, for most of us, that is not the object. We do not like taking fish too easily. We have abandoned with our greedy childhood the practice of catching trout in thick water with a worm. The rules we lay down for ourselves in fishing are all to the advantage of the fish. Spinning, for example, with one of the new spool reels is so easy that a man comes to feel a contempt for his own successes. At first it is exciting enough, but a fisherman soon realises that by spinning with this tackle in 'a good minnow water' he is exchanging the interest of his fishing for the gross pleasure of getting a lot of fish. He comes at last to abstain from spinning with this tackle except in dead low water, in which the capture of trout by this method recovers some of the difficulty that alone makes it worth the time spent in it.

Fortunately for us, in England, fly-fishing for trout is not likely to become as easy as all this. But an American fisherman, Mr Hewitt, in *Telling on the Trout* talks of taking fifty small fish out of a pool in preparation for the attack on the big one at the head of it, whom, if they were not caught, they might warn of his approach.

> It is not hard (in America) to hook and land by far the larger number of those seen to rise, and many times recently I have succeeded in catching nearly all the rising fish encountered. This always seems to be the only real test of a fisherman – how large a percentage of the fish he sees rising can he catch?

He came to England and fished the chalk streams. Not even his fourteen-foot casts stained with nitrate of silver and developed photographically availed him anything. He did badly, and was properly delighted. 'I went home very tired, but feeling that here indeed was the great school for fly-fishermen. It seemed as if there were unlimited possibilities of skill and knowledge to be developed to take these rising fish.' This was admission from the most successful of fishermen that the true pleasure of fishing demands a measure of failure. It will, however, be a long time before any English fly-fisher attains such infallibility as to drive him from continent to continent in search of more difficult fish.

Though not one of us is likely to fish too well, when measuring himself against perfection, we must not forget that this is not the ordinary standard. We usually measure ourselves not against perfection but against each other. And so it happens that even in England and even in fly-fishing it is possible to fish too well. In an old diary of my father's I find a

note that 'The aim of an all-round angler should be to catch his
fair share of fish under the existing conditions.' That definition
can hardly be bettered. The presence in a fishing club of one
man who catches invariably two or three times his fair share of
fish is good for nobody, least of all for the man himself. His
reputation rides him like a nightmare. The poor fellow cannot
afford to have an ordinary bad day like the rest of us. Failure
for us is all in the day's work. For him it is something to
brood upon at nights. Our moderate successes are undiluted
pleasure. His immoderate success is marred by comparison
with his companions'. The best of fishing, even of fly-fishing,
is not a wholly solitary pursuit. Our friend's day is part of our
own, though he may be fishing the beat below the bridge and
we the beat above, so that we do not meet until the evening,
when we turn our catches into the scales at the inn. His day is
ours and ours his. He is a poor sort of fisherman who is pleased
if in the evening he finds that his friend's basket is very much
lighter than his own. In fishing, as in chess, it is best to have a
partner a little, but not much, more skilful than oneself.

A year ago, fishing one of those chalk streams that help to
compensate the South of England for not being the North, I
heard a story of a man who fished too well. Fishing the same
stream this year, and with the same companion, I was
reminded of it. A certain country living was in the gift of the
squire. A parson greatly desired it. His friend, who knew the
squire, recommended him, and he was invited to spend the
week-end with the squire. They had an entirely satisfactory
conversation on church matters. On the Sunday the parson
preached a sermon with which the squire was delighted. On
the Saturday afternoon, on the village green, the parson had
shown that his cricket would be a valuable asset to the village
eleven. His beliefs, his sermon, and his spin-bowling had all
been equally satisfactory to the squire. On the Monday the
squire went off for the day to the neighbouring market town.
The parson missed the morning train. There was no other till
the afternoon, and the parson returned to the house to wait for
it. In happy mood, confident that the appointment would be
his, the parson sauntered through the grounds until, not far

from the house, he came to the river. There was a remarkable hatch of Pale Wateries. In his pocket were flies of his own dressing that seemed of the right shade. He hurried to the house. The housekeeper, who had heard his sermon, was sure that the squire would be delighted to lend him a rod. A few minutes later he was back at the river. His Pale Wateries pleased the trout as well as his sermon and his cricket had pleased the squire. Fish after fish was risen, hooked, and landed. At last the parson looked at his watch. He had but just time to catch his train. He would, he thought, clench the good impression he knew he had made by leaving this handsome dish of fish to greet the squire on his return. He chose but two to take away with him, and left the rest, spread and set out to best advantage upon an enormous tea-tray in the hall. He caught his train and travelled home exulting in the prospect of a delicious life of pious labour and occasional fishing of an astounding quality.

Next day he waited for the postman. There was no letter from the squire, nor was there on the day after that. At the end of a week he sought his friend and begged him to remind the squire that the appointment had not been made.

Two days later the postman delivered a card from the squire with one sentence upon it.

'Sir, I would as soon appoint an otter.'

2 • THE FISHING YEAR

'One Wicket Down; No Score'

WHEN THE FIRST day of the season ends with an empty basket the fisherman feels like the captain of a cricket team who has lost a batsman in the first over. It is an unpleasant feeling, particularly because the fisherman is always in the position of the cricket captain who has put himself in and been himself put out. He is attacked by all manner of doubts. Perhaps this year the thing he has always feared has come to pass and he has forgotten how to fish. Perhaps he has never known. Perhaps he has no right to call himself a fisherman at all, and such baskets as he has had in other years have been nothing but illustrations of 'novice's luck.' Has he set the note for a whole season? Let him comfort himself with the thought that this season at least a great many trout fishermen have had a blank day on their first visit to the river with a fly-rod.

At the beginning of this week there was still ice in many places on the river's edge and huge icicles hung from the rocks, though on the open stretches the sun, that had made me think it might be worth while to fish, was as hot as on many days in summer. The sun had summer warmth, and the river, for all its fringe of ice, was the river of a summer drought. There was very little water. What there was was extremely clear. It was the sort of Eden on which, in summer, the only hope of catching fish is to use a dry fly or to fish at night. And nothing is more useless than to fish a dry fly over fish that are not yet accustomed to take any interest in the surface. I soon began to doubt if the fish were there. If they were, they were taking no interest in Blue Hawks and Light Snipes. From the high banks it was possible in many places to see the whole of the river bottom from one side to the other. There were two or three shoals of grayling, lying as if glued to the bottom. There were several kelts. I did not see a single trout. I saw only two flies. Neither of them was taken by a fish, though both drifted over the likeliest of resting-places.

The question is, How far has the season been postponed? If the conditions on the Eden are the same as those elsewhere it is going to be a late season generally. It is generally said that trout are not worth catching until they have had abundance of insect food. I doubt very much if that is the right formula. Given ordinary conditions, it seems to me that the vigour and fatness of trout must depend less on the appearance of the various insects than on the length of time that has elapsed since the trouts' spawning. This varies in different places, and it seems probable that those trout which are notoriously 'early' are the first to spawn in the autumn, while those which are lean until the end of April are those which spawned late. The hatch of fly marks the progress of the year for us more than for the trout. The old theory of the north that the trout grew fat and healthy as soon as they had had a chance of glutting themselves on March Browns seems to assume that March Browns drop like manna instead of emerging from the river itself, where, if the trout wants them, he can eat them long before, by hatching at the surface, they predispose him to take our flies. But the condition of the river is another matter. Hard late frosts and a long drought at the beginning of the season do seem likely to postpone good fishing and even to hold back the trout. The river during this important time is actually a smaller river, with narrower feeding-grounds. Club waters on the Lune and the Ribble open to-day, but I doubt very much if they will be worth visiting until we get a good downpour, with a southerly wind, to give the rivers a healthy fill of warmer water.

Fishermen will go forth just the same, if only for a dress-rehearsal of a fishing day – something pleasant in itself, even if it does end with the unpleasant feeling of a failure. There is pleasure even in getting together the tackle for the first day, in running through the list and making sure that nothing is forgotten. I went to the Eden without making the list, and I had lost my old one. I forgot two important things. Without a list, going fishing, anything may be forgotten. I knew one man who went pike-fishing and forgot his rod. He cut a branch of a tree and presently landed a five-pounder on it. If he had been fly-fishing his makeshift would not have worked so well. Fishermen, especially on the opening day, have a right to be absent-minded. Their minds have run ahead of them to the river. They need these lists, even if not all of them need a list so comprehensive as that of the old man referred to by Sir George Aston in *Mostly about Trout*. The last item on his list was 'Kiss wife.' In fly-fishing there is not quite so much to remember as in fishing of some other kinds. Even so, there is a good deal – what with rod, net, reel, casts, flies, oil-bottle, line-greaser, scissors, waders, brogues, stockings, and, on a hopeful day, a spring balance. It was a fly-fisher, Pulman, who quoted the delightful rhyme:

> Armed head to foot with baskets, bags, and rods.
> The angler early to the river plods;
> At night his looks the woeful news announce,
> The luggage half a ton, the fish – an ounce.

Until there is a change in the weather it might be as well to leave the spring-balance behind.

'Before the Swallow Dares ...'

WET-FLY FISHING has this considerable advantage over dry, that it is impossible (after the opening of the season) to be quite certain that it is too early to do it. The man who fishes with wet flies can take the winds of March together with the daffodils, whereas he who fishes dry must wait for the swallow, who is careful not to come until he is sure of being able to catch his dinner in the air. The March fisherman may not do much, but he cannot tell how little he will do until he tries. He has an excuse for his day. He can spend it in health, exultation and ever present hope at a time when, fishing dry, he could not in conscience persuade himself that there was the smallest chance of interesting a fish. There are chalk streams in the south beside which no self-respecting angler will show himself before May. Dry-fly fishing is naturally a poor affair until the trout have become accustomed to meet their titbits floating down to them, with sail spread, in Lilliputian fleets. Wet-fly fishing begins as soon as the fish are in condition and ready to take what the stream carries below its surface and so is possible long before there is a hatch of fly. It is less utterly dependent on the season and the day. It is less rigorous in denying excuse to the man who, after the long winter, is almost busting to visit running water with a fishing-rod again.

The early days of the trout season need no heavy baskets to make them delightful. To be at the river is enough. You know that you can hardly hope for more than a few fortunate accidents. You suffer from no moral obligation to make the best of the rise, for there is no rise. Luncheon is a pleasure instead of the nuisance that it becomes later on, when some fishermen make sandwiches of bacon and marmalade, both together, so that they may get through both courses in one, taking a mouthful between casts and never leaving the water. On a cold day in March hot tea out of a thermos flask that numbed fingers find hard to open, potted meat eaten with a spoon out of a cup (much better than any sandwiches) chocolate, and an apple, all these pleasant things are made more delightful by one's need of them and by the abounding leisure given to one by the fish. It is a pleasure to leave the very cold water, to camp in a patch of sunshine, if there is one, in shelter if there is any to be had, and to lunch slowly, watching, on the far side of the river, the sheep munching their way through the daffodils, leaving the flowers as if on purpose and clipping the grass about them to make them show the better. To-day there was a wind you could sharpen a knife on, a violent south-east wind. Starlings were in flocks as if in autumn. The great wind blew them about and chased big splashes of sunshine and shadow across the mountains. But you could see that the clouds had silver linings. A lamb ran silhouetted down the skyline of a little hill, flapping its accidental tail. Although the cold was that of autumn grayling fishing it was March and not October, the best of the trout season was all to come, and it did not matter at all that there were no visible rises in the wind-broken water at my feet, that I saw only three rises all day, and that my basket was extremely light.

In general, the season is late. On the same day last year the sun was warm but not too bright, there was a light wind, a summer's breath, and I had a nice lot of fish nearly all taken on flies imitating the small duns, plenty of which were sailing down the river. To-day a thinly dressed March Brown, with a rather stout body, was the only fly that the fish seemed to notice, and I am pretty certain that they noticed it not because it was like a fly but because it was much more like some of the things they were eating under water. Reports from the Ribble and from the streams farther south suggest that the lateness is more than local. Nowhere, except in some of the smaller streams in sheltered valleys, are the trout in as good condition as they were a year ago.

One thing, however, is certain, and that is that there is no shortage of salmon parr. These little nuisances are all over the place, by no means keeping to the shallows, and the angler who manoeuvres his fly into a nice bit of water that ought to hold a trout is more likely than not to feel that sudden little tap that tells of a parr doing its best to pull his fly to pieces. Still, parr serve their turn, and at this stage of the season there is a sound defence for them. None better than the parr puts a man in training for the season that is to come. Mr Nelson used to say that the best way to give a boy the sense of 'rod touch' was to put him 'among the smolts on a mid-summer evening.' Parr are always ready to do as much for their elders. And these need it, after the winter. Lord Grey, speaking of the need to keep in touch with the flies at the end of a long line and the need to respond instantaneously to the faintest touch at the end of that line, says that the angler 'can only acquire this skill by long experience, and my own opinion is that he can only maintain it by constant practice.'

Now let a man fish never so diligently, unless he have a grayling river close at hand he cannot keep up that constant practice during the winter. A very short absence from the river will lessen his skill even in summer, and after the long winter he returns to the fishing a mere fumbler in comparison with his former self, missing rise after rise. Let him then not grumble at the parr in March, who will sharpen his senses and return him his skill that he may be worthy and ready to meet the trout in April.

Easter Holiday Fishing

EASTER THIS YEAR is likely to bring out more fishermen than flies. The season still holds back. We are still watching for the blackthorn, the free flowering of which is usually a hint that fishing may begin to be worth while – from the point of view of the basket; for several days during March have been delightful enough in themselves to satisfy people who do not weigh their day in the kitchen scales when they come home at night. Hopeful men report a blackthorn in flower here and there, but these can be but rare bushes that share the fisherman's impatience. I have seen none in their full starry glory, but many on the point of breaking out. A day or two of warm weather is all that is needed for them. The rivers need a little more than that. They need a day or two of warmth and a day or two of such rain as is falling at the moment.

This last, I fear, is becoming a permanent need. It is not that the total rainfall over these isles is less. It is that in the general speeding up of modern life even the farmer, supposed to be slow, contributes his full share and hurries the water off his fields in a manner altogether contrary to nature and good fishing. He cleans out the becks and smaller streams, smooths their floors, and would be glad, no doubt, to have them concrete drains. Last year's drought gave him an opportunity which he took, and he busied himself in making one-time excellent becks places no trout would stay in if he could get elsewhere. Weeds and stones alike he flung out on the banks, thinking of the becks simply as means to take the water away as quickly as it comes. The result of this is that rains that should have kept a river in condition for a week raise it to flood height for a few hours and then are gone as if they had not been, while the river drops at once to low summer level. Still, running water is hard to tame, and it has been a delight this spring to watch a beck that had been turned into a characterless canal using each momentary flood and the smallest bends, stones, or tree fallen in autumn to dig out for itself new hollows, to pile up new shallows, and once again to carve its signature. The beck is doing its best, but it can do nothing with the admirable, efficient drainage system of the fields, and until the land slips back to barbarism, drains choke, and fields once more are allowed to be swamps the trout and we shall have to put up with these tropic contrasts between flood and drought. Nothing but steady, gentle rain, a little every night, will nowadays keep rivers at their best. And that we cannot have.

So far, everywhere on the rivers, the main pleasure of fishing has been that of being at the waterside, where, after all, there is much to be seen besides fish. This is the season when a man may see a cloud of longtailed tits blowing through the leafless bushes that overhang the river. Wrens are busy and show the fisherman where they are and what they are about by going into shrill hysterics and scolding him as if they were prepared to drive him out of the river. Dippers are building. Herons, of course, are about as usual, but I have not seen a kingfisher this year. Speaking of kingfishers and herons, the writer of a letter to the *Fishing Gazette* asks for 'the best way of dealing with these vermin'. If herons and kingfishers (members, if rather unscrupulous, of the only angling association to which we all belong) are 'vermin,' what may escape? Most fishermen do not grudge them their share (though herons take rather a big one). Kingfishers can even be useful and give a fellow-angler a tip as to where to find minnows. If any fisherman feels called upon to destory them, let him turn his attention first to more urgent needs. Let him devise means of putting down other 'vermin,' such as holiday-makers in boats, cows watering in the river, bulls, the misanthropic type of wasp, people who put up barbed wire, the stranger's spaniel who proudly retrives your pike float and asks for praise, and perhaps that fisherman I met yesterday who was fishing worm downstream against a howling upstream wind, stamping about in good fly-water, and splashing a monstrous worm like a serpent on a meat-hook under every likely bush. If kingfishers are vermin to be destroyed, there is something to be said for allowing 'justifiable homicide' to cover the removal of a man like that. But I think not. The sight of a man fishing worm in low water downstream against the wind was something to be valued in itself, to warm the heart with laughter in chill days.

Christmas Eve in April

IT IS IMPOSSIBLE to write about the fishing of last week-end without adding one belated note to the chorus of disapproval of the weather. To leave our supposedly bleak north, to travel the length of England for the privilege of fishing a chalk stream in April, to listen for the cuckoo and to hear only the whistling of the wind, to come south for warmth and be waked by the wet snow blowing in at the window, to come downstairs in a Hampshire fishing inn, with the leaves green on the trees, and to be greeted, very properly, with best wishes for a Merry Christmas and a Happy New Year, to look out on the water meadows white with snow, is to realise that one might have fared not so far and a great deal better.

Not that I had anything to complain of (excepting the

weather) on the little chalk stream in Hampshire which I had come so far to fish. It is a very little river, with all the character of the bigger chalk streams excepting that its fish match its size. Everything is in delightful miniature. Quarter-pounders bulge and smut and tail and make good hearty rises, bury themselves in weed beds and require from the fisherman all those delightful ingenuities which make the chalk stream fisher think disparagingly of other waters. The fish are small, but great-souled, ding-dong fighters who are fond of reminding the fisherman of that passage in *The Compleat Angler* where Piscator points out to his companion that a man cannot lose what he has never had. There is a fair sprinkling of half-pounders, and two or three pounders as aloof and un-approachable as the candidates for glass cases who live in larger rivers. Hospitable they are too, ready to encourage their friends. I had twenty-two for a couple of days' fishing, but have seldom had to vary so continually the means of catching them.

For most of the time it was very cold, and there was a howling north-east wind. Very few flies were to be seen, and the signs of life given by the fish were for the most part sudden swirls showing some brisk underwater movement but not breaking the surface. The fish that made such rises came well at the little pale watery nymph of Hardy's, a little dove-grey creature with a turn or two of thin silver thread. This fly served me very well in the same place last year. In the deeper water they were less interested in this fly, but came eagerly to a large black hackle with white silk body and a short tag of peacock and red ibis carried on over the top of the body and tied in at the head. I had made this fly for experimental purposes, but until I lost it in a fish it seemed to be just what these fish were waiting for. I got most of my best fish on it, and the others on a large Tup and a Hirst's Fancy; though I must not forget the rising fish who took my little green palmer, also an experimental tying, so pleasantly that, having already all the fish I wanted, I put him back in return for his compliment.

I saw only two fish whose rises broke the surface. One

refused three different dry flies, but came to the nymph. The other was rising just under a bush, absolutely unapproachable from below, even if the wind had been such as to encourage upstream casting instead of being almost directly downstream. I could not see what he was rising at, but thought that as he lived under a bush he probably would not be much surprised by the arrival of some sort of grub or caterpillar even though it was a little early in the season for such things. I threw a loose line on the water, dropping my oiled green palmer downstream just above the bush. The line straightened quickly. Another second and there would have been drag on the fly, but just as the line drew out straight up came the nose of the charming little fat trout and my green palmer was no more to be seen in the cave under the bush. I tightened, held him very lightly, and that obliging little fellow swam out from under the bush, then, when he was safely clear of it and I hurried him, leapt nobly into the air, plunged into a weed bed, was handlined out, landed, and, being very lightly hooked, was returned with many thanks and much goodwill.

I tried to do the same thing again with another bush, where I thought there ought to be a trout though none was showing there. I lost my beautiful green palmer in that bush, and there it remains. It is gone, but I shall certainly tie some more. There is a place in the meadows just below the Izaak Walton where I have seen caterpillars fall from a bush almost into the open mouths of waiting trout, and among those caterpillars, this year or next, shall fall my green palmer.

Snapdragon

THERE APPEARS TO be the sharpest difference of opinion among fishermen as to the state of the rivers and the fish. Different men, fishing the same river on the same day, exult in satisfactory baskets and complain that the fish are so dour that there is no pleasing them. As for men fishing different rivers, it would be as difficult to make sense of their contradictory opinions as to see at a first glance the picture that may some day be made out of the jumbled bits of a jig-saw puzzle. From the Cumberland Derwent: 'No earthly use for the last week, but the river is falling and should be right at the week-end unless a deluge is in store for us.' From the Ribble: 'Dirty flood on Sunday, cold and blustery weather on Monday.' Yet fish were caught on the cold and blustery Monday, and parts of Tuesday were as good as anyone could wish. It is no use complaining of the Wharfe or the Lune. Baskets have been made on both rivers. The truth about all the rivers seems to be that we have got into a period of snapdragon weather, when the fisherman who lives on the water and can rush down to the river at the first hint of a 'benign moment' can do very well indeed, while he who comes from afar may hit on a bad day and may have the even more annoying experience of arriving on a better day just when the benign moment is over and the day is relapsing into a bad one.

Snapdragon weather of this kind is properly humbling to the good fisherman and encouraging to those of the more ordinary kind (to whom I belong), who are more inclined to rejoice at getting a good day than to resent as unusual the common phenomenon of a day that might have been much better. It makes it obvious even to the good fisherman that his success depends much more upon the fish than upon any peculiar skill of his own. It need hardly be said how pleasant it is for the ordinary fisherman to be given such incontrovertible proof that the responsibility for failure is at least shared.

Consider, for example, what happened yesterday. The day was one of half a dozen weathers. There was sunshine, there were clouds, there was thunder, there was drenching rain, there was an upstream wind, there were squalls that blackened the face of the river and sometimes in long straight reaches drove breaking waves before them. At the same time it was not a March day. Blackthorn has been out for some time. So has the wild cherry. And a cuckoo was calling in the rain. I fished a stretch where I have seldom done much, though it has always tempted me, a stretch well broken with rocks and little pools. For ten minutes I did nothing. Then, suddenly, there was in the air the promise that the benign moment had arrived. I saw a fish come to the surface in rough water. He had my Snipe and Yellow as it fell. For just about an hour I was catching fish, and at the end of it half a dozen good ones were in my basket. One of these took a Snipe and Purple, the others all came to yellow-bodied flies, most of them to a very small fly with a body of dull yellow silk ribbed with primrose and hackled with a feather from one of the many chaffinches that at this time of the year meet their end in battle with their fellows. I had noticed the feathers on the ground at the bottom of the orchard. Next day, wanting a particular shade of hackle to copy a small greenish fly that I had seen the fish taking at the end of the week, I remembered these feathers. Only two were left of the soft feathers I wanted. In nature nothing is wasted, and other birds, busy with their building, had lined their nests with the feathers of the dead. Still, two feathers there were, and with one of them a fly was made which served very well during a bright glaring interval of windless sunshine when the fish would not look at the rather larger snipe.

With half a dozen fish in the basket my fishing came temporarily to an end. I stumbled on a slippery stone and filled a wader. If I had realised then that this was a snapdragon day I would have disregarded it and fished on. As it was, I went ashore and emptied the water out and wasted time over trying to dry a sock. When I began again I caught one more good fish. Every one of my seven had been well hooked. There had been no short rises. Anyone who had watched the catching of those seven trout would have had the mistaken illusion that I knew how to fish. Of course it was not so. The truth was that when fish want to take a fly they can do so, and I happened to be putting flies in their way at the very moment when they wanted them. There, anyhow were my seven fish, and I moved on, planning the distribution of a really tremendous basket. For these seven were easily the best seven I had ever had on fly from this river.

But the tremendous basket was never made. I got an eighth, in the evening, just before a huge black cloud swept all the light from the sky and came down on the river in heavy rain.

In the interval, during what should, normally, have included much of the best of a fishing day, I could not catch a single fish worthy of a place in the basket beside the first seven. I had plucked my raisin from the snapdragon and now could do nothing but burn my fingers. The good fish simply were not to be had. If I had started work at the river an hour and a half later than I did I should have had a few little trout and a poor opinion of the day. As it was, I was lucky enough to get a very jolly bit of fishing and a most encouraging object lesson. During the greater part of that day, when I could catch none but the smaller fish, I was no worse a fisherman than when one good fish after another had risen to my flies and grabbed them so securely that I could not have missed a rise if I had tried.

The fisherman's are negative virtues. He cannot make a trout feed if it does not want to (there is a possible exception to this in minnow fishing and fishing with such flies as are calculated less to resemble food than to stimulate the trout to clean the river from them or to learn them to be such monstrosities), but if a trout is in a mood to feed all that he has to do is to avoid doing something to make it change its mind. Snapdragon weather, such as we are now enjoying, is that of days of which it can be truly said that the part is much greater than the whole. The important thing is to be at the river during just that part.

Whitsuntide Fishing

AT RARE INTERVALS people interested in motor-cars organise an exhibition at which appear not only cars of the latest models, cars in daily use, but cars that have been preserved for old time's sake, cars that illustrate ancient history, cars that have rusted for years in outhouses as roosting-places for hens, cars that have been given a lick of paint and a drop of oil for this occasion, taste petrol for the first time for a quarter of a century, and come out snorting like old war-horses at the long unaccustomed sound of military music. Something like this is seen at the rivers during the Whitsuntide holidays. These holidays fall at a delightful season, and if the weather is all that it should be, as this year it was, there is a great stirring of happy memories and long-laid dust in lumber-rooms. Men who 'used to do a bit of fishing' and see that other men no younger than themselves still fish naturally choose Whitsuntide for an attempt to recapture a half-forgotten pleasure. Why not? The very sunshine seems the same that lit those distant days. Rods leave twill cases that have long been moved only by spring cleanings of the thorough, devastating kind that shake a house from cellar to garrets. Somewhere in a drawer is an old fly-book. There is a reel on which, perhaps, the line is a little sticky. No matter. It will serve. And with twenty years off his shoulders, wondering why he has been wasting his week-ends on other things, the man who used to do a bit of fishing is off at Whitsuntide to join those others who count a free day not spent in fishing as no day at all.

Then there are the young men taking up fishing for the first time, who also make the most of Whitsuntide. They have not yet been winnowed by misfortune. By the end of the season a fair proportion of them will have learnt that fishing, for them at least, is not all that it is painted. A long succession of 'dour' days reduces their numbers, but at Whitsuntide in every year their ranks are filled up. Side by side with the elderly men with their old tackle furbished up for the day are these youngsters whose new rods flash and sparkle in the sunshine where they stride about the river in all the panoply of new-bought harness. I like the old men best, but that may be envy of those whose fishing lives are all before them. Not altogether. There is a ruthless eagerness about these young men that nothing but blank days will mitigate. And them, of course, there are the regular customers who fish every week-end and do not see why they should make an exception at Whitsuntide. They move soberly about their business and are not unduly depressed by the comparative failure that, in these conditions, is almost to be expected.

There is no day in the year on which a light or an empty basket should be easier to bear than on a Whitsun holiday. A heavy basket is unlikely, except on private water. On public or association water the fisherman must be content to fish water that has already been fished over. He must, on that day, welcome, not resent, the sight of another fisherman at almost every pool. All up and down the river fishermen meet and pass and say the right things. No one asks to look in anyone else's basket. 'Magnificent day.' 'Of course the fish are not rising much. Don't blame them.' 'Rather too much water for the upstream worm.' 'Rather too little water for the minnow.' 'Too bright to expect to do much with the fly.' And so on. Meanwhile the fish are laughing in their gills. They have seen a largish crowd of fishermen at Easter, but nothing like this. At Easter they had hardly taken up their positions, but now every fish in the river has a private view of a really astonishing hatch of fishermen. They have so many baskets and bags to choose from that they put off choosing until it is too late, and are still in the river when the fishermen go home.

Whit Monday is not a day on which to fish too seriously. It is not a day on which a fisherman's wife should tell him as he sets out to be sure to bring back a nice dish of fish of even size. (Symmetry counts for more than bulk with those for whom a basket of trout turns quickly, in the mind's eye, into a dish.) It is a day when two or three brace of trout go far to satisfy ambition, a day when it is no disgrace but rather a proof of geniality and good-fellowship to have caught little or nothing. Your overzealous fisherman on Whit Monday spoils his own day and that of others. It is far too good a day to spoil. Fishing on Whit Monday is a salute to the summer. Summer has begun, but there is still spring in the air. Birds are nesting, and we fish to music.

Opening of the Coarse Fishing Season

FOR A GREAT number of men the year begins on June 16. From March 15 until that date they have been existing in a kind of torpor, and on June 16 awake with the stored vitality of butterflies escaping from their chrysalides. All through April and May, two of the pleasantest fishing months of the year, the roach fishers have watched the trout fishers going forth with rod and creel, and have had sternly to turn their faces to the wall and to remind themselves that their time would come, if not yet. It comes decisively, all over the kingdom on the same day; coarse fishing opens with none of the straggling variety of date that obtains with the trout – February in Devonshire, March in most places, April in some, and May in others. On June 16 every coarse fisherman everywhere knows that every other is filled with his own enthusiasm and hope.

For the last week there has been great painting of the tops of floats (orange, I hope), great testings of old casts, delightful purchases of new, testing of gossamer hook-lengths (the coarse fisherman uses finer stuff than ever is presented to a trout), great handling of rods, preparation of every kind. Advertisements of maggots – 'the finest the world can supply,' or 'to suit the angler of discernment and knowledge' – reappear in the angling newspapers, and to those who breed these beasts themselves and wish to gild the lily are offered chemicals that give them gold or emerald coats and other chemicals that make baits magically attractive – oil of rhodium, tincture of aniseed, and the like. Maggots nowadays go to meet their fish prinked and perfumed like Regency beaux.

This week-end once again there will be great gatherings at railway stations, and the general complaint at the shortage of trains will be swelled by a new passionate note, for the coarse fisherman is as gregarious as his roach and does not, like the trout fisherman, demand to have a mile of river to himself. This week-end once again huge charabancs, efflorescent with rods and nets, will carry jovial parties to the rivers. The banks of Dee, Weaver, Severn, and Trent, and many hundred miles of hospitable tow-path will begin again to acquire the signs that help a stranger to know where to fish. In coarse fishing bank-craft as well as water-craft counts for much. Place after place will have its couple of forked sticks, its trodden patch, and to these places successive anglers go and dump their ground-bait until, as time goes on, fish as well as anglers come to know these places as profitable. Indeed, whereas the season affects the trout by making him more shy, the season for coarse fish means for the fish the regular provision of free meals, a few only paying by capture for the gratuitous supply of ground bait to the rest.

Carpe Diem

TWO OR THREE times a year I fish a little river in the South Country which is beloved by many who have never seen it, but feel as if they had from reading the delightful account of it in Mr Sheringham's *Trout Fishing*. The water he fished was mostly below the stretch that belongs to a small group of my friends, but its uppermost limit was the bridge at the head of what we now call the lower water. All readers of that charming book remember the Bridge Pool, in which a monster was to be seen, dimly, in the deep, fastish water just below a bush on the farther bank. On the near bank, the right bank of the stream, is a large and spreading tree at the foot of the pool, so placed that the only effective way of getting a fly on the water is by means of a very long horizontal cast from below the tree and under its branches. To get a fly up across the pool to the deep water by the bush is itself something of a triumph. The pool has in several places a circular motion, which seems to lessen the supporting power of the water's surface. The line sinks there quicker than in other places, no matter how well it is greased. No matter how much loose, wriggling line is tossed up to lie on the water, the various conflicting currents in the pool's surface put an almost immediate tension on every inch of it. Fish will rise short in that pool when they take like starving wolves in every other pool on the river. In Mr Sheringham's time on this water the pool, tempting always, was irresistible on account of its monster, until a period of drought so far lowered the river that he and his friends were able to perceive that the huge trout on which they had been wasting their time was a child's tin steamship sunk to rise no more.

On Saturday we did neither well nor badly during the midday rise. But none of the bigger fish were moving, and after tea I had the greatest difficulty in persuading my friend not to sacrifice my fishing to his chess. He had acquired a disbelief in the evening rise, and was more than ready to leave further fishing till the morrow. However, ruthless insistence on my prerogative as a guest made it possible for me to go down to the bridge to fish the lower water. There was a most interesting fitful rise in progress to a fly which I took to be a large Pale Watery Spinner. In my box was one, and only one, specimen of Mr J. W. Dunne's imitation of this fly, with body of artificial silk on white enamelled hook, which when oiled has the translucent effect that puts quill bodies to shame. It had lain in the box for some three years since the last time I had used it on this very river, and it was already a little the worse for wear. But I twisted the old gut out of the eye of the hook and offered it to a fish. He quietly gulped it, and had got the fly so far down that I had to use a disgorger to get it out. If that fly came anywhere near a rising fish he took it in the quietest, matter-of-business fashion, as if there could be no possible doubt that this particular fly was the one which he had ordered. The fly grew rapidly raggeder. At last it was so ragged that I took it off and tried a very pale variant of something like the same tone. The trout would not look at it, and I was forced for a second time to clean the gut from the old fly and to put it on again. Half the hook was showing bare, streamers of artificial silk hung loose. The hackle itself was no longer what it should be, and yet in that disreputable condition it took the last two fish, one of them in a perfectly still, deep backwater, where the fish had as much time as it wanted for examination of the fly.

I watched the fish come slowly to the surface under the fly. It came so slowly that I had time to remind myself that with dry fly the stiller the water the longer the strike should be deferred. The fish put its nose quietly out of the water, and turned and went down again. When I struck it was already near the bottom. Subsequent proceedings were marred only by an unnecessary conflict between barbed wire and breeches and another between barbed wire and landing net. But the fish had taken that tattered relic of a fly with such finality that these misfortunes were not enough to put the end in doubt. I do not think I need ever ask for a better proof that those men are wrong who say that trout are colour blind. Colour and size were the only qualities in which that disintegrating fly still resembled its original. Its size was approximately right. Its colour was perfect, and I thought with gratitude that night of the many hours that Mr Dunne took from his fishing to match precisely with blended shades of silk the natural fly that for last Saturday was the fashionable evening meal on this famous little river.

Nor could there be a better illustration of the soundest of fishing maxims, which is never to put off fishing till another day. On the Sunday there was a tearing hostile wind and sunshine of the hard, bright quality that makes the countryside look like a coloured photograph, a quality that sometimes goes with thunder and always with bad fishing. It was not a day on which to catch fish, and it was no waste of time to spend an hour or two at Mr Sheringham's Bridge Pool, hoping, of course in vain, that one of those visible, indifferent trout (not toy steamships, for they did sometimes move) would lose his temper and grab my fly to put an end to its recurrent journeys round those eddies. It was a day to drive a man to despair if he had set his heart on making a basket. But the previous evening had fortified me against such reverses and, for all I cared, the day might do its worst. How different would have been my feelings if on the Saturday I had stayed in after tea! I should never have known what delightful fishing I had missed, and I might even have gone away with the belief that the little river was no longer what it was.

On Sunday, after we gave up fishing, we lay in the grass looking at a very large ash tree in the meadow near the top of the water. My friend talked of the great usefulness of ash wood for every kind of farming implement. He told of a Northern farmer's answer to his son who asked when was the best time to cut an ash plant: 'When thou sees one, my lad.' What is true of ash plants is even more true of fishing. The ash plant may not, after all, be gone to-morrow, but there is no catching up with two good fishing hours that have been spent elsewhere than at the river.

Irrelevant Things

LOOKING BACK through the notebooks of some years, I could not help observing that the days I best remembered were not those of the heavy baskets that fall sometimes even to the worst of fishermen. Nor were they blanks, days of hopeless, deadening failure. They were days, neither markedly good nor bad, on which honour had been satisfied but no great sop had been given to ambition. They were days on which the fishing had been just good enough to free the mind for the enjoyment of irrelevant things. For example, I had entirely forgotten what was in my basket when, earlier in the year, walking up a chalk stream and drying my fly in the air, I caught a swift on a Wickham's Fancy.

I see from the diary that I had three brace of fish of no great size. I think my companion had three and a half brace. It had been a delightful day. Competitive ardours had died. The stream had done its duty by us and been fair in the distribution of its favours. Neither of us suffered from the discomfort of having caught much more than his friend and neither of us suffered from a feeling of being wronged in having caught much less. Tension had slackened. We had spoken in admiration of the stream, of the weather, of these plump hospitable fish. Our minds were open, as unpolluted as the stream, fit harbourage for pleasant things.

At the moment, half a field ahead of me, I could see my friend, crouching like a drab toad in the long grass, fishing 'the difficult bit,' where the opposite branches almost reach the hither side of the stream. He was a long way off, but the silent rhythmic switching of his rod, the bend of his back, spoke not of any tense, desperate effort to catch a fish but of the quiet enjoyment of a delicate bit of work. I hoped he would catch another fish, but knew that his happiness would be in no way marred if he did not. And just then, when I was walking quietly some twenty yards from the edge of the stream, my reel suddenly spoke and the throbbing of the rod told me instantly that my fly was not caught in the grass. My Wickham's Fancy had been taken by one of the swifts that were racing up and down the stream and weaving intricate patterns of flight over the meadows.

My first impression was one of extreme wretchedness. I felt a criminal to have hooked this lovely winged thing. I could not forsee how this impression was to be obliterated by its subsequent behaviour. Bringing it quietly to earth, loathing its defeat and my own part in it, I picked it up as gently as I could, while it strugged violently, hatefully. The little tin-selled Wickham was at the corner of its beak. It came away without the slightest difficulty, and I put the bird down. But though a swift can rise easily from a flat surface, it was powerless in the deep grass of the water meadow. As it raised its wings its body sank deeper. It could not get a single free wing-stroke. I bent to pick it up again when there occurred the incident that turned a misfortune into a happy memory.

It had ceased to struggle the moment I took the fly from its beak. Now it made no attempt to escape me. I did not lift it, but placed my fingers immediately before it. It laid hold of them with its long, tickling claws. I lifted it up, clinging to my fingers. It now showed no hurry to escape, but rested as peacefully as if my fingers were a convenient edge of wall, and then, without commotion, launched itself into the air and a moment later had rejoined its fellows flashing up and down the stream. That incident, irrelevant to fishing, will keep the day in memory long after other days with heavier baskets will have faded utterly away.

The Maggot Fishers

THE RAIN brought some colour into the lower reaches of the Leven, and at Greenodd on Monday, 'steadily, shoulder to shoulder,' the maggot-fishers were at work. When I climbed down from the road to the sand I found the club, for this gathering of sociable fishermen can hardly be otherwise described, in full session. Most of its members were Yorkshiremen, and most of them had caught eels. But just as I reached them a very fine fish had been landed and was causing a good deal of discussion. The more generous minded said that it was three pounds if it was an ounce. The others, and particularly those who had caught too many eels, said that it was barely over two. Most of the fishers were Yorkshiremen, so that I was not surprised that so good a chance for a sweepstake was not lost. Everyone hefted the fish and paid his threepence. Then the fish was carried off to be weighed while the club, still arguing hotly on the subject, continued to bombard its floats with handfuls of maggots and sand.

There is a humanity among these maggot-fishers that cannot be sufficiently admired. Two of them noticed that I was without a rod. They promptly fitted me up with a rod belonging to one of their friends, hung his maggot bag round my neck, and moved, one of them two paces to the right, the other two paces to the left, so that I could stand between them and fish without actually elbowing either. Would fly-fishers do as much for an inquisitive passer-by? The water bailiff came along and held a licence parade. A young man carrying a baby picked his way among us, followed by his young wife, who was adjured by everyone in turn not to step on the tips of rods the casts of which were being disentangled after eels. The young man stood behind us while floats and maggots whistled past his ears. He pointed to a float.

'Tell that one to get a fish,' he said, and the baby waved its hands at the float as if it really meant it. Everybody was pleased.

Then the man on the extreme right of the line found that his hook was caught in a rock on the bottom. He walked the whole length of the line to the extreme left, in hopes that it would free itself. He caught some of us, but his hook did not free itself, and in the end, amid general commiseration, he had to break. More eels were caught, one big enough to be landed in the net. There was a discussion on the nature of eels, more flattering to them dead than alive. At last the weighers returned. The original argument about the weight of the big fish broke out lustily again. Some were accused of hedging. Others repeated earnestly their estimates as if, post factum, to influence the weighing. A chorus urged that the result should no longer be withheld. Even in this crisis, as throughout the argument, fishing went seriously on. Men asked, 'Well, what does it weigh?' in the very act of casting. After all whatever it weighed, there were bigger fish in the sea. It weighed 2lb. 10 ounces, and the thought of it will sustain many a patient man who has watched his float all day and caught nothing.

Bank Holiday Anglers

I IMAGINE THAT more fishing tickets are sold and fewer fish caught in August than in any other month of the season. It is the holiday month, and long tradition brings to the country in that month numbers of men who do not fish at any other time. It is a month that offers to the countryman some curious spectacles. There is the man who sees another with a rod and thinks that he, too, will go fishing. He buys rod and reel with a sense of adventure that he has not had since he was a boy, gets the boots in the hotel to dig him some worms, hears from the grocer who sells fishing tackle of a likely stream, remembers vaguely that it is best to throw the worm up but soon discovers that the current brings it down and that it is a good deal easier to let it follow nature's course. I met such a one, who had put his worm into the beck and followed it down three miles through bramble and bracken, keeping as near it as he could, in hopes of seeing a fish take it. He was very hot but rather disappointed.

'Perhaps,' he said, 'this is not the right brook. Do you know if there are any fish in it?'

'Brook' betrayed him for a visitor. Then there was that earnest fellow I saw spinning a Cheshire mere for pike, hurling a heavy bait with the action of a fast bowler, bringing it down with a mighty splash but visibly exultant whenever he got it far enough from his feet to wind in without the tangle of an over-run. Then there is the August fly-fisher who drives the trout before him as with a cart-whip.

For all these fishermen I have a profound respect and some affection. In the first place they do no harm whatever to the rivers. They mostly buy fishing licences (which, months afterwards, in town, found by accident in their pocket-books, give them great pleasure and set them up with their friends). The perfect angling club was described by an old keeper as one with two or three good fishermen, half a dozen lucky ones, and a hundred 'who couldn't catch a trout if you put it on their —— hooks.' All respect the good and, observing the lucky, do not see why some day they should not be as lucky themselves. The hundred are mostly August fishermen and are sleeping partners during the rest of the year. And, after all, the whole fishing fraternity is a huge club, for which it is fortunate that the number of tackle-buying, licence-buying sleeping partners is so large. They fish in August and, if they have been dreaming of fly-fishing through all the good months of the season, they naturally find it hard to wait till evening before they lay their flies upon the water. Their baskets are light, but they can justly blame the time of the year. In this way all are satisfied, the club as a whole is prosperous, and the waters are not depleted.

These, of course, are the fishermen who read tackle catalogues and fishing books, and are useful to fly-tiers and authors. But of all holiday anglers those who deserve the tenderest forbearance in criticism are those who must perforce fish on Bank Holiday. Few of them meet a salmon. They never know a river that is not populous with fishermen or even a canal that is not a silver thread stringing long rows of anglers like black beads. They submit, with astonishing good temper, to the noisy presence of those who have never fished before, and for whom fishing has been an accidental, happy inspiration, like a suggestion to play rounders. Even these, on Bank Holiday, are not to be frowned upon. In England it is not as it still is in Russia, where men on a journey pluck hairs from their horse's tails, cut a rod from beside the stream, and with no bought tackle but a hook are ready to enjoy their evening while the horses feed and rest. But, on the August Bank Holiday, there are places where something like this is to be seen.

On Windermere boats go out bristling with rods of all kinds, including even walking-sticks. The corks from ginger-beer bottles serve as floats. They anchor, and with shouts and merriment the party set to fishing. On this last Monday I heard a boat-load half a mile away fishing in full chorus from a motor-launch that bristled like a hedgehog. Some dangled their feet in the water. Some stood in bow and stern. Others leaned over the gunwale to see if a fish were looking at their bait. And in spite of all these things which are not recommended in the angling books they were catching perch one after another. And, when at last they moved off, probably to litter the shore with empty paper bags, the voice of a small boy rose shrill over the lake, bitterly lamenting. Who knows? In that vociferous boat-load, in those worst of all conditions, he may have been touched by the divine spark, and at the first opportunity will go off, secretly, by himself this time, to fish again, and, presently, to become as quiet and careful an angler as any of us. And, if a man has but fished a few times in earnest, he is already of those who will not, when an angler is at work, stump down the opposite bank to look at the fish or to play ducks and drakes on the water.

That noisy party on the lake on a Bank Holiday may have been the turning-point of a life. Coming home yesterday, I found a small boy leaning over a bridge. He pointed out a trout to me. I asked him if he fished.

'Not for trout yet,' he said, with infinite solemnity, 'but I got three perch on Monday, and a big one looked at my worm and swam away. I've got a rod of my own now, and I'm to have a licence next year.'

O virtuous little boy! There are nearly two months of the season left, and it is a long time till next year.

Trout and Coarse Fishing in August

NOTHING is more unfortunate for trout fishermen than that August should be the month for holidays. In this month they escape for a little from the less serious business of making money and go fishing just at the time when fishing, at least with fly, is at its poorest. More resolves to give up fishing for ever are made in August than in any other month. In July, when there is not such a drought as we have had this year, something can usually be done. In September the trout are almost as philanthropic as in April, though without the suicidal tendencies of their mayfly orgy. But in August they keep themselves to themselves, are wary of a flitting shadow, bolt from a floating straw, and scurry from shelter when the line of a perfectly invisible angler extends in their direction. By the time August comes they have had their memories well rubbed up, and, knowing that in places fished by sportsmen small trout are returned to the water, they take, I believe, an insolent elderly pleasure in seeing the fingerlings leap for the fly that they know too well to be tempted by it, to be lifted from the water, sworn at gently, freed and put back again with a sore lip and a little wisdom.

Fishing yesterday in the Kent, I had over thirty babies from the water and not one fish in my basket to carry home at night. Deep water or shallow, it was all the same. Rippled water or shallow, the grown fish were not to be cozened in daylight with the river so low. And night fishing, though well enough in its glamorous, eery way, is a special kind of enjoyment, not at all a substitute for the fishing days promised to themselves by anglers when, earlier in the year, they snatched a few hours by the river and looked forward to a wonderful fortnight when their holiday should come.

This, of course, does not apply to seatrout, though morts in most of our rivers rarely take except by night, and for daylight fishing for sea-trout one has to go far afield from Manchester. Fortunately it does not apply at all to the coarse fishing which is, after all, the staple of English as opposed to Scottish angling. Indeed, the trout fisherman whose holiday must be in August might well, if he could only forget that wonderful basket he made by the river at Easter, put aside his dreams of trout and with a stiffer rod, though no less light, a different tackle, though no less fine, taste the more sedentary pleasures of the men who fish for so-called coarse fish. He would meet with many surprises. He would discover, for example, that on 4x gut and a light rod a perch, weight for weight, will give him all the thrills of a trout except that of somersaulting out of the water. He would learn for the first time that moment of wild surmise when a carp float tilts up flat along the surface and with hardly a jerk moves out with slowly increasing speed while he watches the loose line pulled through the rings and summons every faculty he has to keep him from striking too soon and too hard lest he break his gossamer on a fish that may rival Mr Andrews's twenty-pounder. If he wants to feel real weight and power at the end of his line there is nothing, save a salmon, to beat your big carp, and no man, except by accident, hooks a salmon on the frail stuff he must use if he would trick a carp.

Pike, too, by August are in excellent condition, though for them you must use a cast strong enough to withstand the hard tug necessary to pull the hooks into their bony jaws. The rod, too, must be stout enough and stiff enough to let you give that tug, though the short rods used generally in America for spinning weigh not more than six ounces. I remember fishing a lake in Esthonia, spinning from the shore with a light trout spinning rod and having my bait taken by a pike who shut his jaws like those of a captain of industry and allowed me to pull him slowly inshore while my rod would not let me give a hard enough tug to pull the bait through his grip and so get a hook into him. When he was so near that we could get a good look at each other he opened his jaws (in a laugh, I believe), released the spinner, turned without undue hurry, and with a stroke or two of his great tail vanished once more into the deep.

Still Water

Trout fishing is over until March next year, and while those of us who are trout fishers only are putting their rods away and resigning themselves to the waste of their leisure in one or other of the many inferior substitutes for fishing, others are discovering anew a different kind of angling, and resolving once again not to let their passion for the trout streams keep them until quite so late in the year from the still waters of the coarse fish. Year after year I leave it too late to go fishing for tench. With the first cold nights the big tench go down into the mud and are not to be coaxed out of it. Year after year those wretched trout keep me in pursuit of them until all chance of tench has gone.

Last week there was some mighty warm weather, and, thinking that the tench might imagine they had gone to bed too soon, I went off to a Shropshire mere where these fish exist in small quantities but of tremendous size. The mere is not a large one. It is unfishable from the shore because of a deep fringe of mud and reeds. It is far from any town, and the only boats upon it are a few ancient punts which are very little used. The foothills of the Welsh mountains rise on either side of it. The houses in the near-by villages are black and white, with intricate frontings of oak and white plaster. The chief industry seems to be the breeding of pigs. The place is remote, serene, and the mere is older even than this ancient civilisation. A prehistoric canoe, a tree trunk hollowed by burning, was taken from it and is now in a museum. It is just the place for monstrous slow-growing fish. But the hot weather did not trick the tench, unless that one terrific tug that left my companion white, trembling, and utterly abased was from one of the fish we had come so far to seek.

It is always more difficult in fishing an unknown piece of

still water to know where to begin than it is in fishing an unknown river. The first day we caught nothing except a few small perch, of which we have plenty at home. Before breakfast next morning I went off to Shrewsbury to get some gudgeon, to try for some of the pike I had seen feeding at the shallow end of the mere in water too weedy for spinning. A coracle man came from his cottage with his boat on his back, looking like an immense turtle on its hind legs. Like all the coracle men he was very small. He came down to the river, launched his coracle, sat himself in it, and with a single small paddle moved it this way and that over the shallows above the Welsh Bridge, through the arches of which could be seen old houses and their reflections in the smooth water, until he found a sunken tin, which he fished up and brought ashore. The gudgeon were very little ones, but the best he had, so I took them and returned to my mere. With the smaller ones we got just one more perch than we had gudgeon, all between half a pound and a pound. The one gudgeon of proper size was thrown into a hole between weed beds to a feeding pike, who took him at once. The pike was a ten pounder and did what I have only once before seen a pike do. He jumped like a salmon, clear of the water, indeed two or three feet above it, the whole length of him horizontal, as it were hanging over the water like a bar of green and gold and olive shining in the sun. He fought with extraordinary dash, and the cast parted at a kink just as I got him into the punt. The disturbance he had made had been enough to put an end to more delicate fishing in that place and we spent the rest of the day in exploring, to find a swim for the morrow. In this we were helped by a pair of birds that I think were young crested grebes. The grebes had a regular beat and came from some distance before they started fishing. One of them came up with a fish near enough for us to see that the fish was not a perch, but a roach. When they came to their fishing ground the grebes worked hard, diving continually and staying under, as it seemed, for very much longer than the moorhen which were feeding near the rushes. Once we saw one of the grebes come up with a fish and make a present of it to his companion. Plumbing the depths here we found that the shallows dropped suddenly to a depth of fifteen to twenty feet, and in this spot, fishing maggot and worm, we caught both roach and perch, the best of the roach taking the balance down to just over a pound. There was just a ripple on the mere, enough to make it a little difficult to detect small movements of our floats. Suddenly my companion's float dipped slowly and steadily and went off under and sideways. A strike, a sudden rush, the end of the rod pulled deep under water, and the reappearance of a barren float illustrated once again the danger of holding the line between one's hand and the rod handle. The reel had not had a chance. The hook had pulled out and the big fish, perhaps the very tench we had come to seek, was gone. 'It felt like hooking a boat that was going in the other direction.' We were not given another chance, but when my companion next hooked a fish no mistakes were made. The reel sang, no finger caught the line, and there came up at last a diminutive roach, wondering, perhaps, why he had been played with such respect.

At evening, night after night, the wind dropped and the surface of the lake grew smooth enough to reflect the extraordinary gathering of the starlings. First there would come a small flock of twenty or thirty, wheeling over the mere. Then, from some other direction, would come another. The two flocks, flying fast, would mingle and be joined by others. There would be at last an immense flock wheeling round the mere, turning altogether with a noise like distant guns. Then, from far away, would come another flock as big as the first, itself, no doubt, made up of many small flocks similarly gathered. There would be two huge clouds of whirring birds approaching, turning, and then indistinguishable, changing colour, now dark, now light, as all the wings of those close-flying birds were shown to us broad as they turned or horizontal in straight flight. And then, at last, the whole huge cloud would go off, and we would hear the noise of their wings when they had passed out of sight. After that the owls would tell us to empty the keep-net and to go home.

And so it was until the wind came out of the north-east with colder weather and our last hopes of tench were gone. Perch and roach up to a pound, pike of ten pounds and ten and a half, but no tench, only a decision firmer than usual that next year we will take a day in the middle of the trout season to fish for these strange hibernating fish that are so much more difficult to catch.

Catch-as-Catch-Can

THERE ARE dry-fly fishermen who look upon wet-fly fishing as poaching. There are wet-fly fishermen who are intolerant of the worm. There are worm fishermen who complain of the use of the minnow. Yet minnow, worm, and wet-fly fishermen walk with their heads upright and are prepared to put up a lively defence of their fishing. Each one of them knows a state of the water in which his method is undoubtedly the right one. There seems to be nothing in fishing on which it is impossible to have two opinions. Most of the men I know, for example, dislike extremely the accidental catching of trout out of season. Yet recently I had a letter from a correspondent in which, without, so far as I could judge, a qualm of any kind, he told me of a friend of his who in a single day had caught and returned over fifty out-of-season trout. That disgusting story shocked me so much that to this day I have been unable to devise a reply even decently polite. Yet somewhere, it is clear, exists a man who does not regard the capture of a trout when fishing for grayling after the trout season as a lamentable happening which, if repeated, is an urgent hint to move on, or at least to take such precautions as are possible to avoid the capture of another. Probably, therefore, there are a number of people who will find nothing reprehensible in the methods used for the capture of salmon towards the end of the season in the upper waters of one of the best of our northern rivers.

The season on this river ended on November 1. It is therefore no longer possible to watch this particular form of sport. Until yesterday however, it was being practised with so little disguise that anyone who went to a certain road bridge over the river on any afternoon when there was no actual flood could have watched it until dusk. Everyone knows about the capture of these fish. In the angling newspapers there appears, every week towards the end of the season, a proud list of the salmon caught in these waters. The licences for the district entitle their holders 'to fish for salmon with a rod and line.' No other conditions of fishing are mentioned, and it must be admitted at once that a rod and a line are used in the capture of these fish. In no other respect does the pursuit of them resemble what is usually considered fishing.

Let me describe what would be seen by a September or October visitor to the bridge. In a broad pool above the bridge he might have the luck to see a man casting an exceedingly heavy spoon with an exceedingly large treble hook across the river, letting it sink and dragging it back again. He might have doubts as to whether this spinner meant to catch his salmon by the head or the tail, but he would be less interested by this exhibition of spinning than he would be by the proceedings which he would find in progress at the bridge itself. On the bridge he would find a few men waiting their turns to fish a small, deep, narrow pool immediately beneath it. Looking over the bridge he would see two men, one working the rod and line, the other standing by with a long gaff. The rod is very stiff (I have seen a stout pike rod used). The line matches the rod. There is no cast of any kind. The end of the line is fastened to a short length of very strong picture cord. On the picture cord are a number of large leads, some of them as much as two and even three inches long, and about two inches apart. Immediately below the lowest lead two enormous hooks are whipped, one above another and facing opposite ways. On each of these hooks is impaled a worm.

The visitor may think the worm unnecessary, particularly if there is no water bailiff about, for whom and not for the salmon he is likely to think that the worm is intended. One visitor did ask, with amazement, if the fisherman expected the salmon to take this monstrous piece of heavy, swinging tackle into its mouth, and expressed the opinion that, if so, he was an optimist. There was a laugh. Then one man said that 'it did happen sometimes,' and gave an example that had occurred some days before when a salmon had actually swallowed the hook while a fisherman was lighting his pipe and letting his tackle dangle in the stream. The incredulous visitor asked whether on that occasion the fisherman was using two hooks and a series of leads heavy enough to brain a man. Well, no, this particular fisherman had been using a single hook on gut. But it showed that there was a chance that the salmon might take the apparatus into its mouth, seeing that there was a worm on each of two hooks. It seemed, however, to the visitor that the fishermen did not trust too much to the chance of so surprising a phenomenon.

It is, of course, impossible to cast this stupendous tackle. Instead it is swung out underhand and dropped into the white water. It is then brought slowly down the bottom of the pool. If this were all it could hardly do more than hit a salmon a shrewd blow with the swinging leads. It is not all. At short intervals the fisherman heaves up his rod, striking with a smart drawing motion. This striking does not depend on the fisherman's perceiving any indication of a fish. I spent some time one day timing the striking, and found that the fisherman strikes, fish or no fish, about nine times to the minute.

A few days ago I reached the bridge just too late to see the capture of a salmon. The fish had been landed and the fishermen were trying, from the top of the bridge, to see exactly where another fish was resting, so that the two hooks and the mass of lead might be dangled and jerked as near to him as possible without waste of time. I asked the lucky fisherman whether his salmon had been hooked in the mouth. He smiled and said that it was hooked 'Back o' the mouth.' I presently climbed down and had a look at the fish. It had indeed been hooked 'back o' the mouth,' and a good way back, underneath one of the pectoral fins. However, there it was, a landed salmon, to appear in the weekly list of captures from this favoured river.

A man caught a salmon in a pool a little higher up. It was too far off for me to see how it was hooked, but not too far off for me to see exactly how it was played. It was brought at once splashing violently to the top of the water. It was held there for just so long as it took a companion to reach the place with a gaff. It was then yanked out. The total time from hooking to gaffing was less than that usually necessary for the landing of a half-pound trout.

Anyone who imagines that salmon fishing demands skill and the outwitting of the fish should visit this river in the last month of the season, to learn that he is mistaken.

November Frosts

A FEW HARD frosts change the character of every kind of fishing. Fly-fishers reluctantly look out the little floats and stiffer rod and put their flies away. If they would make a decent basket of grayling they must swim the worm, until, before this month runs out, we get a belated autumn day or two to help us through the winter. Roach are moving into their winter swims. In the lakes perch leave the pleasant bays where we have fished for them in autumn and go down into the deep water. Pike follow the perch. In the shallow meres, of course, the change is not so marked. But even there the first few days of frost are not good days for fishing. Even in the meres is reflected that general disquiet of house-moving which in other places makes fishing a most uncertain game until the fish have settled in their winter haunts. With the first frosts we think, usually, that this is a good day for pike or that the cold weather will sharpen the appetites of the big roach. But it is not the first frosts that set the roach feeding or the pike on the move. I can tell, or think I can tell, a pikey day in autumn or in winter. But when autumn's nose is only a little red at the tip, when winter is surprised to find that autumn is still lingering about, he would be a very rash man who confidently picked his day.

There are few days (of coarse fishing) that I like better than these Janus days that look both ways and are neither autumn nor winter. For one thing, there is no very great need of hurry either to get early to the water or while you are there. Nothing much is likely to happen before half-past ten. On the other hand, your day lasts until five. The sun is warm for several hours. The benign moment is prolonged and does not, as in winter proper, pass in a flash. You may still have a poor morning and make up for it in the afternoon, whereas next month it is hit or miss, trial, as it were, by court-martial, short shrift, all over one way or other in a shorter time than at other seasons of the year is spent in settling down to the water. In mid-winter fishing is a snapdragon pleasure, though your fingers risk freezing not burning. Just now you can count on a little warmth after midday. It is the right weather for rather desultory fishing by still waters and for roving along a river. You are not likely to be kept so busy by the fish as not to notice the almost hysterical activity of the long-tailed tits in the now almost leafless bushes at the waterside, the kingfisher scattering the hoarfrost as he launches himself from the bough overhanging the water, or the two cock pheasants dancing defiance and presently going for each other wing and claw and merging in a sort of feathery firework. You may catch no fish until the sun has begun to redden and sink into the low clouds. You may catch none at all, but whatever happens, you will not at this turn of the year have a blank day. Such a thing is impossible, properly speaking, though you may well have an empty basket, which is not at all the same thing.

Swimming the Worm

OUR SALMON are busy on the spawning-beds. On one long shallows in the Eden I counted between twenty and thirty fish last Tuesday, some spawning, others forging about in small companies, with fins and sometimes grey, patchy backs well out of water. They were so intent about their immediate interests as to be almost imperturbable, and any scoundrel could have pulled them out with a long-handled gaff. I was grayling fishing, and it seemed that though the river was

crammed with salmon and had a largish stock of grayling, the
two fish interfered very little with each other, each keeping
more or less to his own territory. Now and again the red back
and fins of a great salmon would show, moving up in the
deeper water of a grayling stretch, but in general in the
stretches where there were grayling to be caught the salmon
were not behaving as if they owned the whole bed of the river.
I wondered whether the grayling were profiting much from
the salmon spawn and opened a few fish. I found one egg in
one grayling. There was no sign of salmon spawn in any of the
others. The grayling that had eaten at least one egg was taken
at the edge of an eddy immediately below a shallow stretch in
which the salmon were busy. The grayling in this place were
markedly smaller than those from the characteristic grayling
reaches.

It was a brilliant, sunny day, with a low water enriched by a
slight shower of rain on the previous night. I saw only two
grayling rises, and the fish were not to be caught with the fly. I
had offered them Red Tags and Wickhams and Bumbles, and a
little white fly with a silver body by which grayling are much
intrigued when they are taking fly at all, but they would have
none of them. This was on the afternoon of Monday, on
reaching the Eden. I got only one rise that might have been
from a grayling, and I missed that from not being quick
enough. My father used to say that you should strike, with a
grayling, a quarter of a second *before* he rises. In the evening I
had a talk with one of the best fly-fishermen of the Eden,
extracts from whose diary are given in Mr Nelson's delightful
book. He told me that in his experience it was useless, after
October, to fish for grayling in the Eden with the fly, though a
rare warm spell might bring them up. A fortnight ago they
had been seen rising. Nowadays the only hope was with the
worm, and for that, he thought, the river was too low and
bright. The drop of rain on the Monday night may have just
made the difference. On the Tuesday the fish were hospitable
enough.

In fact they entertained every worm I had to offer them, and
I ended the day with as many grayling as I had had worms,

proof that some worms had accounted for more than one grayling, for the proportion of fish hooked and lost is far higher with grayling than with trout. They can mangle a worm and reject it in a flash. That hysterical, Catherine-wheel, under-water fighting of theirs will free them if they are at all lightly hooked, and every now and then a good fish comes miraculously loose when the fisherman is already thinking that there is nothing left to be done but to lift him out in the net and weigh him. Worms on Tuesday were very hard to get. The boots at the inn in Appleby did his best, and the few that he got were very good indeed – small, lively brandlings and short, stumpy lobs. The grayling preferred the brandlings.

'The time of the take' was from about half-past ten in the morning till three in the afternoon. This makes a short fishing day, but a delightful one. The crisp winter air, the hoar-frost on the morning grass, the last leaves fluttering on the trees, reluctant to leave them, the blue masses of the Pennine Hills picked out with sunshine and shadow, even if the grayling had not been willing, would have made the day a memorable trophy.

Anglers the Enemy of the Human Race

'YOU FISHERMEN are enemies of the human race,' said a melancholy skater to me yesterday when he met me exulting in the change. 'During the summer you did nothing but complain of the hot weather that was a pleasure to everybody, and now when at last we have had a glorious winter month with nothing but sunshine and crisp frost you have gone about with long faces and said you wanted a thaw.'

I told him that in both cases we had only wanted water. I told him that a farmer I knew was very happy because the thaw would save his turnips. But I could say nothing that would make him charitable. He had made up his mind that we were perverse creatures wishing evil to men, and in a way, of

course, he had some evidence (besides the stoppage of his
skating) to support his ill-humour. All through the summer
drought, when other people were delighting in the absence of
rain and welcoming each week of fine weather as an unexpected gift, we anglers were grimly watching our
barometers and praying for thunderstorms at least. And
during these weeks of Christmas-card weather we (except
those limited anglers whose season ends with the trout's) have
been as glum as cricketers watching a football match on their
cherished pitch. But Charles Lamb wept at weddings and
could not trust himself not to laugh at funerals, yet was not
inhumane. And there is a good deal to be said for us who are
inclined to think that the pleasures of skating may be too
dearly purchased and that you can have too much of fine
weather. There is a lot to be said, but I could not think of it at
the moment in the face of this poor skater looking at the
melting ice and wondering when he would have a chance of
putting on his skates again. Yet I need not really have been
sorry for him, for he certainly had had his day, and no one can
say that we fishermen have been any too well treated by 1925.

For a whole month there had been almost continuous frost.
All but the largest lakes had frozen, and the snow (there was no
rain) lay on the frozen land and did not find its way to the
rivers, many of which were below even their normal summer
level. There was tobogganing and any amount of skating, and
enthusiastic persons went about robbing the birds by cutting
holly. There were bonfires by the tarns and high carnival over
the haunts of fish. Fishermen, except in a few most favoured
places, had been having a very poor time. Even the
Macclesfield Canal, which should have been making up to
the roach fishermen in the winter for the very poor sport that
it gave while choked with weed, froze over. Those smaller
rivers which should have been at their best for pike spinning
were so low and bright that the pike found holts untenable that
should have served them finely till the spring. Still waters
were coffined. In the larger lakes that remained open a
migratory spirit seemed to have taken even the minnows. The
other day I could find none in any one of half a dozen places

where they have been regularly for months, and, indeed, but for the timely help of a kingfisher should never have found them at all. I had begun to think that they must all have gone into deep water. It was not so. They had moved from their accustomed shallows but not from all of them, and that brilliant little fisherman was flashing to and fro in the sunlight getting minnows in two or three feet of water along the southern shores of a promontory. Had they shelter then from the persistent northerly wind? The perch were more local than ever and more uncertain. You might anchor over a known perch ground and find that you could catch fish on one side of your boat and have never a bite on the other.

It is, by the way, a curious thing that larger perch are being caught on the 'hill' near the rocky island that seems to be the headquarters of the cormorants than have been caught here formerly. Is it possible that the cormorants, eating perch as well as eels, have been having the same effect on this ground that pike have on a trout river, increasing the size of the fish caught by lessening the total number that have to share a given supply of food? During the past month even perch-fishing has been a poor business. And during all that time my skater and his friends have been rejoicing.

In the lake country the thaw came suddenly. On one day the lakes and tarns were crowded with people skating in bright sunshine under hills sparking with snow. On the next a few enthusiasts were skating in the mist in spite of the water on the ice, and a few, learners, afraid to lose a day, were splashing as they sat them down. Yesterday's gleaming hills were dark. The bright roads were slush, and with the thaw came a great wind out of the south-west, and with it the rain we have been waiting for for so long. Alpine winter was over for the moment, and we had English winter once again, and with it brightening hopes of fishing. For the first time after a month of continual frost and dry weather our rivers have a chance of swelling to something like their normal volume. Rivers and fishermen are plucking up heart together, though the ice was so thick on canal and mere and smaller lake that cold nights will keep them closed for fishermen even if warm days keep them closed for skaters.

Whatever tricks the weather plays us now there should be good river fishing this week-end. The pike will be moving from the retreats to which they were driven by the low water, and may as likely as not be tempted by a blue, silver, and scarlet wagtail. Even if there is a heavy flood something will be possible with spinners of a larger size than usual, a copper Holroyd, perhaps, or Mr Gray's new spoon. Every eddy should be worth searching with a paternoster. If the water begins to clear, the grayling rivers should be in better order for swimming the worm than they have yet been, and it may even be possible to do something with fly. Even if the rain were to stop at once, enough has come down to bring the rivers to life. If the wind holds, I should feel inclined to go after pike. If it drops, it would be pleasant enough to take a stiffish rod, a fine line, a free-running reel, a big float of goose-quill or of albatross, and a bag of good big lobworms and, using the methods of the Trent fishermen, see what could be done with the December chub. Even if the frost closes down on us again and puts into its exasperating glass case all the fish of lake and mere, specimens and fingerlings alike, it will not, as it did a month ago, close down on rivers nearly starved. For a little time, at least, the winter of our discontent is over.

Two Minuses Make a Plus

THE FISHERMAN'S year has two beginnings – one, some day between March the 1st and April the 15th, when for the first time he takes his flies to the river to show them to the trout; the other on the 18th of June, when that season opens in which he offers worms, maggots, hempseed, stewed wheat and bread paste to fish in connection with whom he has come to use the word 'coarse' as a compliment. These are the true beginnings of the fisherman's year. The New Year's Day of the almanac ought not to concern him at all. Yet even the fisherman cannot ignore these arbitary divisions of time.

On New Year's Day he begins a new diary, and he does like

his first fishing entry in it to set a satisfactory tone for all that are to follow. It was therefore very annoying to come to the river in the first week of this January and to fail to catch grayling, or, at least, to fail to catch them in such quantity as the day seemed to promise. There had been hard frosts. On the hills leading down into the valley boys were tobogganing. The mountains were white with snow, and there was a ragged covering of snow on the frozen fields. The cat ice tinkled like broken glass. The outlines of the hills were fairly clear. There was even a little sunshine. The river was at the right height. When I had been here for the last visit of last year the row of piles at the edge of the gravel bank had been surrounded by water. They stood out clear on the day of the first visit of this year. I had good worms, a small float, single hooks the neatness of which it was almost a shame to hide in any worm. Everything promised a good day. There had been no bad omens. I had made no mistakes of which I was conscious – unless it was that in last week's article or in the one before I had published my true opinion of the capricious, contrary nature of these delightful fish. That must have been the reason why I caught only two grayling in the day. The calendar year, accordingly, seemed likely to begin with a failure.

It began, instead, with a lesson on failure in general. Failure it seems, depends entirely on our choice of what we are to consider success. For just so long as I was full of ambition to fill a basket with large grayling the day was a miserable failure. As soon as I abandoned this ambition as fantastic the day turned into success. Until this moment of, if you like, resignation I had not known that I was enjoying myself very much. This was because I had been ruling out all pleasure except that of catching grayling, and these were not to be caught. I was now open to pleasure of other kinds. There was the sight of the hills in snow, which are always to me (if the grayling let me look at them) what the sound of tavern music was to Sir Thomas Browne. I was thus already in a mood to be comforted for my failure, when another failure put the grayling definitely in their place.

This other failure was not mine but that of a wild-fowler in the fields nearby. Bang, bang; I had seen the duck sweep overhead and settle downriver in the reach from which I had caught one of my two poor grayling. As I came up at last out of the river I met the fowler, a sturdy, but disappointed man with a huge empty sack, meant to carry duck in, over his shoulder (just as I had a basket with plenty of room in it for grayling). Exchanging news of our failures we improved each other's worlds. Nor was his failure with the duck all he had to offer me. The generous fellow told me that he, too, was a fisherman, and had been grayling fishing a fortnight earlier, on Boxing Day, in this very place, and had done as badly as myself. We spent a happy ten minutes by the river, within hearing of the fish, discussing the character of grayling unfavourably. We went on to talk of better fishing days. As he talked I grew more and more conscious that this fowler was a very honest man. There was a precision in his reminiscences, a just apportioning of merit, that delighted me. He ranked fish caught on the bustard at night below much smaller fish caught by day. He condemned the garnishing of flies with maggots as stooping from the rigour of the game, but added that 'anyway, he did not think the maggots made a ha'porth of difference.' His dislike of throwing maggots into grayling rivers was as decided as my own. I liked him more and more. And when at last he came, naturally, to tell me the story of his biggest trout I knew that it had been exactly the weight and the length that he attributed to it. This fowler was what we all should be. He had caught, in daylight, on a small fly (Light Starling) and on 4x gut, in this fast-flowing river, a trout of three pounds and a quarter, seventeen and a half inches in length.

'It was the finest shaped fish I've ever seen. And the only trout I've ever had the privilege of eating (I told you I liked this man), the only trout I've had the privilege, the honour, I might say, of eating, that was so big that I had cutlets made of him. Cutlets, and cooked in butter, they were as red as smoked salmon. And now,' he said, 'I'll tell you how it was. That evening, June it was, about five o'clock, just before I went out to the river, I'd said that I didn't believe in these big fish that you read about in the papers. I'd been fishing thirty years and the biggest I'd caught was one pound and a quarter, not because it was smaller than what other folk caught but because I'd weighed it and told the truth about it. And I'd no sooner come to the river, just there, below the viaduct, you know the deep hole there is on the far side, I had this great fish take my fly. It would be the second cast, or maybe the third. And now there are those who didn't see him, and didn't eat those cutlets, that believe in him just as little as I believed in big fish before I caught him.'

Now, strange as it may seem, the fowler and I, today failures both, went our ways in great cheerfulness. He, no doubt, was heartened by the thought of his great fish. As for me, the few minutes of talk with him on the frozen bank of the river, while dusk thickened about the foot of the hills and the cold made my fingers fumble the taking down of my tackle, were more than enough to obliterate the obstinacy of the grayling and to turn my first fishing day in 1929 into a memorable success.

Coxcombs of Fishing

'O, 'TIS a stately occupation,' says a character in an old play, 'to stand foure houres in a colde morning, and to have his nose bitten with frost before his baite be mumbled with a fish.'

That is the way in which I have heard men explain why they do not fish for grayling in the season of the year when the grayling is at his very best. It is a poor explanation, for the grayling fisher who stands four hours without getting a bite is a poor grayling fisher. Nor does it often happen that, fishing pool after pool, driven, almost on the run, by frost and eagerness from one pool to the next, the grayling fisher has so long as four hours to wait with no bob or quiver or hesitation of his float to set his blood tingling.

On Tuesday of this week, however, only those fishermen

who stuck, unrewarded, to their work through a full four hours had their baits mumbled in the end and went home with fairly heavy baskets. I hooked and lost a fish with my first or second cast at about half-past ten in the morning. He slipped away below me into some heavy water where I could not follow and was gone. From that moment until late in the afternoon I saw no sign of a fish. One good pool after another drew blank. Yet it was a grand day. The fields were white and the great hills gleamed in the sunshine. In the sunshine it was not freezing, but there was frost in every shadow and the sun was not hot enough to clear the snow from the fields. I was sure that sooner or later the grayling would come on, though when I looked at my watch and found it after three o'clock doubt crept in.

Doubt had long ago weakened the perseverance of my companion, who, being very young, had not acquired that stiffness of mental habit which makes the elderly go on doing the same thing until darkness or a train to catch makes them leave off, a stiffness which is sometimes mistaken for virtue. Long before three o'clock some desultoriness had shown itself in his fishing. He had taken to walking his float down a pool and then sauntering to another. He had written off as hopeless the pools that he had fished earlier in the day.

The benign moment, when at last it came, found him loitering rod in hand through the snow beside a long and unfishable length of the river that ought to be passed in as rapid a gallop as waders will allow. And the benign moment was a very short one. It lasted for less than half an hour. But while it lasted it was a beauty. It found me at the head of a pool that I had three times fished already, a pool with a green, wintry deep in it. The first fish was under the half-pound, but it was followed by good grayling, one after another, as fast as I could land them. All took in the same place just as the little float, far away, reached an overhanging bough. Each fish came readily aside into water where he did not disturb the others. Twenty minutes or so turned a blank day into a decent one.

My unlucky companion sauntered up, enjoying the sunshine on the hills, just as I landed my last fish. I made him fish the same pool and myself moved elsewhere, but he was just too late. The benign moment was over. I caught one more fish and missed another a little way below, and then cast a shade too far and hung my float in a tree on the farther side of the river. Crossing the river a hundred yards lower down I went back up the other bank to recover my float, and found it together with three other floats and a number of casts, all hung in a tangle together. Evidently that bough on the far side had been for a long time a collector of grayling tackles. There was no more fishing to be done, though, just at dusk, on our way home we saw the only grayling rise that we had seen all day.

That rise in the winter evening, when the sun was already off the water and pouring the rose of its setting on the snow-covered hills, reminded me of a man whom I met on such a night when I had taken a dish of grayling to a friend. He looked at the fish, admiring them as they deserved, and asked me whether I had taken them on a dry fly. When I told him that I had taken them on a wet worm, he remarked, with a loftiness of manner that it is impossible to express by mere narration, that, for himself, he made a point of using nothing but the dry fly. I felt like telling him that he would have to catch a phoenix and tie a fly from its feathers with whisks from the Cheshire Cat if he wished to make a basket of grayling from our northern rivers in mid-winter. I felt like reminding him of Walton's remark that 'winter fly-fishing is as useful as an almanack out of date.' I did tell him mildly that in this river winter grayling do not rise to the fly. He replied that in that case he would prefer not to fish for them. And only a few minutes earlier he had complained that there were too many grayling in the river.

Now this attitude towards winter worm-fishing for grayling seems to me pure coxcombry. It is less excusable than the contempt that the dry-fly fisherman often expresses for him who fishes with wet, because, after all, if a fish can be caught with a wet fly it is usually possible to catch it with a dry, sometimes, indeed, easier to catch it. But the man who despises float-fishing for grayling because it is not dry-fly fishing could not go out with his dry flies and show the float fisher

how to catch grayling in a north country river in mid-winter.
It amounts to this. These coxcombs (no other word will fit)
prefer to grumble at the grayling being in the river rather than
go out and catch them. Theirs is a south-country attitude. In
the south, even as far north as Derbyshire, fly-fishing persists,
because flies persist, longer than in the north. Rivers are more
equable in the south, the quality of fishing more consistent.
But when the south countryman comes north and, remembering May and June days on chalk streams, despises us for
swimming the worm on a January day while he sits at home
reading Halford we may say to him with justice,

> These summer flies
> Have blown you full of maggot ostentation.

It is 'showing off,' and of the worst kind, because, since it is
impossible to persuade the boaster to the river on these cold
days, we cannot put his pretensions to the test. In the north the
grayling nobly prolongs our fly-fishing through October and
gives us now and again a good day in November. But he is in
his best condition precisely during the months when fly-
fishing is a hopeless business. Then, if ever, is the time to thin
the grayling in the river, and swimming the worm, with finer
tackle than it would often occur to the dry-fly fisherman to
use, is the most sporting method with which to do it.

For Going Home

THE FLOODS have gone and the rivers have been for some
days in admirable condition for grayling fishing and,
consequently, for good fishing days, which are, I think,
more surely provided by the winter grayling than by the
summer trout. Swimming the worm is not in itself as delicate
or as interesting an art as fly-fishing, but for a number of
reasons it is more consistent in the matter of good days,
properly so called.

It is rather shortsighted to take the view that a fishing day ends when the fisherman leaves the water. It should be considered rather as a preparation for the evening after fishing, in fact, for going home. It is by the mood on the homeward journey that a fishing day is properly to be judged. This is, of course, the answer to those who cannot understand why some of the most delightful of fishing days are not the days on which we catch most fish. We have all had many a good day without catching any at all. We find, however, that it is safer not to count on this, and to do the best we can to fill a basket.

I do not altogether like catching a lot of fish as soon as I get to the river. When this happens it often seems to mean that during all the rest of the day I shall catch none, so that when it is time to go home the morning's exultation will have been wiped out by many hours of failure. The fish in the basket have already ceased to be those of that day. Your afternoon self has come to regard your morning self as a quite different and more fortunate fisherman, almost an enemy, and it is not the lucky but the unlucky one who will trudge home despondent with the weight of that other fellow's catch cutting into his shoulder. Later on the basket may comfort him a little when it is emptied out upon a large white dish. The fish will be his own once more, but, even so, never in his memories will that day be transformed into a good one. No, it is better at least to begin badly, to feel your hopes dropping and then to have them lifted high by the capture of the first fish just when you had made up your mind that you were going to catch none. Thereafter you may catch as many fish as you like, or as few, on condition that you do at intervals catch one, and that your last fish comes to the net so late that the time between its capture and your packing up is not too long to be bridged without an effort. It is the proper spacing of the triumphant moments of the day that determines the evening mood.

Grayling are far cleverer than trout in giving a fisherman a happy journey home. There is, for example, in winter grayling fishing none of that frantic evening rise with which the tactless trout so often turn the tables on the fisherman who has come at their expense to think well of himself during the day. How often a trout fisherman rejoicing in the steady morning rise, which has been prolonged perhaps till four or five o'clock, has waited for the evening, has seen trout rising all round him, has changed his fly a dozen times, has seen all flies taken but his own, and has at last gone home with his day spoilt, a baffled and discomfited man. Not so with the grayling. You can be too early for them and you can, sometimes, be too late, but even on the days when you catch your last grayling when you can hardly see the tiny float they time their activities well, to send the angler home and happy in the early dusk.

These winter fishing days are not too long. In summer, even if we do not follow Stewart in counting as a fishing day no less than 'twenty-fower hours o' creepin' an' crawlin',' a man can hardly feel he has done full justice to a day unless he has spent a long time on the river. In winter he cannot overstay his welcome if he would. The day is so short, the curtain of the night falls so effectively that the man going home from grayling fishing is never troubled by the uneasy feeling that he might have done better if he had stayed a little longer. Finally, with the grayling the absolutely blank day is rare.

Last Saturday I had what seems to me a perfect day, though people who count their catches in forties and fifties would think that my basket (though full) was a small one. There had been some interest in finding the fish, for the floods, had markedly altered the soundings in some of my favourite pools. The old pool where the water poured out over a steeply dropping lip, close below which it used to be possible to take ten or a dozen grayling without moving, by bringing each fish promptly away from the shoal into a backwater, had been reshaped. The lip had been removed as if by a dredger. The water rushed straight out into the wide pool, and the old feeding place of the grayling was deserted. A new feeding ground had come into existence two dozen yards lower down, where formerly was a bank of shingle. Then, too, it had been interesting to find temporary confirmation of a half-formed theory (all theories about grayling are extremely short-lived) by noticing that if in one pool grayling are feeding near the head of it they are likely to be found near the head of all similar pools, whereas on another day almost every fish will be taken in the smoother water. I moved up river all day, in each pool getting fish in the same place.

The grayling stopped feeding the moment the sun sank in a clear sky behind the big hills to the west. There followed a half-hour of magic. A glow still rested on the eastern hills. The wind dropped. The pool where I was wading was like a sheet of tarnished but polished silver. The only noise was that of water, until a salmon plunged heavily and moved up, his back fin out of water, shattering the reflections of the hills. The ripples were washed away downstream, and the pool was smooth once more. It was very cold. And then suddenly a bird broke the silence with song from a solitary bare tree on the farther side of the river. The song was clear, sweet, and easy, a song of complete contentment. It was without a chorus, for no other bird was singing. For this reason it was more impressive than the general evensong of birds in early summer. It was, of course, a robin, expressing his opinion of the sunset and the day, which coincided with my own. I felt he sang for both of us, and took some little credit to myself for the feeling that we put into it.

3 • A KETTLE OF FISH

Winter Grayling Fishing

THE GRAYLING of the Dove seem to be ready to take an artificial fly even when no natural fly is on the water. A bit of silver and a red tag will bring them up even when nothing living is keeping in their minds the expectancy that makes the difference between the barren hours and those of 'the take.' Perhaps the Dove is so heartily and continuously fished that the grayling in it have come to believe that flies of one sort or another are on the water all the year round. In the Eden it is not so. Eden fishermen agree with Walton that 'winter fly-fishing is as useful as an almanac out of date.' They do no fly-fishing after the end of October unless there comes a belated spell of autumn weather. Indeed, very little fishing of any kind is done during the months when the grayling are at their best. There is much less swimming of the small red worm with the tiny float (that Pritt painted so lovingly) in the Eden than in the Yorkshire rivers. And perhaps it is little wonder, for this, though one of the most delicate and delightful of all kinds of float-fishing, is also one of the coldest of cold jobs.

The winter roach-fisher, with his mittens and his two overcoats and carol-singer's scarf, sitting on his basket, is armed against the cold. Besides, he does not so often have to handle his wet line. The man who spins for pike, walking along the bank, casting and giving his hands turn and turn about in winding in, moves in the warm glow of continual exercise and is more likely to get too hot than too cold. The grayling fisher, swimming the worm, if he dresses warmly, gets too hot in moving from one place to another, and, if he dresses for the walking, gets too cold within a minute or two of beginning to fish. Handling a wet line when you are yourself tingling with warmth on the bank is all very well, but it is a different thing to do it when you are stationary, out of the sun, and thigh deep in the winter river. The actual wading, of course, is warm enough. A very little motion suffices to keep the feet hot when you are wearing indiarubber wading trousers, even when it is so cold that the little ripple which the fisherman involuntarily makes is greeted by the thin laughter of breaking ice as it finds its way to the shores. Handling wet things with cold hands is the rub. Coldest of all is the handling of the fish. The other day, on the Eden, I came almost to resent any grayling who had not the decency and skill to leave me before forcing me to wet my hands in taking him from the net. On this occasion, not only the biggest but also the kindest fish were those that got away.

I had only a very short time of actual fishing, because, unfortunately, the cold affects other things in the angler's equipment besides his fingers. It attacks his instruments. After half a dozen swims, the line, well greased though it was, carried drop after minute drop of water to the agate rings of the rod, there to freeze and presently to turn each ring into a solid little blob on the rod with the line firmly frozen in the middle of it. A tiny icicle formed on the catch of the lockfast joint and the line froze to that. By holding each ring in turn in the fingers the ice could be melted and the line freed, only to freeze again. Then as the line ran out from the rather small reel there came a gentle crackling noise of particles of ice on the line. The line came off for each swim with more and more difficulty. At last, while I was putting on a fresh worm, it froze solid on the reel. I melted it once or twice in my fingers, but I could not melt rings and reel at once, and so was finally defeated.

Only those who have never fished grayling in winter speak of him as a non-fighting fish. Francis says: 'There are two or three times the number of grayling lost after hooking than there are of trout.' Almost all writers speak of its 'exceeding tender' mouth. Yet its mouth is not exceeding tender. Its lips are rather like the chub's in texture, and it owes its frequent escape to its own skill and vigour. It does not put up the prolonged struggle of a trout. In the first few moments, it tries the hold of the hook in every possible way, running amuck and behaving as if scandalised at the insolence of its would-be captor. You feel the indignation of the fish. He has come up perpendicularly from the bottom of the river, with his great fins, red and crimson like a cathedral window, erect, to clean the river from, let us say, a maggot. And the maggot suddenly bites him and fastens to him a long line of gut with an angler at the other end. The grayling is more than hurt. He is outraged. Salmon, trout, perch, roach, pike do not plunge so instantly into battle. There is, with all of them, a moment's almost ceremonial pause. The grayling is the quickest fish that swims. He does not wait at all, but seems to take a flying start. He would break the *moral* of his adversary from the word 'Go.' Right, left, right, left, up and down; no other fish has such a gift for flurrying the angler. A stiff rod transmits staccato the jars of the struggle. It certainly helps the grayling to loosen the hook.

It is true that later on a grayling is inclined to play heavily and trust to his weight and the current. Even this is sometimes strategy. He has a way of simulating defeat just before his final struggle. He has reduced the angler to panic by those first flashing moments of rapier play (quite unlike the prolonged wrestling of the honest trout), and then, suddenly, gives up. The angler, now over-confident, winds in and thinks of his net. The fish comes in a shade too easily, and a moment later the fisherman is examining his barren hook in the hope of being able to put the blame on his tackle-maker.

Grayling Again

A MONTH AGO, in Derbyshire, I had my first day after this most delightful of fish. It was a day of great gusts of wind, stripping the russet trees and blowing fleets of dry leaves across the river. There were leaves everywhere. In the gusts the leaves fell in swirling clouds. In the lulls sometimes a single leaf or a twig dropped into the river, and, if one did not see it fall, contrived to produce an excellent imitation of a rise. In the river, under the surface, were thousands of sodden leaves washed down from the higher reaches. On the surface was a carpet of leaves not yet wholly soaked. Fishing with the wet fly was altogether impossible, but here and there, among the leaves, grayling were rising, and if the wind slackened for long enough to let a clumsy fisherman drop a floating fly in among the drifting argosies, there was just a chance of picking up a fish.

I got a few on Bradshaw's Fancy, but it was disheartening work, as after every cast the fly gathered a leaf on the recovery and the line had to be shortened to allow the removal of the leaf, and then let out again before casting. Nor was it possible to cast at once to a rising fish. A fish would rise, and instantly the place where he rose would be covered by a Turkey carpet of reds and oranges and faded greens, and it was useless to cast at all until that carpet had floated by, leaving a foot or two of clear water to be covered almost at once by the next carpet of leaves floating down behind the first.

Guy Faux's Day, however, brings in a different kind of grayling fishing, and, this year at least, the weather for it and the water. The river is settling. The leaves, all but belated stragglers that resisted the gales, are gone. In a whole day of swimming the worm, I think only two leaves tried to get out of the river by fastening themselves on my tiny hooks. It was cold, too cold for any fly-fishing, and therefore cold enough to let a man swim the worm with a good conscience, but not so cold as to give grayling fishing that almost heroic character that it has later in the season. There was not much sun, but there was always the feeling that it might show at any minute.

There was no rain to matter. It was not one of those crisp early winter days when the really good grayling fisher (such as I am not) has a chance of filling his basket twice over. But it was a day on which it was possible for the grayling to leave no room in the basket for the worm-tin. I regard the transference of that tin from basket to pocket as proof that the day is good enough to satisfy any but a pot-hunter. The fish were both unanimous and uniform. Comparing notes in the evening, we found that on different stretches of the river they had come on the feed at precisely the same time. We each caught our first fish between half-past ten and eleven, and from then on till dusk they were feeding pretty steadily, at least the larger fish. The small fish, apparently, were lying low. Laid out on the grass the fish we caught looked all the same size. The biggest was just over the pound. Nearly all the others were close round about three-quarters of a pound and in the two baskets was only one small fish.

'Always' and 'Never'

GRAYLING have a particular dislike for these two words when used about themselves. Yet no fish so often tempt the angler into using them. They seem at the same time to disapprove of all generalisation and to delight in tricking the poor fisherman into thinking that he has discovered a rule about them. It is enough even to think that you have discovered such a rule to induce the grayling, who have themselves misled you, to disprove it the next time you go fishing.

One of the many amusing spectacles to be found in a fishing inn is that of the man who, taking to grayling fishing, discovers their secret once a week. At last, a humbled man, he learns that they have no secret, or rather that they change it as soon as anyone thinks he has discovered it. He will then sit back silent in his chair and be ready to enjoy the categorical statements of the next new grayling fisher to tread, week by week, the path of disillusion he has followed. For example, taking winter fishing alone:– Week the first. The weather keeping mild, the fisherman, who has read in a book that frosty weather is the best for grayling fishing, stays at home. His friend goes fishing on a warm November day and comes back with a basketful. Week the second. The weather is the same. The fisherman, now convinced that warm weather is the thing, goes out in high hopes and catches not a single fish. Week the third. A hard frost and a low river. The fisherman makes a good catch and announces to his friends that the book was right after all. Week the fourth. Weather and river the same. He catches three grayling. Week the fifth. The fisherman hardly thinks it worth while going to the river, because he has nothing but lobworms. He makes a good catch. Week the sixth. He tries lobworms again. Not a grayling will look at them, whereas he does very well when he gives up the lobs and uses brandlings. And so on, until he makes the wise decision to fish when he can and how he can, and to suppress every effort of his mind to reason on the subject of grayling at all.

This is an easy decision to make but hard to carry out. The grayling, conscious that their mission in life is to humiliate man, are continually tempting him into indiscretion. This they do by seemingly concerted unanimity at given moments. You catch one in a fast stream, and on that day find them in the fast streams all up the river. You catch one in quiet water, and on that day it seems that every grayling in the river has chosen a similar feeding place. They persevere in any kind of behaviour until you notice it and act upon it, when, at once, they change it for another. Even their unanimity is one of their tricks. Now and again they will upset your calculations by being in all parts of the river at once, or nowhere. Long, long Œgo I told myself never to generalise about grayling. Very many times since then, led on by the grayling themselves, I have found myself surreptitiously forming a theory. Every time such a theory has been, as it were illicitly, formed the grayling have taken it upon themselves to smash it just so soon as I had formulated it to myself, and to humiliate me publicly if I have been such a fool as to mention it to anyone else.

Let me give the latest example. For some years now I have been in the habit, when going grayling fishing after the fly season, of making up a few minute tackles, to be carried in a matchbox. These tackles consist of an inch of fine gut joining two small hooks. No. 1 hooks I find big enough. The lower hook is one with a tapered shank, the upper hook is eyed. They are whipped on with red silk. I went to the length of painting the hooks red, but gave it up as an unnecessary refinement. The convenience of this tackle is that it can be put on the cast as easily as a fly and avoids knots and loops in the cast. If the fine whipping wears, as it must after being mouthed by a lot of fish, it is the work of a moment to put on a new tackle. Latterly, day after day, week after week, I could not help noticing that every grayling I caught was held by the top hook and by the top hook only. Clearly, it would seem, grayling always take the worm by the head.

'Always'. There it was. That word has slipped in. The grayling were bound to overhear it. And to clench matters, my friend, using my tackle, announced that his grayling also were always taken by the upper hook and never by the lower one. 'Always' and 'never'. Still, it did seem that the lower hook might well be omitted. I would return to the old single hook. I whipped a small single hook to a length of very fine gut, whipping in the butt-end of a rabbit's whisker on the shank of the hook to prevent the worm from slipping down. The first bite I got I missed the fish and was tempted to give up the experiment. I persisted, however, missed no more, and finished with a fair basket. Yes, it seemed, grayling do take their worms by the head. Just then came my friend, who had also been catching grayling, still using the two-hook tackle. 'It's a queer thing,' said he, 'but to-day all my grayling have been caught on the lower hook.' The generalisation was shaken already. The whipping of my single hook frayed. I tied on one of my old tackles and for the rest of that day and the subsequent day every grayling was caught on the lower hook. The generalisation was disintegrated altogether.

I am not alone in these experiences. There is hardly a book that discusses grayling which does not contain a downright statement to which the grayling have replied on occasion with a downright contradiction. It is said, for example, that it is useless to fish wet fly upstream for grayling. One of the best grayling fishers I know regularly fishes wet fly upstream. The grayling have persuaded some authorities that they have delicate mouths, whereas other authorities, also with wide experience of grayling, compare their mouths to tough leather. There is the business of big and little worms. Pritt and Walbran, I think, advise very small worms, Pritt going so far as to publish a coloured picture drawn to scale of the worm he most admired. Many an hour had I spent carefully picking out Tom Thumbs among the worms until there came the day when I had no small worms at all, but only things like young snakes, and on that day, fishing with those monsters, had as good a basket as ever I had had with the dwarfs.

Remembering all these things, I have at last worked out a rule in which I defy these grayling preachers of philosophic doubt to pick a hole. It is this. If you *never* make a general statement about them and *always* keep an open mind you will catch grayling – *sometimes*.

The Consolation Pike

THE SEASON was such a bad one that it did not seem to matter so much as it might have done spending two of the best months of it in bed, but it did seem like piling one bit of bad luck on another when, after getting out of bed and persuading everybody that the only method of convalescence worth considering is to be found very near a river, some depression or other far out in the Atlantic should take it into its head to move west, bringing with it unsettled weather and so filling the rivers that they were for migratory fish like straight arterial roads through industrial districts with no sort of inducement to them to stop a little by the way and take a bite of something – of my minnow, for example. It was almost enough to send a man back to bed again to wait till next year. Somewhere about the end of March would be a better time for saying good-bye to doctors and nurses and telling them that they have done very well and that you don't feel any the worse for your cure.

And then, when despair had set in hard, there was a fine day, of course with a full programme and useless for fishing. But first thing next morning, drizzle or no drizzle, all roads should lead to the river, and, by way of tempting a salmon, I would fish for sea-trout, and, by way of tempting sea-trout, I would fish for them on the finest tackle I could put together. There is a lot of experience behind this. Anybody who has done much fishing knows very well that one of the good ways of catching the best trout of the season is to lose your landing-net, and that, if all other methods of salmon-fishing fail, it is worth while to take no gaff and to fish for him as if he were a small roach.

The river I was going to is a good river in the parts where it is still a natural haunt of freshwater fish. I was going to fish it where it runs out into the estuary, where its banks are quicksands, where it is affected by the tide, where it has stuff in it that rots the aluminium of my favourite reels and makes the best of lines turn traitor. I thought I might meet down there some good old friends who catch sea-trout with maggots and are accustomed now and again to lose tackle and all in a salmon. It was the odd salmon I was after, though I would not have cared to say so. No. I was going to look at the river and see if my old friends, who are very skilful, and Yorkshiremen at that, had left a single sea-trout in the water.

As soon as I came to the bank, after a much longer walk than usual or than I liked in my present form (due to some new rule made since I fished here last) and climbing some high stiles and getting through some barbed wire, I saw that I had done well. The river had been very high, but it had fallen a little. It was quite clear, and the drizzle did not seem likely to fill it again. Besides, before I was ready to fish the drizzle stopped. And then, just as I walked quietly out on the sand to the place from which I meant to make my first cast, I saw one of those 'salmon.' He was very long, and he had a very large tail, made to seem larger still by another big fin just above it, about where some salmon carry an adipose fin of much more moderate size. And as I watched him this 'salmon' moved slowly without effort on the ribbed sandy bottom and suddenly, taking fright, shot off with a powerful wriggling corkscrew motion most unsalmon-like. This was at the side of a large pool where my Yorkshire friends have been accustomed to feed the sea-trout with maggots. The maggots gather the trout, and after the trout come these curious-looking 'salmon.' I cast well across the river. Nothing happened. I moved on and cast again, and this time, after I had already cast, I saw lying on the sand a little above the line along which my spinner was approaching another of these 'salmon.' I wound in steadily, and just as my spinner was within a couple of yards of the 'salmon,' which apparently had its back to it, the 'salmon' turned and with one motion removed my spinner and disappeared into the depths of the pool.

I rigged another bait, putting a foot of fine wire between the head of the bait and the very fine gut cast. At the third cast it was taken. I did not strike. Any strike would have broken the gut. I simply pulled and left the fish to hook himself. He threw out the bait. I spun slowly on, and the fish followed it in and lay there. Again I spun past him and this time he had it and was off with a rush, and presently was landed a pike of four pounds. Well, there is nothing much in a pike of four pounds in the ordinary way, but this pike of four pounds, being fed on an exclusive diet of sea-trout (for there are no other coarse fish in this part of the river), leapt twice from the water, though I was holding him lightly on the very fine gut, and, moreover, was followed about by a fish three times his size. After a little coaxing I interested this big one. He moved in after the spinning bait. I could not so much see him as see where he was, a shadow that I should have had difficulty in making anybody else see and should not have myself known for a fish if I had not found that by spinning my bait near it I could make it change its direction. The big fish took the bait. I refrained from striking. He let go, took it again, and turned away. I pulled steadily, and the next moment was rejoicing that I had that morning put a good length of backing on my trout reel.

Forty yards of roach line were out and five or six yards of a white line behind it, and the beast was still moving. Happily I had a long stretch of clear sand on either side of me and plenty of clear water in front, and so was able to settle down to a long bout without much misgiving.

The trouble began later when, while playing the pike with one hand, I had to unscrew my landing-net with the other and then screw on a gaff-head which, just in case, I had dropped into my bag at the last minute. The net came off all right, and then I learnt that the screw on the gaff-head was a Continental one that did not fit my handle. It came to an end at last when I gaffed the pike, using my own arm instead of a handle to the gaff. He weighed twelve pounds, the biggest pike I have caught on a trout rod, though I have had salmon bigger on the same rod. After that I got one little sea-trout and then another four-pound pike. Every one of these pike had imbibed so much of sea-trout character by eating them that they leapt high out of the water and by every possible means showed that they felt that it was their duty to be as good substitutes for their betters as they might.

Apart from that, the river was well rid of them. And how will the sea-trout show their gratitude next year for the removal of these unlicensed privateers? They ought, in justice, to reward me with a record bag.

Chub and Elvers

IT IS A LONG way to Tewkesbury, but, apart from the pleasure of meeting many friends at the All-England match, I should have held the journey worth the making for the sake of learning a method of chub-fishing new to me and not described in any of the books. Even Martin, by far the best writer on chub-fishing, who gives a long list of baits for chub, does not mention the elver. This is perhaps because he did not fish the Severn but found his chub in the Trent and the Ouse. I was told in Tewkesbury that the chub show no particular

enthusiasm for elvers in waters in which they are not accustomed to find them in some quantity. There is said to be
a larger run of elvers in the Severn than in any other English
river. These tiny eels, three to four inches long, have come
from the depths of the Atlantic, have survived all dangers
from the monsters of the sea (including the larger eels), and
come up the river in swarms – so that at weirs and such places
they can be seen in black, wriggling masses. Their arrival is
welcomed by chub, perch, and man – who in Tewkesbury has
not forgotten how to make elver cakes. Those who survive
their welcome grow to eels, avenge their brothers by wholesale destruction of small fry, and at last return (some of them)
to the Atlantic to provide more elvers for annual multi-
tudinous pilgrimage. The chub fishermen of Tewkesbury
look upon the elver much as the trout fishermen of Eden and
Lune look upon the creeper and the stone fly.

The elvers are caught below the weirs in fine sieves of
strong muslin. They can, as I proved at the cost of a wetting, be
caught by hand if the fisherman is without better equipment.
They are to be found on the weirs in the soft green weed that
clings to the stones. The fisherman, paddling barefooted,
plunges his hand through the fast water, grabs a handful of
weed and drops it into a tin can; when the elvers, if any are
there, detach themselves from the weed and gather in the
water at the bottom of the can. By this time of the year they are
already scarce, and even the skilled inhabitant of Tewkesbury
who introduced me to the use of them was not able to get very
many. But the more scarce they become the better they are as
bait for chub. Towards autumn the elvers are very rare, and
the chub, remembering earlier feasts, value them exceedingly.
To the chub late elvers are what early strawberries are to man.
I saw two habitual Severn fishers using these baits in the great
pool below Tewkesbury weir. Their method was simple and
must, I should think, work very well when the chub are
actually waiting below the weir for the elvers. They anchored
their punt close under the weir, dropping a stone with a rope
to it in the white foaming water of the weir apron. They then
fished the water on either side of the punt with rather heavy

float tackle. I fished the weir one afternoon, but found the chub a long way from it in the quieter water. Perhaps, with the rapidly growing scarcity of the elvers the chub no longer find it worth while to wait for them. My best day was in the Avon, not far above the place where it joins the Severn.

The place was a pool below a mill which, at the time, was not running, though a fair stream of water was coming through the sluice. Under the sluice, in the soft weed on the stones, there were still a few elvers; and, no doubt, the chub in the pool below were occasionally reminded of their summer banquets by a stray elver washed down in the current. The only place from which it was possible to fish the pool was a brick jetty below the old mill, just so high that, even with my long-handled landing-net, it was impossible to reach the water. Each fish had to be played in the main pool until it could be safely led over a bed of weeds and round to another mill-wheel which also was not running. A nimble lad climbed down through the wheel and reaching out between the blades netted the fish and lifted it up to the jetty from below. The method used, except in striking, was precisely that of swimming a worm for grayling; and it brought me fourteen chub – none very small, none very big, but all big enough to give a most exciting tussle on the fine tackle.

The water ran from the sluice into a broad basin, ending in shallows some thirty yards down. From the jetty it was possible to throw the light tackle to every part of the stream and then, letting the reel run almost free, to allow the tiny float to be carried down to the low end of the pool, when it would be caught in an eddy and carried up again on one side or other of the stream. At the second swim down, with the elver only a couple of feet below the float, I got the first of those chub. The float had danced down the stream and was just sailing into the eddy, when it hesitated for a moment and then shot out of sight. On tightening there was the hard, unmistakeable first plunge of a chub followed by a series of short rushes, rather like the hammer and tongs fighting of a perch.

These Avon and Severn chub are far harder fighters than some I have known in other waters. The next swim I had another fish before the float reached the eddy. Then a chub on the other side of the stream took the float under before it had moved more than a few yards and I lost him through striking at once. With the elver bait you must strike as slowly as with a worm or you have very little chance of feeling your fish. Fishing with wasp-grub, on the other hand, it is easier to miss fish through striking too late than too soon. In elver fishing, with the float twenty to twenty-five yards away and the line slack on the top of the water, following the twistings of the current, there was always time to spin the reel with a touch of the hand to gather loose line before striking. After the first half dozen fish I gave the pool an hour's rest, and found the chub ready for more of my elvers when I came back. A bag of fourteen chub, in waters under the very walls of a town, is such a hint of what might be done with this bait as to suggest that it might be very well worth trying in those of our northern rivers which hold elvers and more chub than the trout and grayling fishermen think should be encouraged.

Perch for a Change

IT IS A HAPPY dispensation that brings coarse fish into season at a time when trout fishing, unless with worm and minnow, is too often an unresponsive business. In May and June the trout fisher is full of loyalty, but towards the end of July he is prepared for occasional revolt against the exclusive tyranny of the trout and the hard work in hot weather which these aristocrats impose upon him. He is prepared to take his ease in a boat and to watch a bobbing cork instead of sweltering in waders flogging a stream which seems in these days to want stocking, though he knows well enough that it does not. Other motives move him. Gone, temporarily, is that lonely ardour of the spring, when running water was itself a sufficient companion. In this hot weather it is pleasant to have someone close at hand to whom he can complain how hot it is. Fly-fishing is, of its nature, not a gregarious activity. Float-fishing is all the jollier for company. It is no accident that it is the Coarse-fisher's Club, and no association of trout or salmon hunters, that announces so humanely on its cards, 'Members' wives are allowed to fish in club waters.' Allowed? They are even invited to enhance the pleasure of a peaceful day. And some of them, whose husbands own a dual allegiance, to trout and to coarse fishing, make no bones about their preference for that kind of fishing which is, at its best, a family affair.

As long as a fortnight ago I saw a reel being given some of the oil that belongs properly to the sewing-machine, a line being greased, and then, in the hot sunshine of last week, a new coat of white paint being given to the inside of a minnow-can. This last touch of thoroughness in preparation showed precisely what kind of a fishing day was planned, for all the world knows that pale minnows are more attractive to perch than dark ones, and that in the whited sepulchre of a minnow-can the blackest minnows blench magnificently. They take their colour from the can, and, dropped into the darkness of deep water, gleam like little beacons to call the perch who see them from afar. It was to be a day's perch fishing. Because, on some days, a red worm is dearer to the perch than the whitest minnow these valuable by-products of gardening had been for some time stored in a bed of moss. The final signal was the discovery of some hooks to gut (square bend for minnow, barbless for worm) soaking innocently in a saucer that I should never have been allowed to borrow for such a purpose. At half past nine the following morning we were netting minnows at the side of the mere.

There was no division of opinion as to where to fish. Perch are conservatives, and the last time we fished this place the best of them had been taken in a little bay which, sheltered as it was from the south-west wind, offered a patch of smooth water. We rowed there at once, laid out our anchors bow and stern (a single anchor will destroy the calm spirit essential to float-fishing), and a minute or two later the member's wife had plumbed the depth, exchanged her plummet for a worm, and was already fishing while she put up her second rod in case the perch preferred minnow. Instantly the float bobbed and went under. There was a moment's delay in putting down the other rod, and in that moment there arrived a competitor for the perch. As she struck belatedly a pike took the perch and the rod bent double. There was little hope of catching him, but he fought as if he were indeed hooked until she had him close to the boat, when he let go. We could see the little perch, and as it was being lifted from the water the pike, a long dark shadow, shot at it again, and the fight was on anew. This time the pike did not hold on for so long, but, after a run or two, decided to abandon a Lilliput perch possessed of such Brobdingnagian strength. With pike about, it is always worth while to put out a bait for them on stronger tackle, and during the day we caught six of them, two of which were caught on the perch tackle, one of them, a small one certainly, falling ignominiously to a worm on a barbless hook. Still, the pike were outside the programme. We had come for perch, and we attacked the pike only because, when one of them was about, the perch warned us by stopping their meal until the pike were either hooked and lost or in the boat. Perch, besides being the handsomest of British fish, conform perfectly to the grosser needs of family fishing. They do not, at this time of year, feed continuously. Nor do they need pursuit singly. Once we have found their feeding-place, the loathsome muddy business of shifting anchors, the unbearable entangling mess of getting out oars, with four or more rods, fully equipped, lying in the boat, is not only abhorrent but actually bad fishing and wholly unnecessary. We do best to stay where we are. The perch, cruising below us, will come again and again to our baits. Bites enliven us, as it were, in gusts or squalls, and the floats all bob at once, like red poppies dipping unanimously to a sudden breeze. When one bobs they all bob, and for a few minutes we wish we had more hands than two apiece. Then there is a period of peace during which, perhaps, the pike float in the offing disappears. Then as the cruising shoal comes our way again there is another frenzy of bobbing floats, of strikes on two rods at once, of playing and landing fish. But some time after the middle of the day there is a definite pause. The perch stop feeding altogether and tell us that it is time for luncheon.

This pause has an easily recognisable character, though it would be hard to say exactly how we know that for the next hour and a half we should be wasting time if we tried to feed perch instead of feeding ourselves. Alone, I should have a sandwich and a banana in the boat, but the member's wife knows better, and we boil a kettle on the shore of the mere and drink hot tea and count our catch (a score of perch, and four pike) and wonder what was the monster that bent her rod double and broke her cast. Then back to the same place, and before long, if we have timed things rightly, the perch are feeding again.

Towards evening we get another brace of pike. At last, at dusk, a stout eel takes a minnow, and after a prodigious struggle comes aboard to be beheaded bloodily and slimily on the bottom of the boat. And so home. The member's wife had chosen her day well. The rain now falling will bring the rivers up again to enable those aristocrats of trout to reassert their challenged dominion.

Worm for the Trout

IT MUST have been well over thirty years since I had fished for trout with a worm in coloured water. In the morning on Tuesday a friend with whom I was going to the Lune spoke of worms and said he was going to take some, and I, rather airily, said he would never need worms in such a good water as we should find. He, however – wise and provident man! – said that you never knew and went off to dig. There never was a better illustration of the local character of the weather among these hills. On our way to the fishing we crossed a number of small becks and rivers. In every one of them was a good fly water, until at last we came to one that was flowing the other way as we climbed over into the Lune valley. This beck, flowing down to join the Lune, had faint traces of colour and was decidedly strong. We were reassured on reaching the river. It was a good height, but still clear, and we thought there was every hope for a good day.

The water I was to fish was some mile and a half or two miles down river. It was raining as I walked through the fields. It was still raining when I came to the shallows where I meant to cross the river. I fished my way across and had two or three small fish, of which only one was worth taking. But during that crossing the river suddenly rose. It was as sudden as if a small tidal wave had come down, and I was lucky to get across dry. Just before this happened I had noticed small fish jumping clean out of the water, as they sometimes do just before a spate. The spate was much nearer than I had imagined. There was a tearing, gusty upstream wind, and I had planned to fish a long flat, which, in such a wind, is at its best. By the time I got there the water was brown and the shallow was almost too deep for wading. The rain poured down and I, unusually, had time to eat sandwiches while I watched the water creep up, over the stones, to the edge of the grass, over the grass, up the bank. There would be no more fly-fishing that day. Nor would there be any chance of recrossing the river except by a bridge.

Sandpipers flew over the brown water, shrilling their long tinkling cry. Two dippers were feeding in an eddy. I spent some time watching their way of entering the water. They did not dive, but flew out over the water and dropped in it feet first while in flight, going straight under, like a man jumping in at the deep end of a swimming bath. By the time I had walked down to the foot-bridge the river was a raging torrent. The high rocks on either side of the salmon pools were all under water. And still the rain poured down. What fools we had been to go fishing on such a day!

And then, as I walked idly up the other bank, the place became alive with fishermen. Rain brought the local worm-fishers out like slugs. Man after man stood close to the edge of the river, his rod-point not a foot above the water. A strange, dull game it seemed to be. And just then I remembered that my friend had gone digging before breakfast. No doubt he was worming now among this multitude of other wormers. Why should not I? I took off my tail fly and in its place attached a couple of No. 1 eyed hooks. I had no shot, but found at the bottom of a pocket a dusty air-gun pellet with a waist to it, which allowed of its attachment by a clove-hitch to the 5x gut.

The next thing was to turn stones for worms. I found a good worm and put him on. Then, remembering long-ago boy-hood, I looked for an eddy or some quiet water on the edge of this raging flood. I found one at the upper end of a long row of now partially submerged willow trees. I dropped in my worm. About ten seconds later something large had taken that worm and gone down into the willows. I did not dare to pull. Suddenly the fish shot clean away from the willows and out into the middle of the flood. With my rod held high up above my head as high as I could reach and the line stretched far across the river, the reel screaming meanwhile, I ran down the bank behind the willows. If that fish had turned and slackened the line he would have had me beautifully with a willow hedge between me and him and my line across the top of it. He did not think of it, and in open water below the trees he came to the net, one pound and a quarter. I went to turn stones to find another worm. The next worm brought a still better fish, one pound and three-quarters. He was lightly hooked and came spattering to the surface within a foot of the bank. The willows were close below, but the landing-net was between him and them, and he was scooped out, still spattering, before he had made up his mind what to do. Do you call this fishing? With mixed shame and greed I turned more stones and found two more worms. I got only one more fish, and that a smallish one.

While it lasted it was an odd experience, this consolation for a ruined day's fly-fishing. I had forgotten altogether what it was like to nurse a worm round a muddy eddy and to be prepared for whales.

4 • FLIES AND METHODS

The V on the Water

FISHING IS a subject on which it is all but impossible to say anything that will not somehow and somewhere turn out to be true and also somehow and somewhere turn out to be false. That is one of the reasons why it is the source of so much pleasant and interminable debate. No fisherman need ever feel that a pet theory of his own has been finally refuted. Somehow, somewhere ... He has only to bide his time. That time may be long in coming. In fishing as in archaeology a theory stated dogmatically enough may keep all others out of the field for years. Now, there have been few writers more dogmatic than the leading theorists of dry fly fishing and on nothing have they been more dogmatic than on 'drag'. A fly 'drags' when it moves at a different pace or in a different direction from the pace or direction of the water on which it floats. It then produces a visible V on the surface of the water, and what the dry fly fishermen said was that this V on the water was to the trout what the label POISON on a bottle is to the human being. They said it very loud and clear and all of us who, with shame, have seen a trout turn from our dragging fly have been ready to agree with them.

'The importance of avoiding drag cannot by any possibility be exaggerated', said Halford, and dotted his 'i's and crossed his 't's by adding, 'The use of the word "drag" was no doubt in the first instance suggested by the perceptible *wake* made by the artificial fly under such conditions.' And listen to this, written by Dewar in his *Book of the Dry Fly*: 'The drag when fishing with the dry fly is not less fatal to the sport in the evening than in broad daylight.'

Hardly a book on fly-fishing has been written in the last fifty years without giving instruction on how to avoid drag, 'one of the greatest protections that Nature affords the trout'. Yet, change one circumstance; let evening light turn to dark, and the V on the water instead of protecting the trout becomes the actual cause of the fisherman's success. The last ten years have seen the development of a way of fishing at night that uses a 'fly' or 'lure' so constructed as to produce as marked a V as possible.

This way of fishing has spread rapidly and on some of the dourest of northern rivers has resulted in baskets of the sort that used to be made in the old fabulous days when there were fewer fishermen and more fish.

Night fishing is a very old game in the north and on many of our rivers people give up day-time fishing after the appearance of the creeper and the stone-fly (our northern Mayfly) and take to fishing in the dark with 'bustards' and similar large lures. Their view of 'drag' and the V on the water has always been unlike that of the dry fly fishermen. Consider, for example, these words from *The North Country Angler* (1800):

> The body of the fly is at least as thick as a goose's quill, and rather more than an inch long, with a great rough head; my line a yard longer than my rod. When I have thrown it out to its full length, I draw it back by little pulls of about a yard, which makes it swim as if alive. When I hear a fish break the water and feel my line stop, I generally strike, though great fish hook themselves by closing their mouths and turning their heads.

That account of an old method is a fairly accurate description of the new. The fisherman of 1800 heard his fish break the water. That big blunt-headed fly of his must have been near the surface if not on it as he towed it along with those lifelike jerks.

Rather over a hundred years later, Dr J. G. Mottram wrote of night fishing that when it was too dark to see more than an occasional faint silver streak made by the line moving on the surface he 'worked downstream, allowing the fly to drag across the lie.' It is quite clear that he was not avoiding but using the V on the water. And, of course, again and again a dry fly fisherman has put on a big sedge, cast into the velvet dark under the further bank and had his rod nearly jerked from his hand when he was in the very act of removing his fly from the water. All of us have had the same experience. Well, a great many people had seen steam lift the lid of a kettle or saucepan before anybody put two and two together and thought of making a steam engine. It was 1943 when Mr Marshall Warhurst, a very successful fisher (alike by night and by day) of the lakes and rivers of West Cumberland, observing that his wet flies seemed less attractive when they had had time to sink and most attractive when they were dragging, set himself to dress an unsinkable fly that should make a better V than most.

'Murder must advertise.' 'Very good', said Mr Warhurst. 'It shall.' He began by making a little Zeppelin balloon from an inch and a half of stout quill, sealed and made water tight. To this he whipped a single eyed hook and found by experiment that the eye of the hook should be rather more than half an inch aft of the point of the quill so that, when attached to the cast and pulled, the Zeppelin should not dive but should slightly lift its bows and plane along the surface throwing a V wave on either side of it. This single hook also acts as a keel. Fastened to it by a short length of stout gut or fine twisted wire is a treble hook that tows astern. The whole is about three inches long from the top of the quill, including the treble hook. Nothing else is necessary but the inventor gives his little Zeppelin a pair of woodcock feathers as wings. These lie close along the quill and mask the treble hook. The thing is too big for any fly but might be the fourteenth cousin of a cockchafer. A well known South country fisherman who likes his flies to resemble identifiable insects said that the thing looked like one of the

Three Blind Mice and suggested that it should be fitted with a tail for the sake of realism as most of the mice likely to be found swimming the river had not yet met the Farmer's Wife and her carving knife. I do not think a tail would in any way detract from the fish-catching powers of the little beast and I doubt if the wings add much to them. All that matters is the V on the water. That triangular wake spreading across the pool first tells the trout that there is something stirring on the surface and then guides them to the apex of the triangle where they find that something, active and in motion, inviting them to close their jaws on it before it can get away. Thus the V not only attracts the fish but also collects and shepherds them towards the lure so that it may well happen that several fish pursue the thing at once and an element of competition is added to the ordinary motives of curiosity and greed.

On one occasion the inventor, invited to demonstrate, found he had left his box of specimens at home. He took a small cork from a medicine bottle, threaded some gut through it, attached a treble hook to the gut, cast the little cork as if it were a fly, towed it across the pool in the dark and caught fish no less successfully than when he towed his Zeppelin, mouse or cockchafer properly equipped with woodcock wings.

Mr Warhurst invented his monster in 1943. By 1948 it was revolutionising night fishing for sea trout in the rivers where it was known. In that year I was present at a demonstration. I came to the river just in time to hear (not see) the beaching of a big sea trout which very much disturbed the pool. Rather unwillingly, because of this, my friend agreed to try again and I crouched low to catch the faint glint of light on the surface of the water. He cast and I thought I saw the wave of a turning fish as the V made by the creature came towards us. 'No good', said my friend. 'The big fellow will have scared them all out of the pool'.

I asked him to make one more cast. He did. I heard that cockchafer, that albatross, go humming through the dark, and I watched the V wave as it was drawn back breaking the reflected light from the night sky. Suddenly there was an explosion in the water and some minutes later another big fish was beached to lie beside the first. Those two fish weighed close on ten pounds each. The second fish turned out to be a salmon, the first salmon ever to be caught in this way.

Have I fished the thing myself? I have and I haven't. I do not like night fishing and fish at night only once or twice a year and then for the sake of the summer night and not for that of the fishing . . . Good night-fishermen have cat's eyes and can see in the dark whereas I stumble about blindfold. Further I would always rather fish with a trout rod and small flies than with the big rod and heavy line these three inch monsters demand. Finally I do not like hearing the loud whirring flight of an albatross (or even a cockchafer) close to me in the dark when I know that the creature is armed with a big treble hook that I have myself sharpened. For all these reasons I cannot pretend to have given the thing a fair trial. But I have fished it enough to have learnt something of what it can do.

In 1948 I was given one of the creatures tied by the inventor himself. I took it with me into Cumberland and with it made one single cast. I had been catching sea trout by day and had tried and failed to catch a salmon and was on my way home when I remembered the still untried monster. The road lay by the river and I stopped at what I thought was a suitable place for the experiment, set up, as instructed, a twelve foot salmon rod, with a heavy line and a stout cast, tied the monster to the end of the cast and from a sense of duty hurled it out into the dark. I began to bring it in. On the instant the end of my rod was pulled hard down into the water, my heavy cast was smashed and two of my fingers were nearly broken. The inventor told me sadly that I ought to have kept my fingers well out of the way. He fishes where possible from the reel, not touching the line at all until after the fish has hold.

I did not try it again until the year before last, when I twice went down to the river at night, taking with me one of the albatrosses and the trout rod I had been using during the day. On each of these occasions I spent most of my time disentangling and untwisting my line. This was entirely my own fault. A heavier line would have lessened the creature's power of spinning in the air. With that fine line it was spinning like a shuttlecock both during the forward and the backward cast. At no point was there any serious reverse spin to put things straight again. A very few casts were enough to twist that line into an intricate mess that took a very long time to unravel with the help of a pocket torch. None the less, during the very few minutes when I was not so engaged and was able to fish, my clumsiness and general lack of faith did not prevent that dangerous albatross from catching on the one occasion a three pounder and on the other a five.

People who enjoy night fishing and obey orders, keeping their fingers away from the reels, protecting their ears with sou'westers and using heavy salmon lines which do not twist, or do not twist so badly, have with great regularity been catching many more and much bigger fish. They owe them all to just that V on the water against which we have been so often warned. There could be no better example of how on matters of fishing it is possible in the same words to tell both the truth and a lie. 'Drag' we were told 'is one of the greatest protections that Nature affords the trout.' So it is in daylight on a Hampshire chalk stream but it is the exact opposite on a sea trout river in a warm July night.

(Broadcast on the BBC Home Service, 12 November 1956)

A Question of Taste

NIGHTLINES and trimmers hardly count as fishing. They rank below the lowest grades of what may be considered as within the rules of the game. Next to them, and just within the rules, comes the business of sitting in a boat, with a boatman at the oars, towing a spinning bait past places where trout or pike may be supposed to lurk. The credit of any fish caught by this method belongs not to the man who holds the rod but to the boatman. The man at the rod is but an extension of the man at the oars. He usually pays him for the privilege of holding this ignominious position.

This business of towing a bait after a boat becomes sport

only when the fisherman does his own rowing. I have not a word to say against the Windermere char-fishers, whose plumb-lining is the only way of catching of char at the great depths which these fish frequent. I have watched a man managing his boat in a wind, with two plumb lines out, each with half a dozen spinners some sixty or seventy feet below the surface and a fish on one of them. To manage a boat in such circumstances, to get in one of the rods, to haul in the line, to deal with the several additional lines that carry the spinners, and at last to land the fish without help, demands a very great deal of skill. But I can see nothing at all in that other spectacle, so common on the lakes, of a boatman rowing at measured pace and a 'fisherman' in the stern of the boat watching a pair of rods and waiting to play any fish that chooses to hang itself on the end of one of the lines.

I think these paying appendages to boatmen are themselves aware that their activities need some disguise if they are to be mentioned in the presence of other fishermen. For that reason they describe this towing, or rather this sitting in a boat when someone else is doing the towing, as 'trolling,' thus borrowing a word that belongs to one of the most difficult and interesting forms of pike fishing. It is as if a man were to say that he was going 'stalking,' when really he was going to knock on the head some rats that someone else had trapped.

The Oxford English Dictionary, that knows so much that it does not mind saying when it does not know, admits that the derivation of the word 'troll' is uncertain, but suggests that its misuse to describe towing a bait after a boat comes through association with 'trail' and 'trawl.' A 'troll' seems to be a little wheel, 'especially an angler's reel or winch.' 'Trolling' is thus a form of fishing with a line on a 'troll.' Its early association with pike fishing suggests that we owe to the pike fishers this important part of our equipment. The earliest known reference to a winch (see Dr Turrell's invaluable little book *Ancient Angling Authors*) was made by Thomas Barker in 1651, who said that 'one of his name was the best Trouler for a Pike in this Realm.' 'The manner of his Trouling was, with a Hazel Rod of twelve feet long, with a ring of wyre in the top of his rod, for his Line to run through; within two feet of the bottom of the Rod, there was a hole made for to put in a wind, to turn with a barrell, to gather up his line and loose at his pleasure; this was his manner of Trouling.' In 1682 was published *The Compleat Troller*, by Richard Nobbes. Trolling in those days was done with a gorge bait (now happily prohibited). The troller swung his bait out and worked it with a sink and draw motion in the likeliest spots. When the pike took, the troller had to be able to let him have line freely, because he did not strike until the pike had pouched. In 1821 Salter published his *Troller's Guide*, 'to those who may be desirous of learning to take Jack and Pike in a fair, pleasing, and sportsmanlike manner.' He says that the art of Jack fishing 'is properly termed Trolling, from the Latin Lucium Pisciculo Inescare,' which does not help us very much. In any case he would have been shocked to think that trolling with its need for extreme-ly skilful casting and working of the bait (it is more difficult than spinning) could be confounded with letting someone else row a boat, and sitting in it to watch two rods which are fishing for themselves.

Float Fishing

I HAVE JUST READ what is probably the first book on float fishing to be published in any language. There are plenty of books on fly fishing, plenty even on the flies and the making of them, but, so far as I know, Mr Ernest Phillips's little book, *Float Fishing*, is the first attempt to deal exclusively with the method of angling used by something like 90 per cent of English fishermen.

It is a defiant little book. Its author speaks of a country squire 'who shared the irritating belief of so many fly fishers that there was nothing in this form of fishing,' but happily became a convert and landed a ten-pound carp. He can afford to be defiant. He is in a strong position as a well-known trout fisherman, and he has the big battalions with him in his affection for the float. Those armies of working men whose love for the water is as keen as that of any renter of a salmon river are as devoted to the use of the float as the trout fishers of Hampshire are to the use of the dry fly. There are other methods of coarse fishing, but none so universally applicable. There is the paternoster for fishing deep waters, though even here the Manchester, Sheffield, and Leeds anglers prefer the sliding float. There is the ledger, a pierced bullet on the bottom of the river, but even this is used nowadays as often with a float as without one. But for all those vast crowds of Saturday and Sunday fishermen, the rigour of the game, in which they most delight, is given by fine tackle and a delicately balanced quill.

Mr Phillips has the big battalions behind him. He has also the knowledge that most of those who scorn float fishing have not tried it, or look back to early memories through a long vista of fishing with the fly. They read their Walton but are ashamed to follow him, and somehow forget that many of the great fly fishermen were keen float fishermen as well. Francis, Jardine, and Pennell, among the dead, all fished with the float, and, if we look among the living, Mr R. B. Marston invented the most popular of the pike floats, and the angling editor of *The Field*, Mr H. T. Sheringham, has written a good book on coarse fishing, and is one of the few men in England who have caught a carp of over fifteen pounds. Trout fishers who are putting their tackle away and sadly thinking that they can do no more fishing till next March should read Mr Phillips and take heart.

Of course there are some fiery implacable spirits who must keep their legs and arms in violent motion to appease the quicksilver in their burning veins and find their nearest approach to calm in wading against a torrent and fishing upstream in rapid water. To them the sedentary pleasures of float fishing make no appeal. But I know one experienced and successful salmon fisher who confesses that in looking back over his fishing life the days that bring back the purest memories of delight are those that he spent in waiting for the delicate curtsy and smooth exit of a small float. Men say that float fishing is without variety. The scene does not change as it changes in fishing down a couple of miles or so of trout stream. Fish are not caught by it in such rapidly changing circumstances. Yet I am inclined to think that the float fisherman, motionless on his basket, may see more than the fly fisher, who, moving continually and waving his rod, drives nature before him, even if he succeeds in remaining invisible by the fish. And there is at least as much variety in the actions of the float as in the rises that come to the artificial fly.

An old angler can tell by the dip of his float what fish is at his bait. There is the almost imperceptible change in the sit of the float in the water which betrays the wise old roach, who knows too well that baits are not always as wholesome as they seem; the hearty, indignant bob and plunge given by the perch who cares for nobody, no not he, and, if he likes the look of a worm, will have it, hook or no; the gentle horizontal movement and slow gathering of speed that shows that the long-awaited carp has been tricked at last; the succession of light dips, the float sinking a little with each one, that shows that an eel is taking the first steps towards the ruin of the angler's tackle; the sharp wriggle of the float given by the overambitious stickleback or minnow; the dip and sideways rush of the float under water given by a trout; the gentle sideslip or mere stoppage of the float when the grayling takes the bait swum in a stream. And then there is that violent bobbing, followed by the disappearance of the big pike float that may presage a struggle with a twenty-pounder. There are men who pale at that moment and have difficulty in controlling the trembling of their hands. Pike floats signal in many ways. I have seen them drop six inches and remain so when a fish has just taken the bait out of boredom at seeing it about. I have seen them slide off along the surface, leaving a wake behind them. I have *heard* them go down with a plop like a bullet dropped in water. And twice I have seen Master Jack take the actual float in his great white jaws, mistaking it for something edible, or perhaps misliking its appearance and wishful to learn it to be a float.

No. Floats show incredible variety in the order of their

going, and though sometimes they stand upon it for a good long time, watching for them to go has an altogether admirable effect upon the mind. No mesmerist can provide such relaxation as is given by that little cork or quill upon the water. In Sir Edward Grey's book on fly fishing there is an excellent paragraph that contrasts the dry-fly fisherman's foreknowledge of the moment when he may expect a rise with the wet-fly fisherman's knowledge that that moment may come at any time in any cast. The float fisherman must be like him who fishes wet fly, ready to respond instantly to a summons the precise moment of which he has no means of predicting. Whatever worries he may have brought with him to the waterside, he can have none as he watches his float. He has no intervals in which he can let his mind run back to politics or the price of shares. Each second asks him Hamlet's question.

The Felon Winds

LAST WEEK, before the holidays, I sketched for the Clerk of the Weather a programme which should ensure his popularity with holiday fishermen. We were to have fine weather on Friday and Saturday. On Sunday night we were to have a little rain for the refreshment of the rivers, and Monday and Tuesday were to be as fine as he could make them. I hardly expected that he would listen to me, but he did. On Sunday night there was just that drop of rain that I had hoped for. Where the Clerk made his mistake and gave us instead of good fishing weather an excuse for not catching fish was in his treatment of the wind. I had said that it must blow upstream, but not too hard. He gave us a northerly gale. Fishermen on the Eden had an upstream wind, but, unfortunately, that was not the river that I had had in mind. I should have named the river. Then, in his eagerness to please, the Clerk somehow overlooked my plea for moderation. Friday was everything that could be wished, in spite of its northerly wind, because that wind was a light one, no more than a caress. Something was done on the rivers, and on Windermere the char-fishers had respectable baskets. But with Saturday the wind got out of hand. Fishermen began to grumble, and the Clerk of the Weather lost his temper. 'I have done my best,' he seemed to say, 'and still you are not content. Blow, blow, thou winter wind, thou art not so unkind as fishermen's ingratitude.' And blow it did on Sunday and Monday till one could hardly keep a fly on the water. March came in like a painted lamb, but it went out with a roar. There were those who got their brace, their brace and a half, and even their two brace on each day, for the most part on Waterhen and Yellow, but no one did as well as he had hoped, and I met one or two who had done nothing at all and were without a good word to say for the Clerk. They did not even seem grateful for the excuse his care-less hurricane had given them.

'A little wind kindles, a big one puts the fire out.' That is so in fishing, nearly always. In North Country rivers at this time of year not many fish are in the fast streams. They are to be found in the smoother water, and if a gentle wind covers the smooth water with a ripple it is a great advantage to the fisherman. But a wind like the wind of these Easter holidays is no help at all. The fisherman who uses an ordinary wet-fly rod and a fine level cast with three flies on it is engaged in a desperate business. Casting up against the wind he will see his flies turn back to meet the line. Casting with such a wind behind him he will spend much of his time in analysing tangles of elaborate design that would take him half an hour to tie deliberately but are made in a moment by this wind that he would think was in too much of a hurry for such fine work.

Sheer strength will not beat such a wind. Old Tod, one of the best wet-fly fishers who have ever lived, advised young fishermen to 'use light clubs daily, to develop wrist power, as I did till I could cast in the teeth of the wind quite easily.' But even Tod on a day with a hard downstream wind was willing to leave the best lengths of the river unfished if he could find somewhere a short stretch on which the wind was not unfavourable. No amount of force will make up for skill in putting flies into the wind. I feel inclined to add that skill itself is less important than the right equipment. Dry-fly fishermen use a heavier line than the line generally used for wet-fly fishing. They use a much stiffer rod. Line and rod alike were evolved to meet the special difficulty of casting into the wind, because the dry-fly fisherman is almost without resource if he cannot fish upstream. Halford thought that of all conditions the most unfavourable was 'a gale blowing in any direction and especially upstream.' He disliked the upstream gale not because of its effect on casting but because it tended to lift the newly hatched flies from the water instead of allowing them the long drifts before rising that kept them within reach of the trout. As for the effect of the wind on casting, that redoubtable authority abashes us with the statement that 'casting against the wind, unless it is a perfect hurricane, will present no difficulty to the man who can cast.' Halford himself, however, with an ordinary wet-fly outfit would not have been able to cast against this Easter's wind. It is worth noting that the strength and direction of the wind are allowed to modify the tackle even of 'the man who can cast.' Halford advised not less than 3½ yards in a calm, four yards with a following wind, reduced against a strong head wind to 2½ yards.

Wet-fly fishermen can learn a good deal from Halford. A little knowledge learnt from Halford is, however, dangerous. It is, for example, no use to borrow his heavy line for casting against the wind and imagine that the use of this line will make easy the conquest of the gale by a 4x level cast with three flies. It will not. The heavy line will go straight into the wind's eye, but it will not transmit its courage to the fine cast. The nearest thing to the fish will be not a fly but the knot on the end of the line. The upper part of the cast must be stout enough to form a continuation of the line itself, though in a different material. The wet-fly fisherman is thus driven to use the dry-fly man's tapered cast as well as his heavy line. The thickness of the upper part of this cast will discourage him in the use of droppers, even though a hard wind makes up for forcing us to use thick gut by lessening the trout's consciousness that it is there. If he dislikes trusting his fortune to a single fly he will

use two, but not for long. He will shorten his cast. Halford
said that 2½ yards is the shortest length permissible, but there
are many dry-fly fishermen who use that length only in the
best conditions and fish a much shorter cast against a stiff
wind. With a cast of a couple of yards or shorter, tapered from
really stout gut, the most hardened fisher of a team of flies will
soon resign himself to fishing with only one. He has come to
use a heavy line, a single fly, and a short cast so steeply tapered
as to seem the natural end of the line.

How much farther need he go? If he wishes to be fair to his
wet-fly rod he will discard it and use the stiffer rod designed
for just this purpose. He has now gone the whole way, and
with a dry-fly outfit is fishing his single Waterhen and Yellow
exactly as in the south in similar conditions men would be
fishing a nymph. With such an outfit he can defy all but the
most felonious winds.

Blank Day

I DO NOT SO very much mind a blank day with the dry fly,
even on one of our Northern rivers on which little but the
character and position of the fly distinguishes dry-fly from
wet-fly fishing. On these rivers we fish the places where we
know a fish is likely to be lying, even if we do not observe him
breaking the surface to pick flies off it before ever we offer him
our own. But when a day shows marked signs of coming, or
rather lasting, blankness we can narrow our rules, stop casting
except to trout actually rising, and so turn our day into a real
dry-fly day, the blankness of which is not so devastating as
that of a day of endless, unrewarded casting.

This straitening of the rules shifts the responsibility from
the fisherman to the fish. If he is not to cast unless to a rising
trout, and no trout are rising, when then a blank day is almost
a feather in his cap. It is, at least, a clear proof that he has kept
the rules. His conscience is as light as his basket, and he may,
besides, have given himself a delightful day, strolling slowly

up the river, watchful always for the bubble or the widening rings that will justify some fishing, free to enjoy the country-side and day, and, best of all, free, if the trout are not rising, from any sort of sense of failure.

With wet-fly fishing a blank day is decidedly blanker. By the time one o'clock is reached the fisherman who has not risen a fish is very well aware that he has been fishing. Supposing that he was on the water by ten, he has spent three hours of ceaseless casting, wading slowly up the stream, and, on a likely stretch of water, casting perhaps six times for every two paces he takes forward. Cast after cast, cast after cast, each one a nervous, tense, delicate searching of the water, ready at any part of any second for the flash or splash or almost imperceptible hint of a taking fish. Down-stream fishing with the wet fly is a lazier business, particularly if the flies are allowed to sweep round. The pull of the stream keeps flies and fisherman in touch with each other, and a far smaller number of casts covers the same amount of water. Even in down-stream fishing with wet flies the fisherman is fishing all the time. In up-stream fishing he works harder, and the tension of his work does not slacken for an instant.

By one o'clock he has spent a great deal of himself, and if by that time he has met with no reward he feels like a man who has said 'Good morning' a great many times and has never once had 'Good morning' said to him in return. And one o'clock, though a critical hour in the day, is only the beginning when the season has run into June. A zealous, worthy fellow will be fishing till nine at night or even later. As the hours slip away the blankness of his day closes round him and acquires an opaque, all-obliterating quality like fog. It is all very well to say, and sometimes to believe (when dry-fly fishing it is easy to believe), that there is no such thing as a blank day for the fisherman because of the many pleasures of the waterside that are always there to take the place of fish. But it is not safe to say such things to a wet-fly fisherman who has been hard at work for ten or eleven hours and has nothing in his basket except a white cloth with which to wrap the fish that he has not caught.

But even the blankness of the blank day of the wet-fly

upstream fisherman is blue sky when compared with the blankness of the blank day of him who has been fishing for trout with bait. The fly fisherman can change his flies, signing a new lease of hopefulness with each new fly, which may, after all, be the fly for which the trout were waiting. Between one vile worm and another there is little to choose. Besides, the fisherman's attitude of mind when using baits of any kind is altogether different from that which is his when he is fishing fly. Trout are known to be moody creatures, and even on the day when his basket is full to the brim and he is daring trouble at home by putting the overflow into his pockets the fisherman still feels that it is something of a miracle that they should ever take so greedily so inedible a thing as a pinch of feather and silk on a bit of steel wire. But when he offers them a bait he is offering a lump of solid food, real food, and he expects them to take it and to take it well. A man fishing fly goes fishing. A man fishing bait goes out to catch fish. If he fails he is without moral consolation of any kind. And bait fishing for trout is a very arduous and difficult business.

I believe it is harder to become a good fisher of the upstream worm than to become good at any sort of fly fishing. The actual casting of the worm is far more difficult than the casting of the fly. I feel myself at the mercy of chance when I try to throw a worm with a fly rod. That lump on the end of a fine cast takes charge. I am no longer my own man, but the worm's. This brings a touch of dogged effort even into the very beginning of the day, long before the question of blankness has arisen. It is the same thing with the creeper. There is no pleasure, at least for me, in the continual effort to drop without a splash a thing as big as a salmon fly while using a light trout rod and a fine cast. There is, of course, the pleasure of doing, or trying to do, a difficult thing. But it is undertaken only because the use of the creeper promises a heavy basket of the larger fish. Well, I have had a blank day with the creeper, the blankest blank day that I can ever remember. In the course of it I met a man fishing wet fly. He also had done nothing, and he little knew how I envied him. He was fishing. I was engaged in a business that is justified only by its results. When the trout have begun their feast on the creeper they eat like guests at an oyster dinner. There is no hanging back. But on that day my creepers came tumbling down the rough water in vain. Nothing touched them, ever. Not a trout seemed to think them even worth looking at. The creepers were all over the river, too. You could find them under every stone.

I had fished just a day or two too soon. The trout had not yet made their annual discovery that these hideous creatures are good to eat. By now, perhaps, great baskets are being made on creeper in Lune and Eden. But when I fished this bait, which is supposed to be more compelling than the minnow, I had a day the memory of which I shall use to console myself for blank days in the future. However blank they are, if I am fishing fly, they can never be as blank as that.

The Dubbing Bag

THIS MORNING there has been half an hour's drizzle, but not enough to do any good, and the sun is already coming through it. For a long time now we have been without rain and fishermen have been inclined to reply sourly to people who ask them to exult in the delightful weather. Only the most determined optimists have been to the rivers, and though now and again they bring home a few fish they have usually lost their optimism before they come back.

So long as this weather lasts fly-fishermen may as well follow the example of an old angler on whom I called the other day. I asked him what he was doing, and he replied, regardless of the damson blossom and the sunshine outside, 'Gone back to winter and the dubbing bag,' and pointed to his table, which was covered with feathers and silks. He was tying flies. Most fishermen, with little time to spare, find flies cheaper to buy than to dress, but in weather like this, which may break at any moment into the weather we need and other folk deplore, there is a good deal to be said for filling up our fly-boxes instead of breaking our hearts walking over the dry stones looking for a puddle to cast in. Fly-tying is one of those crafts, like lighting a fire, poaching an egg, or darning the heel of a stocking; that set a man up in his own conceit by letting him feel that he would not be at a loss if he had no one to do these things for him. Moreover, fish are inclined to encourage the beginner, especially early in the season, by taking his clumsy bunch of feathers as readily as the finished product of the shops. This is profoundly satisfactory to him and brings well to the hither side of idolatory the respectful worship he has hitherto accorded to tackle-makers.

The born fly-dresser is much more rare than the born fisherman, and he, of course, will be tying flies all through the season. But every man who can fasten a fly to a cast can also make one after very little practice, and should be, at least, an occasional fly-dresser. The best flies for a man to begin with and also those that can best be depended upon to catch fish are 'spiders,' tied with a hackle, no wings and a slim body, the end of the hackle being in some of them bound in by the body silk and left projecting at the bend of the hook, the central quill being cut out where it leaves the silk, so that the last of the hackles project and spread on either side.

But it is too much to expect of the beginner in fly-tying that he shall follow accurately anyone's directions. He is not invited to do so by his inclination nor permitted by his skill. He usually proceeds, willy nilly, to the production of 'fancies.' And if he makes those 'fancies' now and tries them between now and the end of May, the fish may almost be counted upon to confirm him in the belief that the monstrosity he produces by accident has been really the result of design. Astrologers will tell you that men of such and such character are born in certain minutes at a particular conjunction of the stars. Into such detail I will not go, but am prepared to affirm that the majority of famous fancy flies fluttered first between the second week in April and the third week in May. During some part of that time the fish are catholic in taste, ravenous in appetite, and still trustful in temperament. The inventor who brings his gaudy creature to the river at this time catches fish.

If (which is not always the case) he is able to make another like it and gives it proudly to a friend, the friend catches fish on it which he would otherwise have caught on other flies, and the new 'fancy' has already the beginnings of a reputation. It needs only that to ensure that it shall be fished with, so that fish caught are put down to its credit. If they are not, their absence is put down to the day. People go on fishing with it, and at last come to believe that it is a conscious imitation of nature.

The other day, looking through an otherwise excellent fishing book, I came upon the statement that in particular months certain 'fancies' would be found upon the water, and that the angler should use 'good artificial imitations of these.' The amateur fly-tyer may thus hope not merely to produce flies that will catch fish, but to add new species to nature and to puzzle future entomologists.

Tup's Indispensable

A CORRESPONDENT complains that there have been too many girds at fancy flies in this column. Perhaps there has been too little explicit distinction between the two great varieties of fancy flies, the monsters created in a fine frenzy or by accident, which resemble nothing in or out of water and catch trout less by deception than by arousing in them a rash spirit of investigation or an indignant desire to rid the river of such nightmares, and, on the other hand, those very different flies which, while not pretending to be copies of a particular insect, are carefully made to suggest a general type.

Of the first variety I will not mention names. Every amateur fly-dresser has his own, which come unbidden, beside the legions of such flies which beguile rash visitors to fishing tackle shops. To gird at these flies is the duty of an honest man. They will catch fish, particularly in the early part of the season, but the satisfaction of catching fish with them is of an altogether lower order than that of clean bowling a fish by presenting him with something which he takes without anger or curiosity in the belief that it is a normal course in his daily dinner. Flies of the second variety earn nothing but praise. The standing example of them is Greenwell's Glory, which, though first dressed to imitate a particular fly, imitates it in such a manner that, this fly being typical of many, the artificial serves the purpose of different patterns and is one that few fishermen would be without. But this is a sober little fly, dull green and gold, plain hackle or with starling or blackbird wing, a fly wearing the uniform of a member of the French Academy rather than the military splendours characteristic of the other variety of fancy flies.

And let us now sing the praises of Tup's Indispensable, fit comrade to Greenwell, a fancy fly invented in the early years of this century by Mr Austin, fisherman and fly-dresser, of Tiverton, which, spreading gradually over the whole of the chalk streams of the South, contributed to the revolution in methods still in progress there and is now finding its way northwards. Halford describes it as 'a fancy hackle pattern dressed with a pale-blue cock hackle and a body of some grey-coloured hair which is supposed to be taken from some part of a ram – hence the name. A few bits of brilliant red seal's fur are generally mixed up with the wool of the body.' He says it is a pattern 'resembling in many ways some spinners' and, with obvious disapproval, mentions that a friend caught a three-pound fish on it before being persuaded to catch others on an orthodox Black Gnat. Mr Skues does not mention its likeness to spinners, but says that 'its resemblance to a nymph induced me to give it a trial upon bulging trout,' and speaks of 'feeling his way via Tup's Indispensable' to the nymph patterns he afterwards invented.

Here, then, is a fancy fly that resembles duns, spinners, or nymphs, and can be dressed to float or sink at the angler's will. It will take fish that are not rising on waters that were long supposed to be unfishable with a wet fly. Strange little thing of primrose and strawberry, it is a fit companion to Greenwell's Glory, a little fly-of-all-work, deserving, like Greenwell, its permanent corner in every angler's box. If it will do in Hampshire it should do on the Dove, and if in Devonshire, then it or a near variation of it should be of use in our North-country rivers.

Art for Art's Sake: A Defence of Match-Fishing

I REMEMBER hearing a discussion between a rabbit fancier and a breeder of fancy mice in which the rabbit-man, praising his pets as good to eat and having valuable skins, said that he could not see the point of keeping coloured mice, which were good for nothing at all. The mouse-man, an omnibus conductor of spirit, replied, with arguments which might have been taken from the art criticism of the nineties, that the whole point of fancy mice was their complete uselessness. He earned a living by collecting fares during the day. He had quite enough to do with handling money. In his off-hours he found in the breeding of oddly coloured mice a pure pleasure free from any sordid motive whatever. For his part he did not know how the rabbit fancier could look his rabbits in the face.

With some such argument the match-fisherman might reply to those superior anglers who heave a half-brick of contempt at the line of patient men, one to every ten yards, seated on baskets beside a canal. For these men care for skill, and for skill alone, whereas there are very few anglers for game fish who are content to return all their captives to the river. I remember a trout angler coming to fish a noted pike water in the South being very indignant that he was not allowed to kill jack under what was certainly a high size-limit. He simply could not see the fun of catching fish which he was not allowed to knock on the head. I wonder what that man would say if he were to go fishing with some of the working-men anglers of Manchester, many of whom make a point of never taking a fish from the river unless it is worthy of being put in a glass case.

Now, in match-fishing this is a universal rule. Keep-nets are compulsory, and at the end of a match every fish is turned back into the water, to use its experience in raising the average level of the skill required for the catching of fish in that place. After a match the waters are no poorer than they were before, but it is, if anything, more difficult to catch fish in them. In match-fishing the satisfaction of a heavy basket on the homeward journey is replaced by recognition of the angler's skill in the shape of a small prize or a medal. (I am proud to know one Manchester roach-fisher who has acquired thirty-nine of these trophies, and is expecting his fortieth.) The skill's the thing. Outwit your fish, but put him back to be more difficult to trick another time. This is art for art's sake, and this is the match-fishing of the Manchester working man.

Under this system of intensive education fish become very hard to catch indeed, and there is no need to sneer at the minute weights which in some of these matches win prizes. Matches are fished in open waters where even an independent angler cannot hope to do very much. And there is besides a very great difference between match-fishing and the fishing of a solitary angler. A match is not like a day's fishing in which the angler starts when and where he chooses, moves from place to place in search of fish, and gives up only when he thinks it is no use fishing longer. The match-fisherman voluntarily limits his opportunities in two essential particulars. He fishes for a limited time. Until the whistle goes at the beginning of a match no man may put his line in the water. No man may throw in as much as a handful of ground-bait. And when at the end of the match, the whistle blows again, all lines must be taken instantly from the water, even when the anglers have hardly had a bite all day and the fish are just coming on the feed.

Further, the match-fishermen have usually to travel some distance to their fishing and must return home at night, so that there are available for fishing only a few hours in the middle of the day, and these hours are not the best, and, indeed, very often are precisely those during which the independent fisherman eats his luncheon, thinks of Izaak Walton, or thinks out letters to the *Fishing Gazette*, not bothering to fish, because he knows that it is almost useless. That does not matter to the match-fisherman, because it is just as bad for his competitors.

But it is often a sound explanation why even the winner of the first prize catches so few fish. An experienced angler knows very well those hours when there seems to be no life in the water at all, and he knows that he might almost as well be fishing in a washtub. In independent fishing he can wait until the moment comes (and he knows it has come before he is warned by his float) when the river comes to life again and he may expect another bite. In even the worst days there comes 'the benign moment' when it is as if a spell had been cast on water, trees, sky, fishermen, and fish, the moment when, if at all, fish will be caught. That moment passes sometimes before a match begins. Sometimes it comes just as a match is ending. Most often it seems to come just after the match is over, and it is then that the independent angler, smiling in his heart and profiting by other people's ground-bait, takes in an hour more than the whole catch of many score of more skilful fishermen than he who have had to fish through the worst of the day and withdraw their lines before the moment came. If trout anglers were restricted to the middle of the day they would make even poorer baskets than they do in July and August.

The other limitation imposed by match-fishing is that of place. The man fishing in a match cannot move surreptitiously along a river or canal and use his watercraft to choose his swim, and afterwards choose half a dozen others if his luck is out. He must fish at the peg the number of which he has drawn out of a hat. He must fish nowhere else. This means that whereas an average fisherman can do pretty well by fishing those places only that he finds easy, a match-fisherman must be capable of adapting his methods to any sort of water that may fall to his lot.

Even if match-fishing were not the favourite sport of an enormous number of working-men anglers it would be justified by its influence on the technique of fishing. Roach, once the sheep of the river, have become as cunning as the fox. The angler must strike at the faintest movement of the float, and for this reason the roach rod is not a pliable wand like a trout rod, but stiff, remorseless. Yet, though his rod is without the flexibility that tempers the strike to the fine gut, the match-fisher uses much finer tackle than is used for trout. When fish are biting anything will do, but when you have to catch fish at moments when they are rather disinclined to bite than otherwise, you must fish as fine as your neighbour if you are to have a chance. Your sea-trout, hearty fellow, fresh up from the sea, thinks nothing of a length of 2x gut. Your brown trout will usually forgive you for using 3x. Your old roach, who has survived many matches, is far more particular; 4x gut is the coarsest that can be used for him, and most match-fishermen use 5x, and would user finer if they could get it.

Last Days of the Salmon Season

THERE ARE FEW more enjoyable sports than that of salmon fishing on a day with winter in the air, white frost on the ground, a bright sun, a delicate clear sky, and not too much wind. These are the conditions of late autumn and early spring. In the autumn the fish are not at their best, nor are they so willing to collaborate with the angler in providing the ultimate excitement. But it is in itself an exhilarating experience to stand well out in a strong river on a really cold day, leaning back on the rush of the water (sitting on the stream, as a friend of mine admirably describes it), exercising every muscle, and knowing that at any moment may come that bang, silent it is true, but seeming to have a deep bass note, as if suddenly someone were to press heavily on a key far down the piano, when a salmon takes hold. In most of the English rivers the autumn season is over before this thrill of cold which gives perfection to the exercise and is in its way comparable to the pepper which Keats put in his mouth in order to enjoy to the full the coolness of his claret.

On Tuesday, I had to melt my waders before I could get into them, for the water of the day before had frozen hard in them, and they might have been made of iron. Yet, after a few minutes in the water, I had to take my coat off and leave it on the bank. And there are people who consider fishing a game for lazy men! Grayling fishing in winter has some of this pleasure, but the rod is lighter, the work easier, and the fisherman can be unpleasantly conscious of the cold. In salmon fishing, when hands, arms, body, and legs have, all of them, plenty of work, he could easily do with another degree or two of frost.

Nor is the capture of fish essential to the pleasure. I spent two days and only hooked one fish, and him so lightly that I lost him at once. The actual business of casting a salmon fly is like that of batting, using a tennis racket, a fives glove, or a golf club. A cast a little better than another will set you up with yourself, and a failure leaves you only the more anxious to recover your self-respect by a good one. And who can compare tennis court, fives court, cricket ground, or golf course, with the setting of a frosty morning, a clear river, gulls, like the salmon, up from the sea, the sun glowing on the last of the leaves, the continual music of the water?

Those two days of mine were well spent in learning, under the tuition of a master, the special cast of the Derwent, in which, instead of lifting the line to the top of the water before making the backwards cast, the fisherman uses the water to pull against his rod, sweeping it almost horizontally up river so that when the suck of the water is conquered the line flies back like the stretched elastic of a catapult, when, after a moment's pause, with a turn of the rod (the thing I found hardest to learn) the angler brings it easily forward again and across. It is a beautiful cast to watch and a valuable one, as it makes the angler almost independent of trees. At the end of the second day I could do it with a shortish line. But, as 'G. W. M.,' who was teaching me, showed, it can be done with as long a line as can be thrown by any other method. If I do not die too soon I shall learn it.

The End of a Dry-Fly Day

UNLESS THE RIVERS are stirred by some rain that is really worth having those who go fly-fishing by day in our northern rivers should make up their minds before they start that they do not really expect to catch any fish. They will thus secure themselves from disappointment and increase the enjoyment of possible windfalls. Even the best of wet-fly rivers are now in such a condition that he has best chance of a decent trout who takes things easily, abjures continual casting, and skulks slowly upstream watching for a rare feeding fish to which he may offer a floating fly. Most of the decent fish seem to be in retreat, waiting for rain, and letting the fingerlings have things all their own way. The little fellows were dimpling everywhere on Monday, but at the end of the day I came to the old bridge with only a brace of sizable fish in my basket and the memory of one surprising boil by a sea-trout at a No. ooo fly. With this slight reward I was well content and ready with the utmost goodwill to leave the river to the bustard-fishers for the night.

The first of the bustard-fishers strolled up on the bridge soon after I arrived. He had a long ash-plant with a net at the end of it, a fine old hickory rod, and a cast of stout gut with three enormous bustards upon it, tied on salmon-hooks, with soft brown owl wings and heavily dubbed bodies, local tradition in every fibre of them. For some time we talked on the bridge.

'River's too low to begin till it's dark,' he said, and I had done my fishing and was looking down from the arch of the high bridge hoping to see a friend. It appeared that the bustard-fisher knew him too. 'There's a rare big eel under this bridge,' he said.

'There is,' I replied, and told him how, three weeks before, I had walked right on top of the eel in the mudbank below the central pier.

'All of two pounds, he'll weigh, I reckon. And there's a smaller one with him, a greenish one, very light-coloured indeed. And then there's a third one, middle size, that's sometimes about and keeps out of the way of the others.'

He knew as much about those eels as I did, but he did not know that once already that night I had seen the big eel, the biggest I have ever seen in that river, and that I had hurriedly taken off my fly and put on a hook, turned stones till I had found a worm, and then waded in under the bridge to offer it to the eel, only to find that the eel had decided not to wait for it. I was waiting on the bridge to see if he would come back.

We both stared down into the clear water. If the eel were to appear again I had a new plan for catching him. I would lower my worm to him from the top of the bridge. I had already pulled off the right amount of line and had fastened an airgun pellet to the cast with a clove hitch. Everything was ready for that eel.

The bustard-fisher whetted my excitement. 'I never ate eels,' he said, 'till last spate. I got a good one then, and my daughter cooked it, and she talked so much while she was eating it that I took a bite, and it was good meat – better than a trout's. And all these years I'd laughed at old Billy Robinson. Thirty years ago I used to go fishing with him when the water was a bit dirty, and at the end of the day he'd always give me a trout for an eel. Many's the trout I've had from him for an eel that I'd have thrown away. He had the best of the bargain, and me laughing at him all the time. It's good meat, eel's meat, and I never knew it. There he is . . .'

A dark, undulating line showed on the white stones of the base of the bridge pier. It slid off into deep water and worked slowly up on a shallow bank of gravel.

'That's the middle one, the black one that keeps to himself. You'll never get him from here.'

I let go my coil of line, and the worm dropped into the water. It was already too dark to see it from that height, and we could tell where it was only by lifting it and seeing it dimple the surface. It was extremely difficult from the top of the bridge to get it anywhere near the eel. Excitement grew.

'Plunk it in above him,' said the bustard-fisher. 'Then he'll smell about and find it. They're rare ones for smelling about.'

'There's an eddy where he is. Water's going the other way,' said I, who had spent the afternoon in fishing dry fly.

'Where's the worm now?' said the bustard-fisher. 'It's that dark.'

'Somewhere near him,' said I. 'If he takes it he takes it, and if he doesn't . . .'

At that moment the eel for the first time made a movement that was not altogether leisurely. A few inches of the head end of him suddenly straightened and shot forward a distance not greater than the breadth of my hand. But there had been purpose in that sudden jerk, and I had half a hope – no more –that he had seized something and that the something was my worm.

Staring down into the dark I saw the eel lift and wave his head. Or was it his tail? I struck, and the stillness of the evening was broken by a yell from the bustard-fisher. 'You've got him. You've got him. Hang on to him!' Far down below us there was a great commotion in the water. The eel was on, thirty or forty feet below us, attached to a particularly fine dry-fly cast.

'Have you got a knife?'

'I have that, and a good one.' The bustard-fisher dropped his rod and net, ran from the bridge, got into the field and rushed out into the river. 'Don't touch the line,' I shouted after him. 'It won't stand it.'

'Bring him up on the grass,' he shouted back. 'Don't give his tail a chance among the stones. Keep him up.'

The fly rod (J. J. Hardy, No. 1), surely never yet put to such a purpose, did its work well. Letting out line, I crossed into the field. The eel, closely attended by the bustard-fisher, approached the grassy bank and slid out upon it. There was a desperate step-dance as we both tried to get a foot on him. It was done. In a flash the knife of the bustard-fisher descended, and the eel shared the fate of King Charles.

'Sharpened it this morning,' said the bustard-fisher. 'Well,' he added, 'that was a rare bit of sport. There's nothing like clear-water fishing after all. I don't care if I don't get a fish tonight.'

It was indeed, for all but purists, the perfect end of a dry-fly day.

5 • AT HOME AND ABROAD

Fishing through the Ice

WE ARE THREATENED with another spell of severe frost, which, in this country, means an end of fishing, at least in still water. In England no one dreams of fishing through the ice. In Russia, where the frosts begin in October and last till May, fishing through the ice is the most normal thing in the world, and every tackle shop keeps the special instruments for it. Otherwise, the fishing season in Russia would be short indeed. The rivers freeze up as well as the lakes and even in the comparatively warm climate of Riga I have sailed an ice-yacht as late as the twelfth of April. One cold spring I went fishing for the first time on the first of May and came back to Petrograd to find a heavy fall of snow and sledges plying in the streets. But keen Russian fishermen do not let the winter interfere with their sport. I think there are more fishermen in winter on the frozen water under the Kremlin walls than there are in summer. Ice makes boats unnecessary. The angler can walk over the water to the likeliest places. Even netting is carried on through the ice. Holes are made at regular intervals, and one end of the net is fastened to a long pole which is used as a needle, pushed along under the ice till the end of it reaches the next hole, seized there and pushed to the hole beyond, until finally it is brought back again to the starting-point, when it is taken out and the two ends of the net are in the fisherman's hands. But netting hardly concerns those who fish with rod and line.

Nor can they consider with anything but reprobation the abominable method of fishing that I have seen practised in Moscow, which may be described as intentional foul-hooking. For this two holes about five feet apart are made in the ice with a pointed, iron-shod weapon. The fisherman stands between the holes holding in each hand a short stiff rod. From the end of each rod on a strong cord hangs a sort of wheel covered with upward-pointing prongs. This lies flat on the bottom of the river in a place where fish are known to shoal. It is allowed to rest there a minute or two and then jerked upwards in the hope that unlucky fish swimming over it will be impaled upon its prongs. Roach and perch are caught in this way.

A more sporting method needs a similar preparation of two holes in the ice, but is real fishing in that a bait is used in the form of an artificial spinner. The fisherman stands between the holes and holds two short rods with some spring in them. His lines are of the exact length necessary to reach the bottom of the river, spare line being wound round a couple of nails on the handle of the rod. The spinners are heavy metal minnows, brightly polished and usually decorated with a tassel of scarlet worsted. The hook is in the head of the minnow and the line is simply knotted to a hole in the tail. The fisherman keeps warm by jerking first one and then the other so that both are in constant motion, and the moment he feels that a fish has taken the bait he strikes hard and, dropping one rod, grabs the line with the fish on it and hauls in hand over hand. In principle this is much like true trolling with a drop minnow, except that the fisherman cannot move about but must agitate his minnows in one place and depend on his knowledge of the water for choosing the right place in the beginning. It is a very considerable labour hacking a hole through the thick ice, and once a pair of holes have been made at the beginning of the season they are usually reopened daily, either by the angler who made them or by another who wishes to save his own time and muscles.

Perhaps the favourite method is that of the ice paternoster. The rod used is about six inches long, never more than a foot or a foot and a half. It is made of a small flexible twig or the tip of a bamboo and is fastened to a sort of stand, shaped rather like the wooden sole of a clog but so that heel and sole are in one plane, about the same size and perfectly flat. It would be a good deal easier to draw this thing than to describe it: not that its shape matters very much, except that it must serve as a holder for the rod and be so formed that it will easily be frozen to the ice. It will stand well enough without freezing, but I have noticed fishermen dipping it in the water before putting it in position, when, of course, the frost grips it at once. The twig just holds the line taut when the plummet is at the bottom. The tackle is an ordinary paternoster, and when a fish takes the bait the twig responds and the angler grabs the line and hauls in.

This, of course, is a mighty cold business, and I have seen the fishermen light little fires on the ice to keep themselves warm as they crouch on their heels wrapped in sheepskins, and, of course, wearing felt boots. The slightest wind is almost unbearable, and they rig up windscreens of old sacks on sticks, the end of which they allow to freeze into the ice. On a good piece of ice known to cover a regular feeding-ground I have seen as many as twenty of these little camps, all within hail of each other. The usual bait is a bloodworm. The hooks are of very fine wire, three or four bloodworms being put on a hook. Ordinary worms would be hard to get with the ground frozen so hard and so deep, and even in summer the Moscow fisherman, however poor, manages to buy bloodworms, which he prefers to any other bait. They can be had in the market winter and summer, and before the Revolution there used to be a little shop in a street called Lazy Street (because it is so short) where all the tackle for this kind of fishing could be bought, together with the bloodworms, which are not worms at all but the larvæ of various species of *Chironomus*.

There is yet another way of fishing in winter, which,

however, is not done through the ice but from its edge where a swift current or the condensed steam from a factory prevents the river from freezing. It is not a profitable method, but it saves the labour of digging a hole in the ice and is therefore popular. There is nearly always a short, narrow stretch of open water under the Kremlin below the Stone Bridge, and here, all day long, stands a row of fishermen. In the interests of science I watched them once for four hours. At the end of that time one of them caught a small perch. Thereupon all the unsuccessful crowded together towards the place where the fish had been caught, there was a loud crack in the ice, the whole party flung themselves on their faces and crawled back to safety, the successful fisherman abusing the others at the top of his voice for having spoilt the fishing for the day.

The Russian Walton

SERGEI AKSAKOV, who wrote the first book on fishing to be published in the Russian language, was born in 1791 and died in 1859. His fishing-book was published in 1847, just twenty years before the appearance in England of Francis Francis's *A Book on Angling*. Yet when we read Francis we are hardly conscious of any great difference between the fishing in his day and the fishing in our own, whereas when we read Aksakov we are back at once not merely in the nineteenth but in the seventeenth century. If we ask ourselves why this is, we are led inevitably to the conclusion that the character of fishing depends very closely upon the tackle used for it. The invention of reels, for example, shortened our rods and changed the manner with which we set about landing a large fish. The invention of the heavy casting line has made us more or less independent of the wind. The invention of the spool reel has changed the character of spinning.

Now in Russia, when Aksakov lived, fished, and wrote, the tackle used would have been recognised by any English fisherman of the seventeenth century. If Aksakov and Walton had gone fishing together neither would have found anything surprising in the methods of the other. They would have suited each other very well, for Aksakov, like Walton, was chiefly a lover of fishing with a float. Of fishing with artificial flies he wrote that he could say nothing, because, often as he had tried it, he had been always unsuccessful. Besides, he found trout-fishing in swift streams 'sufficiently unquiet and tiring.' He knew two ways of fishing without a float, but did not like them, chiefly because 'fishing without a float is deprived of much of its delight.' Coarse-fishing was what he liked, a combination of peace and passionate excitement. A mill-dam was his favourite fishing place.

> The sight of a dam and a mill, the tapping of the machinery, the noise of the falling water move the heart of the old fisherman to a sweet and quiet agitation.

His rod was of birch or hazel, cut in springtime before the opening of the leaves. There were artificial rods to be had, but he decidedly preferred the natural. To take 'an artificial rod' to pieces carefully and without hurry was 'contrary to the nature of a Russian.' The first of the sixteen points of a good fisherman which Aksakov enumerated was that he should know how to pick and to prepare a suitable rod, to make a line that would not twist, to tie neat, small knots, and to keep his hooks sharp. To keep his hooks sharp he must avoid the common practice of sticking them into the wood of the rod for convenient carrying. His line was of white horsehair, and he preferred it plaited. He had seen and tried gut, but did not think much of it. 'Its only virtue lies in its transparency and lightness ... fit for fishing for small fish without a float ... strong when new ... With care and a good rod one can catch even a four or five pound fish on it ... but it presently frays, and for good fish is untrustworthy, even dangerous.' Gut casts that came to Russia from abroad he thought were meant as lines, and attached his hook to the end of them by a length of fine green silk. He was accustomed to use this green silk for his hook length unless he had a tapered horsehair line, when he fished with double or single or treble hair. The best hooks he knew, I am happy to record, were English, long-barbed, with a sneck bend. He preferred them with short shanks. The shank ended in a little spade. This was because they were not whipped to the silk or hair but knotted. Such hooks are still used for sea-fishing and for night-lines. It was necessary to look to your knots each day, because the hooks rusted the silk, though they were slower in damaging horsehair. The line was fastened to the rod with 'a double loop,' which must, I think, have been a clove hitch. The spare end of the line was twisted round the rod, so that if the rod broke you still had a chance of coming to terms with your fish. Aksakov's floats were of light wood, or of wood stuck into the lower end of a goose-quill, or of cork with a wooden peg. He preferred floats made of black poplar. As for shape, it was a matter of taste. 'I have seen floats very artistically carved from black poplar to represent a bird, a fish, and even a man; but in general floats are fattest at the middle.'

Much of his advice is dictated by the character of this simple tackle. The good fisherman does not slap his rod into the water when making a long cast. Nor, in striking, does he use great force, lest he should lose large fish and be unable to find small ones that he has hurled over his head into the grass. He must not fish with many rods at once. When fishing on the bottom he may use three, otherwise not more than two, and when fishing for small free-biting fish one rod is enough, and it should be held constantly in the hand. This advice is still much needed in Russia, where within the last few years I have seen men using as many as twelve rods at once. The good fisherman does not let his line sink *much*. If a big fish goes straight away so that the fisherman cannot hold up the point of the rod the 'only salvation is to drop the rod in the water.' The good fisherman does not lay his rod in the water while waiting for a bite. It is better to lay it on the reeds or to push the butt-end of it into the bank. Of course if you can hardly reach the deeper water, fishing over a weedy shallow, you cannot help yourself. In getting out a big fish the good fisherman never touches the line with his hand unless he has broken his rod. Aksakov wrote a delightful poem on the loss of a big chub by a fisherman who took hold of the line at the last minute. If a fish goes to weed the good fisherman slackens line, when the fish will usually come out. If it does not come out, then wade for it and at least save your tackle.

Others of Aksakov's 'sixteen points' are of a more general character. The good fisherman must know when and where to find the fish. In the hot Russian midsummer he must be at his post when the first pale streak shows in the eastern sky. By the time he has set up his tackle the dawn and the fish will arrive together. By six o'clock, when the sun is already hot, he may go home to sleep until the evening. In cooler weather he begins later, and fishes all day. He must know when to strike with different fish. Nor does Aksakov forget to add that there is much luck in fishing. 'It would otherwise be impossible to explain the undeserved success of some and the undeserved failure of others.' Whatever happens, he says, it is important to keep one's temper and bide one's time.

Chinese Fishing

CHINESE FISHING is a disappointment and, as fishermen, the Chinese are a decadent race. I went to China eagerly, primed with the knowledge that some five hundred years before the Christian era Confucius, whose philosophy is to this day the most influential in China, had fished with rod and line, refusing a net. Surely, I thought, if China is full of Confucians, they must follow their great teacher in a matter obviously more important than mere philosophical theory. Old Chinese pictures frequently represent men fishing in a worthy manner. Barbless hooks were known to these people two thousand years before they were introduced to us. I came to China as a pilgrim to the cradle of a religion. I expected to find followers of the true faith seated, bamboo in hand, by every ditch. I was as disappointed as must be those Mohammedans who come to Mecca and find there an elaborate system for fleecing the pious instead of an edifying spectacle of pure religion.

The whole time I was in China I saw only two men fishing with rods, and they were not Chinese, but Japanese. I did, however, see a great many fishermen. All, without exception, would be instantly expelled from, for example, the County Palatine Association. The object of the Chinese fishermen seems to be the capture of fish with the least possible expenditure of energy or skill. On the Yangtze the commonest method is as follows. A huge bamboo framework supports a wide, shallow net, which is lowered into the stream close to the bank in places where the fish swim, and is at intervals lifted, when fish that happen to be passing over it are caught. Neither fish nor fisherman is called upon to use more judgement than is necessary in choosing a lottery ticket. Nor does the fisherman use a particle of unnecessary energy. The net would be difficult to lift directly from the water. It is therefore suspended from a balanced pole. The fisherman lies comfortably upon the bank smoking his long pipe. When he chooses, he pulls down a light cord, the pole swings up, the net is lifted with so little effort that he can hold his pipe in one hand and hand up the net with the other. If there are any fish in it he scoops them out with a long-handled landing net. If not, he lets go the cord and the net sinks again under the water. And that is all there is to it.

Another method is the setting of long lines of a hundred hooks. These are lowered away over the stern of a boat, which is then anchored, while the fisherman sleeps. When he wakes he hauls in his catch. In the lake of the Summer Palace outside Peking I saw men using four-pronged spears. A more interesting method, but one in which the fisherman earns even less credit, is that of making cormorants do the fishing. Going up the Yangtze, I saw three cormorants flying low over the water and presently settle and dive. In a narrow boat, with perches along its gunwale, a fisherman waited a little way down stream. The cormorants catch fish and bring them back to the fisherman, who suitably rewards them. It is as if in England in a low water an angler should sit on the bank and employ little boys to tickle trout for him. O monstrous degradation!

The chief fish to be caught in China are members of the carp family. There are, however, small trout in the becks in the hills not far from Kiukiang, and, I believe, plenty in Manchuria, where there are too many bandits to leave to anglers the peace of mind their sport requires. There is good sea fishing in many places, particularly at Wei-hai-wei and Pei Ta-ho, where the bass are of a good size and take a fly heartily. On the way to China, by sea, I fished at Aden, Penang, and Singapore with a tiny rod made for me by Farlows, which I carried in my suitcase, and at all these places caught something.

At Aden, sweltering in terrific heat under a sun hat on the 1st of January, I was rowed with a friend in a rough boat full of blackamoors to an anchored lighter to which we tied up. Here I got catfish on raw meat. When the tide turned, the lighter, which was very low in the water, swung, and there was a sudden yell of 'Fish, big fish!' from the blacks. Something big had been sheltering under the lighter and had been disturbed by its swinging. There was a mighty swirl in the water on the far side of it. I had just caught a catfish, and, jumping from our boat to the lighter, I dangled it at my feet in the place where we had seen the swirl. Suddenly a fair-sized shark, seven or eight feet long, shot up so near that I could easily have kicked his back fin as he turned. He came right up under my feet, turned over, and was gone. I tried desperately to tempt him with the catfish. He would not come again. But at least I had seen a shark, and nearer than I am ever likely to see one again. At Penang, also fishing with raw meat, in the evening, after going to the top of the hill and seeing butterflies as big as soup plates and a centipede a foot long and thicker than my thumb, I tried in the inner harbour under the light of an arc lamp and got a fat fish striped and brightly coloured, which was appropriated by a Japanese, who said it was very good to eat. Also another catfish. At Singapore I fished from the top of a stockade built out into the sea to form a bathing enclosure free from sharks. Here the bait was prawns. I caught two curious fish about half a pound each and then a sea-serpent. A naval lieutenant was sitting on the top of the stockade with me at the time, and as soon as I was able to bring the brute to the top of the water and he saw what it was he ran round on the top of the stockade to the shore and came back with a stick and a kitchen knife. By the time I had the snake on the stockade the navy had not left much of it. There are plenty of these sea snakes about, and they are said to be poisonous. They certainly have ugly heads.

The only fishing I had actually in China was one afternoon in the Hong-kew Park in Shanghai. My steamer postponed sailing by a few hours, and I took the chance. The pond in the Hong-kew Park holds nothing but carp, and the day was not a carp day, but one of hard wind and biting cold. It snowed at night. I found there two Japanese, who showed me a photograph of a carp of some eighteen pounds that one of them had caught in the summer. We fished through the afternoon. Each of the Japanese was fishing with six rods. I had one. The total number of rods was thirteen. So that perhaps we should have caught nothing anyhow. One must not always blame the weather.

Devils of the Sea

FOR A DAY or two there had been preparations. Karl F. had bought a great ball of thread, and triple hooks, and made heavy paternosters of bent stout wire weighted in the centre with lead, with a hook bound to thread with copper wire hanging from each arm. He had cut and peeled neat sticks of juniper wood, on which he had coiled his lines, and at each meal told us how on previous occasions friends of his had filled a boat, fishing with similar instruments. He had, although Esthonia is a dry country, got a bottle of vodka. We took with us a kettle of cold tea, meat, cheese, butter and black bread, and beside that a basket full of stromming, small silvery fish to be used as bait. At half past eight we started.

The bay is extremely shallow for a great belt round its edge, and we had to use fir logs as rollers, and, barefoot, shove for a couple of hundred yards before our boat took the water fairly.

She was a regular fishing boat, built in a primitive manner with as few planks as possible, pointed and raised bow and stern, with a pair of wooden rowlocks, pegs of wood, in the extreme bows, and another single rowlock in the stern. There were thwarts in bow and stern, and a sort of box for fish amidships. He who rowed in the stern had to backwater, while he who rowed in the bows pulled in the ordinary way. None the less, the boat was very light, and we made a pretty fair pace out into the bay. We had some five or six versts to go, call it three miles to the point where there were said to be fish. Wild duck, so tame that for last six years of war no one can have worried them with a shot-gun, settled in the water close before us, rising and flying a short distance as we approached and settling again. Gulls swung overhead. We changed oars from time to time.

At last, taking our bearings from the Packerort lighthouse on the western point of the bay and from the last rock of a group that run out into the sea from Cape Lohusaar on the eastern side, we anchored in some twenty metres of water about one third of the way between the two points. The sun set curiously in a thin straight line, leaving a glow that did not disappear but moved imperceptibly eastwards until it turned into the dawn. There were however two hours of comparative dark in which we could hardly see the shore, from which came an extraordinary roaring and howling, not like that of dogs, nor like the noises made by the most fantastic of humans. I should have recognised it, but did not, and it was not till morning that we had the explanation.

Four of the party baited their pairs of triple hooks, and dropped their paternosters overboard. I have however a great distaste for hand-lines and had brought an old pike rod, and fixed up a simpler tackle, consisting of a heavy ledger lead slipped on my line, and, below it a single pike hook. I fished this hook, just as the others fished their paternosters, finding the bottom with it, and then lifting it a couple of feet. There was this other difference between our fishing that they used a considerable mass of silvery fish to cover their triple hooks, while my single hook was amply disguised with a very modest mouthful. For two hours nothing happened. The moon looked down at us, like a pale prisoner through a window of green glass barred with lead. We prophesied rain, and drank the vodka and ate the food, and rejected the cold tea, and suppressed the desires of one who wished to desert the fishing ground and investigate the howling on the shore.

At about one fifteen, I thought I felt something, but hardly believed it, and waited for a better tug. There was little to feel with a stout rod, and well over twenty yards of line swinging loose below, and the boat gently rocking. However I wound in quietly, found my bait had certainly been touched, put on a fresh one and lowered again, saying nothing to anybody, lest I should be unable to prove my bite by a fish. At 1.20 I felt another touch, struck at once, and wound in. He came up without difficulty and was in the boat before anyone knew there was hope of him. Then, in the dark, he was passed from hand to hand. A creature all head and horns, with a short tail mottled red and white below and brown above, with a huge square mouth, and mottled fins sticking out below beside a couple that fringed his back like a newt's. The Esthonians knew him at once. 'Meerekuraht', they said, 'The Devil of the Sea,' and conversation stopped, while each man fingered his line with new attention. But whether it was that their baits were too big, or that they could not feel the bites at such a depth I do not know, but they caught nothing. With my single, less obtrusive hook, I caught two more sea-devils, bigger and beastlier than the first, and those three were the sum-total of our united catch. I could have wished it had been otherwise though I could not but approve the demonstration that at sea as on land, fishing line is the better way than main force and grapnels. However everybody was very good tempered.

We finished the vodka, and then, as the sun rose, we learned that we had not been fishing alone, and learnt also who it was that it had been howling so dismal and vigorous among the rocks of Cape Lohusaar. Fifty yards from us, shining in the morning sun, was what might have been a round flat topped black rock, if it had not blown and puffed like a city merchant bathing. It was a seal. Presently he dived, and his broad black back shone above the water as he went under to come up again many yards distant, blowing and enjoying himself, no doubt, and taking no notice whatever of his fellow fishers. It was agreed at once that his presence was more than enough to explain the lack of fish, since who could expect them to interest themselves in being caught on hooks, when they had a more immediate task to avoid being caught by seals. And with that we weighed anchor, and came home easily with a very light wind behind us, rippling the waters of the bay.

(Unpublished manuscript, Brotherton Collection,
University of Leeds Library, May 1920.)

England for Fishermen

'PEKING is a fine city, but it's not like home,' says a Chinese proverb. And perhaps one of the advantages of seeing that fine city is the violence of the desire that it creates in the traveller, in the fisherman particularly, to be somewhere else. There is no fishing anywhere near Peking, and, indeed, there seemed to be very little anywhere in China barring sea-fishing, which hardly counts. I was told by long-established residents in Peking that for as far back as the memory of living man can reach the politics of that city have been so exciting and have produced so rapid and continuous a stream of dramatic and unexpected events that it would be impossible to take much interest in fishing even if there were any. I do not believe it. Indeed I am more inclined to believe that the real reason why Chinese politics have to be so continuously exciting is that they have to make up for the lack of the healthier stimulus of fishing. A perfect desert of a place. But it is unfair to pick out Peking for censure. Shanghai is nearly as bad. And, thinking it over, I am not at all sure that even if there were fishing in these places, and if it were extremely good, it could make up for the wretchedness of being there and not in England.

In Latvia I have known really excellent trout and grayling fishing, but half the pleasure of fishing those delightful little rivers was that here and there they reminded me of the rivers I had known in England as a boy. Pike-fishing in Esthonia and Russia has given me plenty of pike, but the pleasure of it would have been much less if it had not been closely interwoven with memories of reedy meres and weir-pools at home, at the other end of Europe. The pride of catching a big rainbow trout in New Zealand must be marred by the thought of how much greater the pride would have been if the big fish had been caught in England. These foreign fish do not count in the same way. They are somehow unreal. We may catch them ourselves, but at the bottom of our hearts we know them to be not much better than photographs, substitutes for English fish, with a flavour of artificiality about them, margarine instead of butter; more of them, perhaps, but not the same thing.

Four months of exile have confirmed me in the opinion that England is the place for fishermen. The four months were those of the butt-end of the year, the four that one would choose to lose, if one had to lose any. Yet they included the month in which the biggest pike are caught, the month in which the fortunate rich get at their spring salmon, and that exciting, tantalising month at the beginning of the northern trout season. For nearly three weeks before I got back people had been making good baskets of trout on fly in Windermere. Yet after leaving the Pacific coast, coming home overland, because it was the quickest way back to my rivers, I saw only one patch of open water before getting into Poland. All the rest was ice. Sledge roads were running down the Siberian rivers. Only just where the Angara flows out of Lake Baikal there was a mile or two of shallow, open, fast-running water. There, anchored in midstream, were two boats with fishermen busy with long rods over the stern. The river had opened only a day or two before. Those men had been waiting to fish it since the previous October. And in England there is not a day throughout the year when there is not fish in season and fishing to be had.

Ours is the most humane and civilised of climates, though it must be admitted that we do not deserve it and do our best to spoil it. We fill the air with smoke to cover with a vile film the surface of our lakes. We cut down our trees without planting new ones, to lessen the equability of the supply of water to the rivers. We poison the very rain itself by covering the roads with tar so that when the rain runs from them to the rivers it carries with it death to the fish. We behave generally like ingrates and noodles, and yet, in spite of the worst that we can do, England is still for the fisherman the finest country in the world.

Consider that in coming from Peking to Manchester the wretched traveller has spent fourteen days and nights in the train, that he has crossed Asia and crossed Europe, and that during all but three of those days he has seen nothing but frozen water and rivers that for half the year are valued mainly as sledge roads. Then consider the remaining four hours of his journey, from London to Manchester, and the extra three hours of exultant flight (it can hardly be called travelling by train) that take him from Manchester to the hills. He can hardly look away from the window without missing a fishable river. The very names of the rivers are a poem – Colne and Ouzel, Tove and Ouse, Avon and Anker, Tame and Trent, if we go one way, and if we go the other we approach Manchester by way of Wye and Derwent and the fair trout streams of Derbyshire. And in thinking of the rivers, I am in danger of forgetting the canals, mile upon mile of them, with rare slow barges that do but keep the fish awake. Then, on leaving Manchester for the North, apart from smaller streams, there are the two great rivers Lune and Ribble, rivers so attractive to fish that the salmon and the sea trout brave the human foulness at their mouths to go up to Whitewell and Newton-in-Bowland to Kirkby Lonsdale and Lowgill and Tebay, where we shall meet them when they come. Compare for a moment those fourteen days and nights of barren railway travelling with the continuous excitement, the generous wealth of memory and hope packed into these little English journeys that are so short that, after coming from Peking, it scarcely seems worth while to settle the luggage in the rack.

The crowning glory of all this is that it would not have mattered if these little journeys had been made at another time of year. If it had been mid-winter, then the trout streams would have been fair memories and distant beckoning promises, while there were pike and roach to be caught presently in the more sluggish streams and those miraculous canals. Now, in April, while the Trent brings memories of J. W. Martin and his books and the canals are for float-fishing several months hence, the blackthorn in the hedges beacons the news of the opening of the trout season. The whole horrible jumble of Chinese politics is swept away in a moment as, on leaving the train at the long journey's end, I meet a man who tells me news of real importance, that there is a good hatch of March Brown on the lake and that grouse and claret has been the taking fly.

6 • CONSERVATION

Tar

THE WARMER WEATHER is bringing the motor-boats out on Windermere, and the fishing is consequently going to the bad. The Windermere trout season seems likely to be limited to the first six weeks after the opening day. Towards the end of April motor-boats appear, and now, when the fishing should be really worth while, these monstrous creatures with a crew of one or perhaps two are roaring up and down the lake, creating a vibration that can be felt from one side of the lake to the other and making the surface of the lake a patchwork quilt (there is no other way of describing the effect of the oil they exude). On a day with a good ripple on the water that ripple will be broken by long streaks of oily smoothness. And it often happens that the shore on which the ripple should be breaking, the shore that should be good fly-fishing, is instead belted with a wide border of oil-film. One at least of the fast boats can be smelt in a light wind from Rawlinson Nab to Storrs. A day's fishing on one of the more distant lakes, neither better situated nor naturally better for fish, but happily free from motor-boats, shows to what extent the few who race their boats for an hour or two at a time (they go so fast that even for themselves they exhaust all the pleasures of Windermere, except the possibility of unnecessary speed) have destroyed the beauty of our finest inland water for all who come to see it and the pleasure of those who in old days were happy to spend a day upon it.

But the motor-boats on Windermere are less harmful to fishing in general than the eagerness with which the road surveyors poison the becks and rivers throughout the country. These people seem to become addicted to tar in the same sort of irreclaimable manner in which Chinese become addicted to opium. You may point out that an official authority has publicly and definitely declared, after exhaustive experiment, that tar in any form whatsoever is fatal to fish, and the surveyors will listen to you, go on using tar, and, on further protest, reply that the tar they are now using is a carefully purified product – as if purified potassium cyanide was any less poisonous than the same chemical diluted. They will twist and turn in all directions rather than be done out of the use of their favourite stuff. They are as good at excuse and subterfuge as drug-fiends. One of them even defended the use of tar on the grounds that it was 'supporting a British industry'!

It is difficult to understand why tar should be used on any roads that drain into streams and rivers holding fish when there is in bitumen at least one substance which makes as good roads and has been certified as harmless to fish. It is not as if the tar companies were in a position to appoint the road authorities. It is not as if the road authorities could profit personally in any way by using tar. Is it that there is a new form of mental disease, *piscophobia*, vicious hostility to fish, and that persons affected by it seek the post of road surveyor in order to be able to indulge their secret propensity? This would at least explain their evident desire to push their horrid practices farther and yet farther into country hitherto free from them. Crummock and Buttermere are lakes still unspoilt, but early this week I saw the ominous black barrels along the road that skirts Crummock's very shores. Masses of tar have just gone down along the road on the western shore of Windermere. This year there were reports of surprisingly good fishing in Ullswater. What happens? At once the road surveyor with his 'Yo Ho Ho! and a barrel of tar' sets about putting down a new lot of poison on the road that runs not more than a yard or two from the banks of one of the becks up which the fish run to spawn. Not far from where I am writing there is a delightful beck flowing into Morecambe Bay, full of decent little trout and frequented by salmon in the spawning season. A few days ago, thanks to the road authorities, there was so much new tar on the roads that the rains blackened the stream, in the words of a local postman who actually saw the dead fish floating down it. If this sort of thing is to go on unchecked it will not be long before our trout and salmon rods will be treasured in museums as 'instruments used in the early twentieth century in the capture of now extinct aquatic creatures.'

Humanity for countless ages has held in contempt the poisoner of wells. Some forms of pollution are old established and difficult to prevent. Tar is a new one. The poison is only now being put down. It is known that it is a poison. It is known that there are harmless substitutes for it. Its use is without excuse of any kind. There are those who think that, as an overdose of sweets will cure a child of gluttony, the best use of tar would be for the coating and subsequent feathering of the road surveyors who are unable to restrain their taste for it.

Licensed Nuisances

THE BOARD OF TRADE has, it appears, handed over Windermere to the small group of rich men who find pleasure in moving on it at very high speeds. South of the Ferry and north of Belle Isle, the Board of Trade sees no reason for any restriction on speed, and these few people are to be allowed to drive their boats as fast as they can. This is a serious blow to those who look to the lake for their fishing.

The question of whether there is any pleasure in moving at frantic speed through beautiful scenery (foolishly raised at the inquiry) is altogether irrelevant. The question which ought to have been considered, but apparently was not, is how far any man is justified in spoiling the pleasure of great numbers of other people for the sake of his own. By the decision of the Board of Trade it is clear that in this matter Windermere is to be in a worse position than a public highway. There at least there are some restrictions. Here there are to be none. All the other pleasures of the lake, fishing, boating, and yachting, are compatible with each other. This one, alone, of excessive speed, is destructive of all the rest. There is no escape from the man in a fast motor-boat. The noise and vibration of his passing fill the air for miles. There is no getting away from him. One man, in a boat moving at 24 miles an hour, can in thirty minutes inflict himself on every other human being from end to end of the lake. He is in possession of an instrument which, like a loud-speaker, multiplies enormously his power of making an impression.

One would imagine that his first care would be to make that impression as little objectionable as possible. If the man in a fast motor-boat (there are seldom more than two persons in such boats) thinks at all, he will hesitate before driving his boat along the shores during the fly-fishing season. In the middle of the lake, however, are the charfishers, and the least that he can do for them is to give them a wide berth and to reduce speed and vibration in order not to lessen their already meagre chances of sport. Even if he disregards the fishermen, he should surely remember that a good many people live on the shores of Windermere and on the surrounding hills. It is a little hard on them that because a man is rich enough to put a powerful engine into a boat he should be licensed to turn the peace of the lake into a deafening, insistent roar. In fact, if he measures up his own pleasure against that of the many others involuntarily concerned he will, if a person of normal kindliness and decent instincts, save his own petrol and other people's happiness by being content with a speed low enough to be silent and to let him enjoy those qualities of Windermere which are not dependent on trying with a tremendous accompaniment of noise and thrum to run away from his conscience.

The Price of Fish

THE TROUT FISHERMAN who during the close season is apt to acquire some reserve of bad temper should not waste it on his family or his friends. He should use it for the public good. Let him keep it for the polluters of streams. Let him not forget that whereas he does not fish from October until March these miscreants know no close season for their activities. If he leaves his river alone during the whole of the winter he may return to it in the spring to find it already ruined. A little righteous indignation properly applied and not applied too late is much more useful than a desperate protest after the evil has been done. The trout fisherman who in the winter of his discontent visits the scenes of his summer happiness will often find that he has a chance of doing something that will make a great difference to his next year's fishing. The chance is sometimes slender, but the more active fishermen are in defence of their rivers the more likely it becomes that here and there that defence will be successful.

Let me give an example of the sort of thing that such a fisherman may find. During those dreadful days when even grayling fishing was impossible, when the floods were out and the gales such that the best a man could do, in the country, was to persuade himself that the trees blown down were not those he valued most, I happened to go along the road which closely follows the small river on which I count for some of the happiest of the year's trout fishing. I do not propose to name the river, because it is rather too well known already. It is fished by the local inhabitants and by men who have for a long time been in the habit of visiting the valley during their holiday escapes from the neighbouring towns. The road, until recently, was a narrow and winding road, with sharp turns, compelling careful driving, a lane rather than a road, never very far from the river and for long stretches within a stone's throw of it. There came an evil day when this road and another that crosses the river at the bottom of a steep incline were tarred, though at many points the men who did the tarring had only to look over their shoulders to see the rising trout. After rains the stream has been seen flowing black with the poison, and dead trout have been picked up. But after each poisoning there was some sort of recovery. A good deal of fresh water comes down, and in some of the floods that bring the sea-trout up there was probably little to warn them that their old spawning grounds were threatened. The fishing has been growing worse, but I imagine that occasional tarrings of the narrow little lane might be continued for a number of years before the sea-trout run would be finally brought to an end. The fishing would gradually deteriorate. At last it would be not worth bothering about, and as a fishing stream this pleasant little river would pass unnoticed out of existence.

So far as I know, no protest was made against the tarring of the lane. But now a far worse thing is threatened. When, the other day, I went down the valley I found great works in progress. The road is being widened and straightened. It is no longer to be a country lane but a road for heavy motor traffic. Much of the engineering has been done, and, from the look of things, it would seem that the new motoring road will be completed by the spring. Between now and the beginning of the trout season a surface will be put on it, and, since no compunction was shown in tarring the old lane, it is pretty certain that, unless protest is made at once, the new wide road will be similarly tarred and repeat in a far more decisive manner the minor poisonings of which we have already had experience. The new road is wider than the river and drains in many places directly into it. A more useful winter hobby for a trout fisherman could hardly be found than that of making things as uncomfortable as possible for the council responsible for tarring such a road.

There is no explaining the affection of surveyors for tar. Other materials for road surfaces can be had, and official intimation has been given that poisonous stuffs should not be used for road surfaces in the neighbourhood of rivers that contain fish. It is our business to see that the surveyors have not the excuse of saying that they did not know there were fish in the river. The sight of rising trout means a good deal less to these people than a formal warning from a Fishery Board. We can, and should, make ourselves a nuisance to the Fishery Board concerned until it sends a warning to the surveyor or to the council that employs him. We can, and should, harry the lives out of individual council members until, by the time the Fishery Board's warning comes along, we have got them to see that there is some public opinion behind it. It is no use talking to these people of the delights of fishing, of the wickedness of poisoning water, or anything of that kind. There is, however, one argument that will at least attract their attention, and that is a reference to the actual value of fish.

It will be found in most cases that it has not occurred to them that fish have any value at all. We can show them exactly what it would cost to replace any fish that they destroy. The Howietoun and Northern Fisheries, which were founded by Sir James Maitland, who did much in introducing game fish into New Zealand, have recently sent out a pamphlet on fish-stocking, which, extremely interesting in itself, gives the actual prices of young fish in the United Kingdom. Yearlings cost, delivered at the nearest railway station, £4 per hundred. They would, of course, cost rather more than that by the time we had put them in the water to make them justly comparable to the fish we are trying to defend. According to Halford, a good yearling would be six inches long. It would hardly be so big in a northern beck. That is to say that the little trout not yet fit to catch are worth about 9½d. each. Two-year-olds, which, in such a river as I have in mind, would be takable fish, cost £10. 15s. per hundred. That is to say that the ordinary small trout of takable size is worth about 2s. 1d. Now tarring turns live trout (replaceable at 9d. to 2s. apiece) into poisoned dead trout worth nothing at all, except, perhaps, as manure. It lessens the river's power of restocking itself. In a quite small natural river the yearling trout (to say nothing of the larger fish) can be counted by thousands, and it is easy enough to demonstrate that the actual value of the fish (expressed by the cost of replacing them) is so high that there can be no possible justification for allowing a tar-loving authority to use the public money in destroying them.

The Story of the Wye

NO MAN EVER WROTE a bad book about a river that he knew well. Every fishing river in England deserves its own portrait and its own biography, and it is surprising that so few of the fishermen who write ensure a value for their books by limiting them to accurate accounts of the single river that each man knows best. Writing about rivers is like writing about men. Better far an accurate account of one man than a general account of humanity.

The Wye is a particularly good subject for a fisherman. Here is a river, the distressful state of the fishing in which was notorious for more than half a century, which has within the memory of a young man become one of the finest salmon rivers in the country. Here is a river in which the stock of salmon had fallen so low that the netsmen in it found their work unprofitable, and a river in which only a few years later one man, on a length formerly alleged to be useless for rod-fishing, caught over 500 salmon in a season. No more magnificent example of what can be done by proper river preservation can be found. To read the story of how this remarkable change was brought about should encourage the work of conservators everywhere and, not less important, should encourage riparian owners to believe that conservators are worth supporting.

Mr H. A. Gilbert in his *Tale of a Wye Fisherman* tells the story of the Wye from early times to the present day, and I can well imagine a meeting of riparian proprietors of certain other rivers at which, with malice, the upper river owners would bring a copy of it to present to the owners of the lower reaches and find that the owners of the lower reaches had also brought a copy for presentation to those unreasonable fellows from upstream. For, so far as man is concerned, the story of the Wye is the story of a long series of faction fights between groups of people who in order not to do good to each other did harm to the river as a whole. One group gripped by the feet the goose that laid the golden eggs, another had her by the head, and between them they succeeded in all but wringing her neck. It was a long struggle, and until quite recent times its motives were the same – jealousy and greed.

In 1588 the fishermen above a weir rioted and pulled it down because they thought it gave too large a share of the salmon to the fishermen below it. It was rebuilt, and in 1825 the battle over the weir in that place was still going on. The improvement of navigation in the Wye got rid of the weirs, to the advantage of all fishermen, but even then it was not realised that the netsmen on the lower reaches stood to lose if an insufficient number of salmon got past them to the spawning grounds, and the fishermen on the upper reaches killed the fish on the spawning-grounds without realising that by doing so they were in the long run damaging themselves. All legislation protecting the fish was regarded as a wicked infringement of somebody's rights for the benefit of somebody else, and the Rebecca rioters, who had come into existence to protest against the toll-gate system, continued their activities in protest against the fishery laws and undertook wholesale poaching raids, with the support of public opinion and even some of the magistrates, until near the end of the nineteenth century.

The curious thing is that through all this time the local men were ready to resent anything that they thought might damage their river. Mr Gilbert has not referred, perhaps from wealth of other material, to the struggle of the men of Hereford against the introduction of gas-lighting in the town for fear lest it should result in harm to the salmon. This at a time when numbers of men were making a living out of catching and selling salmon parr and when nets up and down the river were being most ruthlessly worked. The netsmen were, of course, chief obstacle to the river's recovery, but in the end made that recovery possible by so depleting the river that there had ceased to be a run of salmon sufficient to make the netting a commercial proposition. The netsmen destroyed their own livelihood on Loch Lomond in the same way.

From the seventies until 1924 the struggle to free the river from freshwater netting continued. In that year the last of the netting rights passed into the hands of the Board of Conservators under the chairmanship of Mr. J. A. Hutton.

Since 1909 it had been possible to prohibit all netting above
Brockweir Bridge. Such netting as is done now is done by the
permission of the conservators and in the tidal water. It is
sufficiently successful to pay the interest of the money
borrowed for the purchase of the netting rights and even to
pay off the bonds as they fall due. In the opinion of Mr Gilbert
it does no material harm to the fishing. The fate of the river did
not depend on the treatment of the estuary netting but on the
river above the tidal level. It was the netting that reduced too
far the number of the river spawning fish. It does so no longer,
but Mr Gilbert is aware of a new danger in the possibility that
pollution may decrease the river's power of feeding baby
salmon. He mentions his suspicions that tarred roads are
responsible for the disappearance of the one-time enormous
hatches of fly.

Poachers

THERE WAS JUST the beginning of light in the sky and the
thick mist over river and meadow was already white.
When we came to the Marron Pool nothing was visible more
than a few yards away.

'Where are we?'

'You'll find the big stone just before you. The thirty yards
below it are the best.'

Our voices were low, but in the windless quiet were enough
to give warning. Somewhere in the mist below us there was
sudden loud splashing. An otter? Then angry low voices.
More splashing. Poachers! There was a minute of silence.
Then a shrill whistle between the fingers produced a thund-
erous splash some forty or fifty yards off. Someone had been
startled and missed his footing in the river.

We moved along the bank to Marron Foot, watching the
ground. The poachers, however, had crossed the river and
taken to the high wooden bank on the far side, from which
they have been known to stone anglers in the water. The pool

was useless anyway, and as we walked upstream again, while the light grew and the mist rolled up, we found the tracks in the wet grass showing how the men had come. There could be no fishing in the Marron Pool that dawn.

Poaching in the Cumberland Derwent is not what it was five years ago, nor what it is today in Wales, but the long drought has worn out the watchers, who have had to be busy protecting the fish from every kind of disaster, and, after all, watchers are few and poachers know that they must rest sometimes. The poachers had probably seen us fishing the pool at dusk, and, when we went off to brew coffee in the fishing hut and to talk the darkness out of the sky, they must have made sure that the place was left to themselves and others on the same bad business, like the heron who, when we disturbed him, went off with loud indignant curses, most unlike the muffled anger of the humans. His attitude towards us was probably like ours towards them. He looked upon us as poachers creeping quietly along his river to disturb by our crude methods his private skilful fishing.

Most fishermen have a softness for the heron, as they have for the kingfisher and as they have not, usually, for the otter, though 'G. W. M.,' of the Derwent, who knows the otter more intimately than most men know their household cats, assures me that the otter is a harmless, not too successful fisherman – fit almost to be a member of an exclusive angling club. The poachers and the heron may have done better than we, but we found the sea-trout at their dourest, hooked one and lost it, rose another, but otherwise, except for the brown troutlings, might have been fishing an empty river. They were not feeding. That was all, for the river is full of fish.

River-Watchers

GOOD RIVER-WATCHERS are worth their weight in gold, but do not get it. I do not speak of the river-watcher on a private fishery, whose task is easy, but of the river-watchers on club waters which may be fished by some twenty members or even more throughout the season. The good watcher on such a water needs to be a diplomat, a fly-dresser, an entomologist, and a weather prophet. He must have a wonderful memory for faces. Some of the members will fish only once or twice in a season, when they will come for the sake of bringing a friend in whose eyes they wish to raise their standing. It does not do, on such an occasion, for the keeper, 'our keeper,' to come up to the proud host and demand to see his membership ticket. Not at all. He must greet him by name and, whatever sort of a duffer he is, ask him what he thinks of the water. It is remarkable how much intimacy with a river-watcher raises one fisherman in the opinion of another. Not only must the watcher know each one of the members, but he must also know a good deal about each member's skill as a fisherman.

There is the man who needs to be encouraged by being shown an easy fish to put in an empty basket. There is the other who comes along with basket already full but is glad enough to know if the particular fish called Didymus at the bend above is feeding and what flies the keeper has seen him take. Now this means that the watcher must know not only the fishermen but also the fish. He must know all about the suspicious Didymus, and, up and down the river, he must know the fish that feed in places that make their capture easy for anybody. He must know the river. The watcher who has spent twenty or thirty of the most active years of his life watching a particular length of a particular river does, of course, come to know that length in a way that no single member of the club can know it. He knows the character of every pool and stream at every height of water, at all positions of the sun, and under all winds. He comes to know these things without having to reason about them. He has come to be the river, and when he speaks on that subject it is the river itself that has found a voice. Such a man improves the fishing of every member of the club. Every member, it is to be hoped, has some little knowledge of the river himself, but in the river-watcher there is the greater part of the club's knowledge of the river walking about on two legs. No single member fishing one or two days a week during the season can hope to know so much, but the more each member knows the better use he is able to make of the river-watcher's twenty or thirty years of continuous, accumulated experience.

It is a mistake to think that the business of a river-watcher is simply to be here, there, and everywhere on the river looking out for poachers. His business is to improve the fishing, and patrolling the river is only one of the ways in which he does it. Indeed, if his duties are to be limited to patrolling the river will be badly watched. If, for example, it is known that he will on every day go from one end of the water to the other and back again, it may be said that the river might as well not be watched at all from the poacher's point of view. The presence of the keeper will become as easily calculable as the passing of the Royal Scot or the Clyde and Thames Express. The least intelligent of poachers will be able to allow for it and to work his wicked will accordingly.

Fortunately the other duties of the river-watcher, of the good river-watcher, make his presence here or there along the river free of any time-table. His progress along the banks should be as full of digressions, of loiterings, of dallyings here and there as any essay. His business is to increase the satisfaction of the members in their fishing. With his knowledge of the river he can hardly fail to help their fishing, but to do that he must stop and talk with those members whom he meets. Not all members can be on the water at once, and to insist that the keeper shall not stop to talk with a fishing member is merely a dog-in-the-manger policy on the part of those members who are away in town. I can hardly remember a river I have fished on which I have not had a blank day turned at least into a pleasant one, or a good day enhanced by a half-hour talk with the local river-watcher. Nor was the river worse watched because the keeper spent half an hour in one place letting me share some of his much greater intimacy with the water. Such dallyings made his presence an uncertain thing. No poacher, if there were any, could tell precisely when the keeper would be at any particular pool, even if he had

known at what time the keeper started on his walk. Absent
members did not suffer in any way. When they in their turn
visited the water, they too found the river-watcher, the
major-domo of the river, dispensing, on behalf of the river,
hospitality and entertainment.

There is hardly need to say that the best river-watchers are
men who have themselves been anglers from their youth up.
There is no way of learning a river so thorough as that of
fishing it. Every one of the best keepers I have known has been
himself a good fisherman. It is good policy as well as sound
humanity to encourage a river-watcher now and then to fish
the water he watches. It is asking too much of a young
fisherman that, on becoming a river-watcher, he shall
abandon his favourite pastime altogether and spend the rest of
his life helping other men to good fishing without ever
handling a rod himself. Waiters are paid to give people their
dinners, but they are also allowed to eat. A river-watcher
cannot restrict himself to an eight or a ten or a twelve hour
day. There are times when even in twenty-four hours he can
hardly do all that needs to be done. But he must rest
sometimes, and if, when he rests, he spends a few hours with a
rod he is at the same time enjoying recreation for himself and,
from the point of view of the club that employs him, is
actually, though on holiday, still at the riverside, and therefore
serving them instead of finding relaxation somewhere else.

Fishermen's Complaints

I SHOULD LIKE to think that fishermen were perfect, but I
have to admit that ours is a complaining nature. We complain in turn of rain, drought, wind, calm, heat, cold, flies
(too many), flies (too few), flies (biting ones), fish, and other
fishers, furred, feathered, and human. Complaint has become
a habit with us, and we complain like parrots, not always
apropos. For example, this week the rivers I fish have been
low, the wind has been blowing the wrong way on the best

reaches, it has been very hot walking about in waders, and it has been a great deal easier to see what magnificent fish there are in the water than to catch them. (I am not complaining. I am telling you.) The fisherman has laboured under quite a number of handicaps. But this week there has been one thing of which nobody could fairly complain, and that has been the hatch of flies. I have never seen so many Little Yellow Sallies in my life, nor have I often seen so fine a dance of Ginger Spinners over the pools in the evenings. And throughout the day the trout have been ready to feed, though it has been difficult to come near enough to help them without sending them in a desperate hurry somewhere else. Yet on the river bank, in the middle of the best part of the day, I met a man not fishing but wagging a fly-rod and looking as if he would like to use it to cut buttercups.

'It's no good fishing to-day,' he said at once; 'fish not rising.'

While we talked I saw martins picking flies from the river, and here and there a disturbance of the surface that was not made by a bird. When we parted I went down into the water and caught a few fish and had opportunities (missed) of catching a few more. I frightened most of the fish, but any that I did not frighten rose most eagerly. If that disheartened man upon the bank had complained of the low water he would have had some reason. But he complained of the mood of the fish, which deserved nothing but praise. Either he was complaining just from habit or he was of those who have learnt that the most ingratiating way of meeting any other fisherman is to meet him with a complaint that may serve as an excuse for him if he has done nothing and will flatter him if he has done well. Another man's complaint about difficult conditions is equally good sauce for a full basket of fish or an empty one. His complaint may therefore have been tactful. Even so, it was badly chosen.

The very next day I was given a more serious example of careless complaining, in a lament that the Mayfly fishing on Windermere is being ruined by the black-headed gulls, who are eating the Mayflies. This complaint is the more regrettable

in that it diverts attention from a serious to a frivolous
grievance. On the rivers, one of the first signs of a hatch of fly
is the sight of swifts and swallows and martins hawking over
the surface of the water and picking off the flies. It is a beautiful
sight, and a welcome one, that hurries the fisherman to his
work. The appearance of the gulls on the lake and the sight
of them picking the big Green Drakes off the water would
not be disturbing at all if it were not that for other reasons the
hatch of Mayfly is not what it was.

Has it not occurred to these complainers that since the
Mayfly spends almost the whole of its life in the water and
only comes to the surface to spread its wings for its brief
experience of flight the trout have an infinitely better chance
than the gulls of eating them? The complaint should be
directed against the causes which have so lessened the supply
of Mayflies that we grudge a few to the gulls. The complainers, it appears, want to shoot at the gulls. It would be
more to the point if they sought leave to shoot at the motor-
boats. If there were no oil on the lake the flies would have a
better chance and the Mayfly fishing might once again bring
fishermen to Windermere.

In looking for reasons for the deterioration of fishing 'the
proper study of mankind is man.' Complaints about gulls and
otters and herons and cormorants do but distract attention
from the real culprit. It is man who upsets the balance of nature
to his own disadvantage. I do not think that I see more herons
busy at the river than I used to see when I was a boy. There are
certainly fewer kingfishers. The pike in Windermere eat more
perch than trout. The same thing is true of the cormorants.
The otter, who gets his share of fishermen's complaints
because of his free-handed way of helping himself to trout as
an occasional reward for his valuable work in destroying eels,
earns his keep in many a river where the eels are too numerous.
When there is talk of the deterioration of fishing there is
always the assumption that once upon a time it used to be
better. But gulls, cormorants, otters, herons, and pike are not
new inventions. In the old days, before the fishing needed
improvement, they were taking, probably, a larger share of

fish and fish food than they are taking to-day. Such damage as they do is negligible in comparison with the damage done by man. They depend, like the fisherman, on their own skill and dexterity. They do not use the destructive methods of modern warfare. They do not use chemicals. They do not establish artificial-silk or beet-sugar factories without proper means for making their effluents harmless. They do not use rivers as open drains. They do not rush about on inland waters in high-speed motor-boats emitting noise and oil. They may attack fish and flies, but they do not attack water. The celebrated Dr Dolittle, when approaching the moon at the end of his daring flight on the back of a gigantic moth, perceived through his telescope a tree.

'If it is,' he cried to his faithful follower, 'we're all right. It means water, Stubbins, water! And we can manage to exist here. Water and Life!'

In these times and on this earth, whatever may be the case in the moon, water does not always mean life. It may mean washings from a tarred road, or a scum of oil, or the refuse from a factory the owner of which may be rich enough to live too far from it to smell it. When, as fishermen, we complain of the weather or the fish we are within our rights and do no harm. When we complain of our furred and feathered competitors for damaging the fishing we are on most uncertain ground. When we complain of pollution we are doing a service to humanity in general. Since ours is a complaining nature let us satisfy it by making the right kind of complaints.

Fishing Books

DELIGHTFUL as it is to pursue chub with Nottingham tackle, watching the great goose-quill float slip down the current past the scraggy, leafless bushes, to spin for pike while the cat ice on the sodden, half-frozen meadows crackles underfoot, to wade for grayling in the long, gravelly pools, thereby thawing the waders that stiffen the moment we leave the water, there is no doubt that for most fishermen the winter is the lean part of the year. Trout and salmon fishermen, of course, put their rods away altogether, and, of the fishermen for coarse fish, the greater number are content to limit their fishing to the season Walton loved, the season when a fisherman can, if he will, sit under a tree for shade's sake without fear of catching a chill. Even the resolute fellows who fish on every day they can throughout the year find that (whatever may be their intention) they do, in fact, get less often to the river during winter months. Short days, bad roads, rain, snow, and howling gales conspire to keep them from it. What are they to do? Make tackle and read fishing books.

Now, a man cannot wisely make an unlimited number of casts and flies. The one will rot, and the knowledge that he has too many of the other rapidly reduces the enthusiasm of the fly-dresser. He can, however, read fishing books without end.

To read a fishing book is next best thing to fishing. It is like talk in the fishing inn at night. Considering the year as a single day, the months as hours, we may fairly describe these winter months as the evening during which, after a long day, say March to November, on the water, it is exceedingly pleasant to rest in chairs about the fire and to hear ourselves and other people talk on this inexhaustible subject. For the authors of fishing books seldom have things all their own way. We do not often give them the chance of a long monologue. The dullest man, if he is really a fisherman, has tough ideas on many things, tough because founded not on hearsay but on his own experience. He is no mere patient sponge to soak up other men's views, but is for ever critically comparing them with his own. He quarrels with this, heartily agrees with that, tastes in memory or in hope his own fishing in accounts of the fishing of other men. He is an active, not a passive, reader, and since good readers make good books it is not surprising that no sport has so rich a library as ours. And since we use that library mostly in winter it is not surprising that it is in winter that the publishers most often make additions to it.

Fishing Diaries

LORD WALSINGHAM's delightful little book, *Fish*, is another proof of the wisdom of keeping a fishing diary. We are not all going to write books for other people, but we may just as well seek precision in the one that we spend our lives in writing for ourselves. Among the objects of youth is that of storing memories for old age. Yet how many old men there are who remember little more than that the fishing was better when they were young. The whole detailed delight of the days they can never have again has faded into a rather sulky comparative.

Perhaps even that is based on an illusion. Perhaps one of the uses of a fishing diary is to prevent the posthumous growth of fish. There are those who laugh at anglers for stuffing their

best fish, just as there are many anglers who laugh at their
brethren for bothering to keep a journal. They laugh at men
wiser than themselves. A stuffed fish, even a fish poorly
stuffed (and I have seen some that looked like punctured
footballs), is better than any crystal globe for evoking visions
of the past. There it is, to restore the fisherman's self-respect
after a blank day. There it is, to be caught a thousand times in
the study when there is no chance of getting to the river. There
it is, to put the clock back from any despondent moment to the
year, the day, the hour, the tremulous minute when it was a
question whether or no it was to come out of the water. There
it is, proof against credulity or unbelief, incapable alike of
growth and diminution.

Every fisherman knows that his best days, his most
interesting days, the days he would wish to remember are
often not those on which he has the good fortune to catch a fish
worth putting in a glass case. They may be days when he fills
his basket with worthy, respectable, but in no way remarkable
fish. They may even be days when his basket is by no means
full. There is no definite relation between best days and best
fish. Both are delightful things to remember, and if the fish-
stuffer preserves one, a properly kept fishing diary is the best
of glass cases for the other.

Sometimes, of course, it will seem that there is little to enter
in the log but the number of fish caught, nothing particularly
memorable in one way or another. Be not too sure. Twenty
years hence you may be looking back through your diaries to
compare the efficacy of new with that of by then outmoded
flies, or to seek for evidence to support an argument on the
inexhaustible subject of fisherman's weather. You cannot tell
now what you will be seeking then. So, if you are wise, you
will put down on each fishing day other things beside the
number of fish in your basket and the weight of them. There
will be the direction of the wind, the character of the sky, and
the state of the water. These three matters are important in any
fishing day. If you are fishing fly, you will note what flies you
used and what fish you caught on each, the time of the take,
the natural flies that you identified on the water. You will find

after only a year that you look back with interest to see what flies you were using this day last season. If you tie some of your own flies, you will have favourites. Nothing but an accurately kept record will prevent you from nursing the most fantastic illusions as to the execution done by particular flies. Whatever you are fishing, fly, worm, or minnow, you will note with care exactly where your best fish took hold, and thus in the course of time will come to have a more exact knowledge of your river than ever you could have if you trusted to your memory alone. The habit of noting such things strengthens the habit of observing them, and much writing in your diary of your own river will help you surprisingly in reading any other river that you are fishing for the first time.

Nor is it only with trout or salmon fishing that there are things to be noted. Never catch a pike without writing down the time at which you hooked him. This will save you much early rising in some seasons of the year. Note when your roach came on the feed. Set down exactly the times at which you caught your best perch. Note your baits. Treat your spinners like your flies, so that you may have solid grounds for your choice of blue wagtail in one kind of water, copper spoons in another, and silver Holroyds in a third. Note the depth in which you found your fish. The noting of every one of these things, besides helping to preserve fishing days that are past, will help towards better fishing in the future.

There is, by the way, with this object, another thing to note which is usually neglected, and that is the weather, not when you were fishing but afterwards. And then, besides all these utilitarian notes, do not scruple to put down things which have little connection with fishing but much with fishing days. Set down the kingfishers, cormorants, and herons, the weasel that watched you from a hole in a stone wall, ducking when you cast but constrained by curiosity to bob up instantly after, owls and moonlight on the way home, on which trees the buds showed in spring, the first red leaves in autumn, and those drifting leaves that in the back end of the year take the place of parr and keep you both impatient and alert. Even human beings are worth mentioning sometimes, though not often.

Fishermen's Letters

O NE OF THE REWARDS of writing these weekly articles is a continually increasing fishing post-bag. Perhaps half of this post-bag is of a utilitarian kind – 'Can you tell me of some really good fishing within easy reach of Manchester?' To which I have to reply, 'If you find any, please let me know.' But the other half is made up of letters which I am very glad to get. In these, fishermen of all kinds, knowing by some happy instinct that they have a willing listener, tell me of their own fishing, good or bad, and let me share a hundred fishing holidays besides my own.

Fishermen's letters, no matter how ill written, have in the reality of their feeling at least one thing in common with the greatest literature. Their authors do not have to go to school to learn to write. No rules of 'polite correspondence' hamper the man who writes to tell a friend how well the trout rose to his ginger quill. Fishing, like love, will find out the way, through no matter what thorny hedge of syntax or orthography. Here, at least, all men are equal, not because they all write badly but because they all write well. Even your professional word-spinner is at his best when he writes of fishing, but no better than the blacksmith who writes of the same thing. In Kingsley's letters there is the mottled pattern of sunshine and shadow that there is under trees, but all the passages in which he mentions fishing are among the sunlit spots. 'Now to business, Tommy, which is fish,' he writes to Tom Hughes. 'Oh that I could go to Lambourne Monday! But I preach in town Sunday, and have three good fellows a-dying in my parish, so that I must be at home Monday afternoon. . . .' And, two pages later, 'Sell your last coat and buy a spoon. I have a spoon of huge size. I killed forty pounds of pike on it the other day.' That is the real stuff, but it is no better than the letters I get every week from men who would never think of comparing themselves to the author of *Westward Ho!* and *Water Babies*.

There is the man who writes of the sea-trout that take his fly, play him for a while, and then depart without waiting for the landing net. He writes to know why they depart, and does not dream how often, fishing for sea-trout, I have envied him when the morts would have no truck with me at all. There is the small boy who takes forty years off my back and gives me once again the excitement of pulling out my first trout when he writes, 'I lift them out of the water and then they drop off. Please write and tell me why they drop off.' Then there is the man who catches his first salmon on a trout fly, describes it as a freshly run cock fish, and sends me as illustration of his letter a photograph of a decidedly not freshly run hen. No matter. A salmon it was, and he caught it on a trout rod, and played it for an hour that was certainly worth an age without a name, and through his letter I can feel the trembling of his knees as at last he got that fish to bank. One man sends me quite casually in the middle of a letter about flies the best account of grayling spawning that I have ever read, described exactly as he had seen it. A clergyman, worthy descendant of Izaak Walton's reverend friends, wants to know how to colour maggots. Then there is that kindly fellow who, on my return to England and to this column, wrote to hope that 'I had had a good day among the sturgeons while I was away.' There are also those who never go for a fishing holiday without writing afterwards to describe weather and water and the fish they had and the flies they used each day. Whether the sport described is good or bad, these are among the most valuable letters in the bag. Lastly, and, of course, best of all, are letters which suggest that if I should like a day on this or that water I can have it.

In today's post there are rejoicings from men who were fishing at the weekend, which kept its promise on the Ribble and elsewhere. There is also the story of the killing of a cannibal trout in a most unusual manner. My correspondent puts the story in inverted commas, so that I am not sure whether he or another was the fortunate fisherman. Here is the story.

Fishing the Dove on the 4th inst. I hooked a small trout about seven inches long on the Mayfly. Whilst reeling it in the small trout was seized by a large one. After playing it for some minutes I saw my Mayfly was in the mouth of the small trout, which was held crossways in the mouth of the large one. I made sure that the big trout would sooner or later release its hold, as I was putting considerable pressure on. I made two attempts to net the fish, but owing to high bank could not quite reach. Eventually I sat down on bank to get nearer, and on the third attempt I got it in the net, and it was not till then that the trout relaxed its hold and the two trout lay in the net apart. The sides of the small trout were deeply cut. It took me between five and ten minutes to land. The large trout weighed 2lb 8oz.

My correspondent asks if this is not an unusual event. It certainly is. It is not unusual for a pike to grab a trout or a roach while it is being played. In 1924 a man hooked a 13-inch pike on a 9-inch spinner, felt the weight suddenly increase, and at last gaffed a 15½lb pike, which had seized the little one and not let go until too late. I heard of a case in which someone fishing with worm caught a minnow and left it in the water, when it was taken by a perch, which was taken by a pike, which was landed. Two years ago a pike seized a trout that I had hooked and allowed itself to be played to my feet, when, if the net had been big enough, I might, perhaps, have landed it. In this case also the larger fish swam about with the smaller gripped across the middle. But the story of the big Dove trout is much more remarkable. It must have been caught by its teeth, have got the small fish well back across its jaws, and been played by a skilful angler who, keeping a steady pressure on it, never gave it a chance to let go. Greed alone could hardly be sufficient to explain its hanging on until the third and successful attempt at netting it. In any case, the fishermen of that length of the Dove ought to be grateful to its captor. Here, at any rate, is a cannibal caught and executed in the very act. Or had the little trout dashed in and stolen the Mayfly to which the big trout had addressed his more leisurely mind? But the teeth that made the deep cuts on the little trout's sides, and were in the end the big trout's undoing, had not grown on a diet of insect food alone.

Farewell

IT IS TIME to bring these weekly articles on fishing to an end. They were begun in August, 1925. They have run on continuously, except for their author's short absences from England, for over four years. Judging by myself, everybody must be heartily sick of them. Besides, I want to enjoy my fishing like other people, and so long as there is a 'Rod and Line' article to be published every Friday I have to fish for subjects instead of for fish. Pleasant enough it is sometimes, when subjects rise like trout in a good water. It is a good deal less pleasant when subjects are as dour as trout in a July drought. Even after you have risen your subject, you have but begun. And while you are playing it this way and that, watching lest it run from you into some thicket of weedy doubt, or away altogether to leave you to wind up a barren line, your fishing day has ceased to be a fishing day. You are fishing for the pot, the ink-pot, and that is no sport but hard business.

But I will not pretend that I have not enjoyed 'Rod and Line', even while putting it on paper, even while thinking of it at the riverside. There is nothing like writing them down to find how vague thoughts are. And experimenting, as every fisherman does, now with dry flies for sea-trout, now with a spinning reel, now with float fishing for chub or carp or perch or roach or, best of all, for winter grayling, the writing that has accompanied these four years of fishing has driven me into taking pains that perhaps would not otherwise have been taken. Now and then some kindly, encouraging person has written to say that he has learnt a hint or two from 'Rod and

Line', but no one has learnt so many hints from it as its writer. Writing it has forced him again and again to turn surmise into certainty, suspicion into something like belief. It has made him grab notion after notion by the scruff of the neck instead of merely letting it nod at him in passing. Some of the notions turned out to be rubbish, some not, but this compulsory pursuit of them, this pinning of them down, has, I think, made him less of a bungler than he was. Not that he claims to be anything but a bungler now, but at least, in a great many cases, when he bungles now he knows why and how.

Perhaps the greatest pleasure I have had from 'Rod and Line' has been the friendships it has made for me with other fishermen. Two of the many who have helped me in it are dead. The first was Mr Nelson, whose name will be for ever associated with the Eden. The second was Mr Fearn, with whom I fished the Border Esk and the Wye in Monsal Dale only a few days before he was found dead from heart failure on the banks of Esk, with a fresh-killed salmon at his side. Of the living there are too many to name. I think of a group of Yorkshiremen on the Wharfe, of two fishers of the Dove, of half a dozen names well known on Ribble and Hodder, of friends on the Cumberland Derwent in spite of whose efforts I have never yet caught a salmon there, of a crack roach-fisher in Oxford who spent a day in teaching me that Thames style of which he is a master, of a great pike-fisher in the same place, of my constant companion on the sweetest of the chalk streams of Hampshire, of other Yorkshiremen whom I have met by the chub-haunted Avon and the breamy depths of the Lincolnshire drains, and, perhaps most often, of the working-men fishers of Lancashire who year by year have taken me to fish with them and have been tireless in suggestions for this column. I hope that I am saying farewell to none of them in bringing to an end the series of articles to which every one of them has in some way contributed.

The winding up of 'Rod and Line' will not mean that there will be nothing on fishing in the *Manchester Guardian*. There will from time to time, as hitherto, be articles on fishing. The only change will be that this weekly article will be no more.

And that, for one fisherman at least, is no unpleasant thought. Tonight I write this after coming back from an afternoon's visit to the river. There was something particular about this visit, because it was the first for over four years made with the knowledge that, whatever happened, no 'Rod and Line' was to come out of it. There was another thing particular about it too. I caught today the best brown trout I have ever had from the river. He ran me down an awkward place, got away on the far side of the river behind a sharpedged rock, and there 'jiggered' so that I could feel the rasping on the stone and knew that the gut was wearing through. There was only one thing to do, and that was to let the line go slack and to go far down before tightening again, in the hope that the gut would come clear of the rock. This was done, and when I wound in again the fish dashed off into open water, and some time later was netted. I had been right about the cast. Three inches of it were furred and so thin that it broke at once. But the fish weighed 2lb 9oz. He was a beautiful fish, well shaped and in fine condition. I was surprised that when he was cut up two small trout were found in his belly. He looked as if he had a better character.

It was not of his character, however, that I thought as I tried in vain to stuff him into my basket. No, I thought of something else. This was a fish that for several reasons (not mentioned here) was of considerable interest. He was the best brownie I have ever had from the river. He was the answer to a question that I had several times asked myself about the place where I caught him. He had given me a much better fight than some salmon. Yet I thought of none of these things. I looked at that fish, and I looked at him again and I said, 'Well, thank goodness, there is no need to write an article about *you*!' Henceforth when I go fishing I shall take my rod and take my line and a few other necessaries, but at least I need not think that I must remember a fountain-pen. And so farewell.

The World's Whopper

THEY LOOKED at the big pike rod, lying in a rest on the cockpit coaming. They looked at its big porcelain rings, its dark varnish, its enormous reel. Six feet of the rod were poking out over the river and from the end of it a thin green line was pulled out straight by the tug of the stream.

'Where's his float?'

'Gone,' said Joe. 'No. There it is. Away down by them reeds. That's a likely holt for a big 'un.'

'He say we could go aboard,' said Pete.

Joe climbed aboard and stood in the cockpit. Bill followed.

'Aa, you,' said Joe. 'Step easy. You'd scare every fish in the river.' He pointed to the ripples running across the water after Bill had got into the cockpit. 'Now then, Pete.'

'Wonder if the bait's died on him,' said Bill.

Twenty yards downstream, two small pilot floats and a big white-topped pike float swung gently on the top of the moving water, tethered by the thin green line that ran from the tip of the rod. They lay so still that it was hard to believe that anything but a dead bait hung beneath them. Pete watched them as keenly as if he were fishing himself.

Joe was fingering the reel. He gave a gentle tug at the line above it and heard the reel click as it turned. He looked at the back of the reel and touched the brass catch.

'That makes it run free,' he said.

'It's not like the ones on our reels,' said Bill.

Joe pressed the catch, gently at first and then harder. Suddenly it slid back and the reel began to turn, faster and faster as the line ran out.

'He say not to touch the rod,' said Pete.

'He'll have the liver and lungs out of you,' said Bill.

For a moment Joe could not get the catch to move back. He managed it and the tip of the rod dipped and straightened. Far away down the river the floats that had been moving with the current stopped dead.

'Gosh!' said Joe. 'I thought that were going to run right out.'

'Don't you touch it again,' said Bill.

'The bait's waked up,' said Pete suddenly.

The big white-topped float bobbed sideways, twice, and then swung back into line with the pilots above it.

'Will it be an old pike after him?' said Bill.

'Fare to be,' said Joe. 'See if that bob again.'

For some minutes they stood silent in the cockpit, looking away downstream at the two little floats and the big one rippling the water a yard or two out from the reeds. Joe and Bill soon tired of that.

'Let's scout along the rond,' said Bill.

'Come on,' said Joe. 'He say to keep anybody off.'

'Float bobbed again,' said Pete.

The other two, who were just going to jump ashore, thought better of it. The floats certainly did look as if something might be going to happen.

'What do we do if an old pike take him under?' said Bill.

'Yell like billyo,' said Joe. 'Nothing else we can do.' He

stopped short. 'He'll have a horn, being a motor cruiser. Here you are. Press that button and it'll wake the dead.'

'That's the starter,' said Bill.

'It might be,' said Joe. 'Well, he's bound to have a foghorn. You keep your eye on them floats, Pete.'

Doubtfully, he opened the cabin door that the fisherman had shut to keep the mist out of the cabin. He saw the glow in the neat enamelled stove. He saw a comfortable bunk, not yet made up after the night, and breakfast things ready on the table. Then he saw what he wanted. There it hung, just inside the door, so as to be within easy reach of the steersman, a smallish brass foghorn. Joe took it from its hook and put it to his mouth.

'Don't you do that,' said Bill anxiously. 'He'll think something's up.'

Joe blew gently into the horn. Nothing happened. He blew a little harder and a sudden 'yawp' startled them all.

'Float's bobbed,' said Pete.

'Don't jump like that,' said Joe. 'Look at the wave you make.' He put the horn carefully back on its hook and closed the cabin door.

For some minutes he stood still, looking now at the floats and now upstream along the reedy bank, half expecting to see the fisherman coming on the run. But the floats did not stir again. It was as if they had gone to sleep. And the fisherman did not come. Joe decided that it was all right. It had sounded pretty loud in the cockpit but, after all, it had been the very shortest of 'yawps'.

'Who's coming scouting?' he said at last.

'I'm coming,' said Bill.

They stepped ashore as quietly as they could.

Pete, his eyes still on the distant floats, said, 'I'm coming too.'

'Come on then,' said Joe.

Pete had one more look. Was that float stirring? No. The others were already moving off along the rond. Pete had another last look at the floats and joined them.

'Knives in your teeth,' said Joe.

'We needn't open them,' said Bill.

Scout knives are awkward things to hold in the teeth on a cool misty morning and it was as well that these had been well warmed in their owners' pockets. Stooping low, and muzzled by their knives, the three set off along the bank. The reeds already hid the boat from them when Joe, the leader, stopped short and took his knife from his mouth.

'Password's "Death and Glory",' he whispered, and then, startled, 'What's that?'

A harsh 'Krrrrrrrrrrrr', like the cry of a corncrake, sounded from behind them. Pete's knife dropped from his teeth. He fumbled for it on the ground. Bill, his knife in his hand, listened, gaping.

'Krrrrrrr . . . Krrrrrrrrrrr . . . Krrrrrrrrrrrr. . . .'

'Out of the way, Pete,' shouted Joe. 'Look out, Bill. It's that reel. . . . It's a pike. . . .' He rushed back the way they had come, followed by the others.

'Krrrrrrrr . . . Krrrrrrr . . . Krrrrrrrrrrrr. . . .'

The rod was jerking. The reel spun . . . stopped . . . and spun again.

'Krrrrrrrrrr . . . Krrrrrrrr. . . .'

The rod straightened. The reel stopped spinning, as Joe climbed aboard.

'Quiet,' he whispered as the others dropped into the cockpit beside him.

'Floats have gone,' said Pete.

'All three of 'em,' said Bill.

'He's off with the lot,' said Joe.

'Look where the line is,' said Pete.

The line no longer stretched down the river. It disappeared into the water a little above the *Cachalot* and about half way across. There could be no doubt that a pike had taken the bait, gone downstream pulling at the rod and had then turned and swum up.

'He's weeded it,' said Joe. 'Weeded it and gone.'

'No, he ain't,' said Pete. 'Line's moving.'

The line, though still slack, was pointing further and further upstream.

'He's still on,' said Bill.

'There's a pilot,' cried Pete.

One of the small pilot floats showed well above the *Cachalot*, moving slowly along the surface of the water. Another showed ahead of it. The big white-topped pikefloat came to the surface.

'He's thrown it out,' groaned Joe.

'We ought to have struck him,' said Pete.

'Better wind in, I reckon,' said Joe.

And then, suddenly, the floats dived again, the line pulled taut, the reel screamed and Joe, grabbing line and rod together as the rod jerked, struck with all his might.

The rod bent nearly double. The top of it slammed down into the water. The line raced out, cutting Joe's fingers.

'He's on,' shouted Joe, getting the point of the rod up. 'He's on. Hi! . . . Hey! . . . Let go with that foghorn, somebody. Go on. Quick. . . . Keep at it. . . . Hey!'

Bill had the cabin door open in a moment, seized the horn, blew and kept on blowing.

'Geewhizz, he is a big 'un,' said Joe, hanging on to the bent rod, and bruising his fingers on the handles of the spinning reel.

'Wind in,' said Pete. 'He'll have all the line out if you don't stop him.'

'Keep on with that horn,' panted Joe. 'No. Stop it. No good. He's gone after all.'

'Wind in,' said Pete.

The line had gone suddenly slack. Joe, finding it very difficult to hold the heavy rod and wind in at the same time, rested the rod on the cockpit coaming. He wound and wound and still the line was slack and came in as if there was nothing on the end of it.

'Shut up,' said Joe. 'No good hooting now. . . . We lost him. . . . And that was a big old pike too.'

'There's a float,' cried Pete. 'There . . . Under water. . . . It's moving. Coming downstream. Wind in. . . . Wind in. . . . He's still on if he ain't broke the line.'

Joe wound and wound. The curve of the line slowly

straightened. It was cutting the water almost opposite the *Cachalot*. Suddenly the rod dipped, the reel screamed, and the spinning handles nearly broke Joe's fingers. He let them spin and held the rod up.

'Give him the horn again, Bill. He's still on. Up on the cabin-top, Pete, and see if he's coming. Hey! Hey! . . . Hey!'

Twenty yards down the river it was as if there had been an explosion under water. Just for a moment they saw an enormous head, a broad dark back and a wide threshing tail, as the big fish broke the surface and dived again.

Bill was blowing the horn. Joe, holding up the rod and feeling the heavy tugs of the fish, was shouting at the top of his voice. But still there was no sign of the owner of the *Cachalot*. The big fish turned and came upstream again. Joe, desperately winding in, saw the line cutting the water only a few yards from the boat. Again the pike rushed away upstream. The reel screamed. Joe tried to brake it with his thumb and nearly had the skin taken off.

'Hang on to him,' said Pete.

'Ain't I?' panted Joe. 'Why don't that chap come. Hey! Hey! Hey!'

The reel stopped spinning. Joe began winding in again, getting a few yards, and then having to get his fingers out of the way of the spinning handles when the pike made another rush. And then again the great fish came downstream, this time deep in the water, so that they did not see the floats as he passed. The line tautened again. There was another sudden, long rush, on and on, as if the pike were making for Yarmouth. It stopped. The floats showed on the surface far downstream opposite a big clump of reeds, in the place where they had been lying before the pike had taken the bait. They rested there a moment, bobbed, and came up again close to the reeds.

'He's going back to his holt,' shouted Pete. 'Stop him! Stop him! There he go. . . .' The floats shot suddenly sideways into the reeds.

Joe pulled. It was as if he were pulling at a haystack. He wound at the reel till the rod top was on the water. He tried to lift. The line rose, quivering and dripping. Joe let the reel spin to ease it. It was no good. Deep in the reeds the pike lay still and, for the moment, the battle was at an end.

'Lemme have a go,' said Bill.

'You can't shift him,' said Joe. 'No good breaking the line. We'll lose him if you do. Gosh, I wish that chap'd come.'

Bill tried to wind in, while Joe blew frantically on the horn. Suddenly he stopped. 'We can't let him lie there chewing and chewing till he throw the hooks. We got to get him out of that. Where's Pete?'

From behind the reeds, far downstream, came Pete's voice. 'Where is he? This the place?'

The tops of the reeds waved violently.

'Further down,' shouted Joe. 'That's it. Hang on there whiles I bring the boathook. Here, Bill. No good winding till he come out. You keep blowing. I'll be back as soon as we shift him.'

Joe took the long boathook from the *Cachalot* and ran to join Pete behind the reeds. Just there the reeds were very thick and they could see little of the water. Joe poked this way and that with the boathook. The foghorn from the *Cachalot* sounded in long gasps. Suddenly there was a clang as it dropped on the floor of the cockpit.

'He's moved,' shouted Bill. 'He give a tug just now. . . . No. He's stopped again.'

Once more the foghorn sounded its desperate call for help.

'May be right in under the bank,' said Joe. 'Come on, Pete. We got to drive him out. Make all the row you can.'

He stabbed away with the boathook, while Pete, standing on the very edge of the solid bank, kicked at the water sending wild splashes through the reeds.

'Touched him!' shouted Joe. 'Gosh, he is a whopper.' There was a tremendous flurry in the water. Waves ran through the stems of the reeds.

'He's close in,' shouted Joe. 'Go on, Pete. Splash! Splash!'

Pete, in his seaboots, took a further step, stamped in the water, slipped, tried to recover himself and fell headlong. His struggles made a bigger splash than ever he had made with his boots. Reeds swayed this way and that as he fought for foothold in the soft mud, for handhold among the slimy roots.

'You all right?' said Joe. 'Take a grip of the boathook.'

'All right,' spluttered Pete, spitting river water from his mouth. 'Ouch!' he yelled suddenly, and came splashing out of the water on all fours. 'Joe,' he said. 'I trod on him.'

'He's out. Joe! Joe!' Bill yelled from the boat. Joe raced back with Pete after him.

'What's all this row about?'

The fisherman, hurrying not at all, with a full milk can in one hand and a full sack in the other, was coming back along the path. He saw Pete, muddy and dripping, on the bank beside the *Cachalot*.

'Hullo,' said the fisherman. 'Fallen in?'

The foghorn sounded again. 'Hey! Hey!' shouted Joe.

'They've a pike on,' yelled Pete. 'We just chase him out of the reeds.'

The fisherman darted forward.

Joe, in the cockpit had grabbed the rod from Bill's trembling hands. Far away, out in the middle of the river, a great tuft of reeds showed above the surface, moving slowly across the stream. Joe wound in, and the reeds came upstream, jerking now and then, as if something were tugging angrily at their roots. Bill blew and blew.

The fisherman spoke from the bank behind them.

'Ever caught a pike before?'

'No,' said Bill.

'You take him,' said Joe, looking over his shoulder.

'How long have you had him on?' asked the fisherman.

'Year or two,' said Joe shortly.

'Carry on for another month then,' said the fisherman. 'You're doing very well.'

'He's a big 'un,' said Joe.

'Been all over the place,' said Bill. 'Most up to Kendal Dyke and back and then he go into the reeds.'

'How did you get him out? He seems to have taken a good bunch with him.'

'Chase him out,' said Joe. 'Pete tread on him.'

The fisherman turned to look at Pete, who was standing dripping on the bank, thinking of nothing but the fish. 'Look here, you,' he said. 'We don't want to have you dying. Kick those boots off, and get out of your clothes. Go into the cabin and . . . don't let that line go slack! Wind in, man! Wind in!'

The pike had turned and was coming back towards the *Cachalot*. Joe was winding for all he was worth. 'You take it,' he said. 'You take it.'

The fisherman, who had come quietly aboard, put out his hand to take the rod, but changed his mind. 'Not I,' he said. 'You've hooked him. You've held him. You've played him. I'm not going to take the rod now. Hullo. He's a beauty. . . . Go on, Pete, get into the cabin. Never mind the wet. It'll drain into the bilge.'

'Lemme see him caught,' said Pete.

'He's coming now,' said the fisherman and reached for the long gaff that lay on the top of the cabin. 'Wind in a bit more, you with the rod. Now, lift him. . . . Gently. . . .'

For the first time, they could see how big the pike was. A huge fish, mottled light green and olive, rose slowly to the top of the water. He had shaken free of the reeds, which were drifting away. He opened a wide, white mouth, shook a head as big as a man's and plunged again to the bottom of the river, making the reel whizz.

'He's all of twenty pounds,' said the fisherman quietly. 'I was sure there was a good one about. Don't lose him now. Bring him in again. That's the way. . . .'

'There's the float,' said Pete. 'He's coming. There he is.'

'Keep still.'

The fisherman leaned from the cockpit with the long gaff deep in the water. The big fish was coming to the top once more. The fisherman suddenly lifted.

'Look out now,' he shouted, and in another moment the big fish was in the cockpit, threshing its great tail among their feet.

'How are you going to kill him?' said Bill.

The fisherman lifted a seat in the cockpit, took a short-weighted club from the locker beneath it and brought it down heavily, once, twice, on the pike's head. The great fish lay still.

(from *The Big Six*)

Poaching and Poaching

THERE'S MORE than one sort of poacher. It's the same with men as it is with beasts and birds. Hawks now. I'd never shoot a kestrel for taking a pheasant chick once in a way. He's earned it by keeping on with steady work among rats and such. But I'd shoot a sparrow hawk at once and know I was doing good to the wood. An old badger, too. I'd never touch him. But I'd have no mercy on stoats. Mean beasts they are. Live with the rabbits in the same burrow, play with them, watch them, and then pick the best and fattest of the young ones, and run it to death. You'll have seen that if ever you find a stoated rabbit lying dead, it'll always be a good one. Too many stoats, like too many foxes, will kill a bit of woodland altogether. That's the way the keeper looks at it. His business is to do the best he can for the wood, or the moor, or the river, and that's why he has a blind eye for some chaps and a pretty sharp eye for others. And his eye is sharpest of all for those who don't play fair, and come poaching not just once in a while to pick up a rabbit for their dinner, but are there to make money, and if they can clean a wood or a warren right out in an evening, will do it and think themselves clever. Then there are the men who don't wait for the twelfth of August but sneak up the moors on the eleventh, to have a lot of other folk's grouse for sale the day the season opens. I think very different of those chaps from what I do of the farmer who shoots a brace of grouse on a corn stock from behind the sheepfold wall, and sits down to his dinner with his missis, and the both of them finding a sauce to the birds in knowing that he'd best say naught about it. That same farmer'll be the first to let the keeper know if there are folk about driving the birds into nets.

It's the same with the river as it is with a wood or a moor. There's no great harm in the man who comes down to the beck and throws a fly for a trout, and in these days, now that there's an association for the fishers, there's less work for the keeper. The man that doesn't fish fair has an enemy in every man that does and no man's happy long if he knows he's misliked by all the others. And if they catch him at it and put him in the river, and break up his tackle all by accident on purpose, and send him home with a wet jacket and a black eye he'll get no sympathy, no, not even from his wife, who won't like it when other folk's missises are saying 'Serve him right'. Nowadays every local fisher's a keeper on the water, and take it all round things are a lot better for the river.

Not but what there are bad spots yet. They tell me that at High Brig, that's on the Lune, the same thing's going on that I saw near eighty years ago, when my father took me across there to see an aunt of mine who was a great hand with Eccles cakes. Her cottage was not that far from the river, and my father took me down the brig to see if there was salmon leaping the weir. It's a late season up there, and this was well into the back end, and the fish were coming up ready to spawn. I mind now seeing the fish in the smooth water above the weir, the cocks with beaks to them like parrots', and mottled about with colour like an old carpet.

Below the bridge there's a narrow place where the river pours out deep between two rocks. I dare say a lish lad could jump from one to tother, though I doubt few would like to try. We went down to the bridge, and my father lifted me up on the wall so that I could see over. There was one man fishing and a parcel of others sitting on the rock beside him. It seemed funny fishing to me. He'd a rod near as thick at one end as tother, and a line you could rope a bullock with, and his line went down into the deep water between the two rocks, and every so often he'd lift it a foot or two and drop it again but never take it from the water.

'Dad,' said I. 'When's he going to cast?' For I'd often laid on the bank watching and seen the rod bend and lift, and the line fling up straight in the air over my head and out again across the water to put a fly where it was wanted.

I didn't ask twice, and my father did not answer. Never a word. He just stood there on the brig, watching with a face as black as a thundercloud.

'Time!' one of the other men sang out, and the chap with the rod didn't lift his line from the water but gave up his rod to the next man, and sat him down on the rock with the rest of them. The chap who'd called out 'Time' had a watch in his hand. There was room for no more than one to fish, if you can call it fishing, and they were all taking their turns.

The man who had the rod now was doing like the first, lifting the end of his pole with a sharp hard lift and then lowering it again. Up and down. Up . . . and down. And he'd not been doing it above two minutes before he had a fish. Play it? Not he. He just hauled it straight up the side of the rock. Hooked in the belly. We could see that. One of the others knocked it on the head and put it in a sack, and before it was in the sack the chap had his line in the water deep at his feet and was going on with his up and down.

My father stood there on the bridge, and watched while they hauled out four fish, hooked in the belly, in the tail, in the side, anywhere but in the mouth. And we were near enough to see the tackle they were using. A great heavy weight on the line and a couple of big hooks below it. In that narrow place there fish had but the one way through, and they were dropping their hooks to the bottom and lifting them dropping and lifting again till they got a hook into a fish and then up and out with it and ready for the next. With that pole and the line they were using, they'd nothing to do but haul.

(from the unfinished typescript of *The River Comes First* Brotherton Collection, University of Leeds Library.)

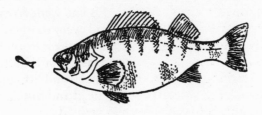

Acknowledgements

One of the pleasures of writing about Arthur Ransome is the encounter with a fellowship of enthusiasts, many of them members of the The Arthur Ransome Society (TARS), who respond helpfully and efficiently to requests for help. Among this band, I would like especially to thank Brigit Sanders, President of TARS, Dr Christopher Birt, David Carter, John Cowen, Elizabeth Drury, Hugo Eastwood, Jeremy Gibson, James Hawkins, Ian Hughes, Dick and Desmond Kelsall, Brian Ridsdale, Keith Skilleter, Rod Welch, Dave Stewart, Margaret Taylor and H. B. Whittam.

Thanks to gifts by the Ransomes and later by his literary executors, a comprehensive selection of his papers are in accessible collections in Leeds and Kendal. I am in great debt to Christopher Sheppard and especially Ann Farr, the enormously knowledgeable and helpful curator of the Ransome archive deposited in The Brotherton Collection, Leeds University Library; and to Edward King, Vicky Slowe and Janet Dugdale at the Museum of Lakeland Life and Industry, Abbot Hall, Kendal. I am also grateful to The Brotherton Collection and to Abbot Hall for permission to quote from material in their possession. My thanks also go to Mrs Lydia Spurrier and to Mrs Audrey Spurrier for permission to reproduce the drawing of Roger and the pike on page 71, and to Penelope Renold, Roger Wardale, Ann Farr and John Bell for permission to reproduce photographs. The Gilroy portrait of Ransome opposite page 96 is reproduced by courtesy of the E. T. Archive and the Garrick Club, and Eric Fitch Daglish's woodcut of a salmon on page 89 with the permission of J. M. Dent, publishers of Viscount Grey's book *Fly Fishing*.

Many other people have helped with memories of Arthur Ransome, leads, information about fishing, and comments on the manuscript. I particularly thank Dr Ron Broughton, Chairman of the Grayling Society, Peter Cresswell, Uig and Hamanavay Estate, James Shaw Grant, journalist and local historian of Lewis, Leslie Magee, Caroline Moorehead, Penelope Renold, Tania Rose, Taklit Temolo and Anthony Wilson.

I owe much also to Christina Hardyment and Roger Wardale, whose books have been a mine of facts about Ransome's influences and his boats; Christina Hardyment has also generously supplied much useful additional information. Hugh Brogan's biography is a major work which touches on all the main themes of Ransome's life, including his fishing, and I acknowledge my considerable debt to him.

John Bell and Sir Rupert Hart-Davis, Ransome's literary executors, have generously allowed me to use the Ransome materials, and John Bell in particular has been a source of enthusiasm, contacts and help. I owe him an important debt of gratitude as do all Ransome fans. Tony Colwell, my editor at Jonathan Cape, and Carol Heaton at Greene and Heaton have provided support and encouragement for which I am grateful.

J.S

Sources and Bibliography

Quotations from and references made in the text to the published works of Arthur Ransome are as follows:

Pond and Stream, Anthony Treherne, 1906
Bohemia in London, Chapman and Hall, 1907
A History of Storytelling, T. C. & E. C. Jack, 1909
Edgar Allan Poe, A Critical Study, Martin Secker, 1910
Oscar Wilde, A Critical Study, Martin Secker, 1912
The Elixir of Life, Methuen, 1915
Old Peter's Russian Tales, T. C. & E. C. Jack, 1916; Cape 1984
Six Weeks in Russia, George Allen and Unwin, 1919
Racundra's First Cruise, Allen and Unwin, 1923
Rod and Line, Jonathan Cape, 1929
Swallows and Amazons, Jonathan Cape, 1930
Swallowdale, Jonathan Cape, 1931
Winter Holiday, Jonathan Cape, 1933
Coot Club, Jonathan Cape, 1934
We Didn't Mean to Go to Sea, Jonathan Cape, 1937
The Big Six, Jonathan Cape, 1940
The Picts and the Martyrs, Jonathan Cape, 1943
Great Northern?, Jonathan Cape, 1947
Fishing, National Book League Readers' Guides, second series No. 2, Cambridge University Press, 1955
Mainly About Fishing, Adam & Charles Black, 1959
The Autobiography of Arthur Ransome, edited (with a prologue and an epilogue) by Rupert Hart-Davis, Jonathan Cape, 1976
'The River Comes First' in *Coots in the North and Other Stories*, edited and introduced by Hugh Brogan, Jonathan Cape, 1988

Sources unattributed in the text are either Ransome's *Autobiography* or as follows:

page 20, catching trout in a tin can: Ransome, typescript 'Notes on the Lincoln imp', Saturday articles for the *Manchester Guardian*. The Brotherton Collection, Leeds University Library.

page 31–2, Stevenson quote: from Christina Hardyment, *Independent on Sunday*, 27 March 1994.

page 23, Ransome's first story: from Peter Hunt, *Approaching Arthur Ransome*, pp. 22–24.

page 38, from a letter to his mother on finishing the first draft of *Old Peter's Russian Tales*: Brogan's *Life*. p. 103.

page 40, information on Piscator and his Phillida from Brogan, *The Life of Arthur Ransome*, p. 110.

page 42, letter to his mother: Brogan's, *Life*, p. 142.

page 44–5, quotes from Lockhart, *Memoirs of a British Agent* (pp. 266–7) and *My Rod My Comfort* (pp. 40–43).

page 45–6, Petrograd during the revolution: Ransome, *Six Weeks in Russia* (p. 133) and *Mainly About Fishing* (p. 112), and Saturday article in the *Manchester Guardian*, 19 July 1930.

page 51–2, letter to his mother: Brogan's *Life*, p. 223.

page 56, train ride from Peking to London: Ransome, *Mainly About Fishing*, pp. 111–12.

page 57, February 1933 version of the signal code provided by Dick Kelsall.

page 59, Ransome and the Kelsalls: address by Dick Kelsall to the Arthur Ransome Society, Bowness-on-Windermere, 15–17 November 1991, and personal communication from Desmond Kelsall.

page 61, Arthur Ransome, 'On the writing of Saturday articles', *Manchester Guardian*, reprinted in *Mixed Moss* (The Journal of the Arthur Ransome Society) 1 (p. 3) 1992.

page 62, Halford on kingfishers: Halford, *Making a Fishery*, p. 79.

page 63, attack on noisy boat-owners, *Manchester Guardian*, 23 September 1927; also quote from *Rod and Line*, p. 182.

page 68, perch soup: Christina Hardyment, *Arthur Ransome and Captain Flint's Trunk*, p. 41.

page 74, description of Low Ludderburn, reprinted in *Mixed Moss* (Journal of the Arthur Ransome Society) No. 3, pp. 11–12.

page 74, parrot footprint: extract from the diaries of Lt Col T. E. Kelsall, R.E., provided by Dick Kelsall.

page 75), eel fishing: quoted from Wardale, *Nancy Blackett*, p. 117.

page 83, Francis Hirst: Ransome, *Mainly About Fishing*, p. 93.

page 83–4, Charles Renold: quoted from Ransome, unpublished typescript of *Autobiography*, The Brotherton Collection, Leeds University Library.

page 84–5, salmon flies: quoted from Ransome, *Mainly About Fishing*, p. 121.

page 87, Tom Stainton: Ransome, unpublished typescript of *Autobiography*, The Brotherton Collection, Leeds.

page 90, 'gummock': Ransome, unpublished part of typescript for *The River Comes First*, The Brotherton Collection, Leeds.

page 91, Younger, quoted from *Mainly About Fighting*, p. 43; swans and geese: unpublished typescript from the Collection of the Museum of Lakeland Life and Industry, Abbot Hall, Kendal.

page 92, sailing for char: Ransome to his mother, from Brogan's *Life*, p. 401.

page 93, salmon chew gum: quoted from *Mainly About Fishing*, p. 20.

page 94, letter from Ransome to Morritt (unsent), 1 September 1948, The Brotherton Collection, Leeds.

page 95, guineafowl hackles used in a hat in Vermont: Ransome, *Mainly about Fishing*, p. 24.

page 96, Desmond Kelsall and guineafowl feathers: personal communication from Desmond Kelsall.

page 97, letter from H. E. Morritt: May 1952, Ransome's 'Fishing Notebook', The Brotherton Collection, Leeds.

page 98, Estonian refugees in Stornaway: James Shaw Grant, *Stornaway and the Lews*, p. 144.

page 99, sea trout for the porter's cat: the Fishing Diaries of John F. Eastwood, OBE, KC; personal communication from Hugo Eastwood.

page 99, 'grumbly old bugger': personal communication from Anthony Wilson.

page 99–100, Ransome hating abroad, from *Mainly About Fishing*, p. 112.

page 100, the Dobsons at Uig: Evgenia Ransome, quoted in Brogan's *Life*, pp. 402–3.

page 103, advice to Morritt: Ransome, unpublished letter to H. E. Morritt, 5 January 1955, The Brotherton Collection, Leeds.

page 105–6, quoted from *Mainly About Fishing*, p. 109.

page 106–7, letters between Ransome and Hartman, and poem on salmon: unpublished manuscripts, The Brotherton Collection, Leeds.

Bibliography of other published works mentioned:

Hugh Brogan, *The Life of Arthur Ransome*, Jonathan Cape, 1984

R. H. Bruce Lockhart, *Memoirs of a British Agent: Being an Account of the Author's Life Early in Many Lands and of His Official Mission to Moscow in 1918*, Putnam, 1932

—— *Retreat from Glory*, Putnam, 1934

—— *My Rod My Comfort*, Putnam, 1937

W. G. Collingwood, *Thorstein of the Mere, A Tale of Viking Life*, Edward Arnold, 1895

Negley Farson, *Going Fishing*, Country Life Publications, 1942

James Shaw Grant, *Stornaway and the Lews*, James Thin, 1985

Viscount Grey, *Fly Fishing*, J. M. Dent, 1923.

F. M. Halford, *Making a Fishery*, Vinton, 1902

Christina Hardyment, *Arthur Ransome and Captain Flint's Trunk*, Jonathan Cape, 1984

Robert Hartman, *About Fishing*, Arthur Baker, 1935

Peter Hunt, *Approaching Arthur Ransome*, Jonathan Cape, 1992

Andrew Lang, *Angling Sketches*, Longmans, Greene, 1891

T. E. Pritt, *Yorkshire Trout Flies*, Sampson, Low, Marston, Searle and Rivington, 1885

Richard Waddington, *Fly Fishing for Salmon: A Modern Technique*, Faber and Faber, 1951

Izaak Walton, *The Compleat Angler*. The first part by Izaak Walton, 1653. The second part by Charles Cotton, 1678. The two parts together with introduction by John Buchan, Oxford University Press (World's Classics), 1935; also republished by Dent (Everyman Library), 1953.

Roger Wardale, *Nancy Blackett: Under Sail With Arthur Ransome*, Jonathan Cape, 1991

Other works mentioned in Ransome's 'Rod and Line' articles:

Sir George Ashton, *Mainly About Trout* – origin unknown

George A. B. Dewar, *Book of the Dry Fly*, Lawrence & Buller, (London) 1897

F. M. Halford, *Dry Fly Fishing in Theory and Practise*, Vinton, 1889; *Modern Development of the Dry Fly*, 1910

Edward Ringwood Hewitt, *Telling on the Trout*, Scribner's Sons, (New York) 1926

Charles Kingsley, *The Water Babies*, Macmillan, 1867

Charles Kingsley, *Westward Ho!*, Macmillan, 1874

J. C. Mottrain, *Fly-Fishing*, Second edition The Field Press, 1915

Richard Nobbes, *The Compleat Troller*, T James for Tho. Helder, 1682

The North Country Angler, (London) 1786; Third edition John Smith, (Leeds) 1800

Ernest Philips, *Float Fishing*, Allen & Unwin 1925

Thomas Frederick Salter, *Troller's Guide*, John Wickstead, (London) 1820

Hugh Sheringham, *Trout Fishing*, Hodder & Stoughton, 1920

W. J. Turrell, *Ancient Angling Authors*, Gurney & Jackson, 1910

Baron Walsingham (John Augustus de Grey), *Fish*, Philip Allan, 1926